ACKNOWLEDGMENTS

THIS IS a subjective book, reflecting the author's tastes, opinions and predilections. And yet the first person plural which crops up occasionally has a meaning beyond the editorial. This book owes a great deal to a great many people, and it could not have been written without them. A loyal legion of personal friends with differing interests and specialties rallied around, supplying leads, suggestions, notes, and criticisms. Scores of San Franciscans in all walks of life patiently answered questions and supplied essential information. Dr. Stanley Louie, Frank Quinn of the San Francisco Council for Civic Unity and James Warnock, Joseph Haughey, and Nancy Henry of the San Francisco Chamber of Commerce were kind enough to read the manuscript and offer suggestions for corrections, additions, and improvements. I, of course, take full responsibility for the errors of both omission and commission.

My daughter, Nora, spent a summer in researching historical and background information, typing up scores of index cards that seemed later to fall miraculously into place. My wife, Eva, devoted several months to intensive legwork, wearing out several pairs of shoes in the process. She wrote copious notes which formed the basis for the whole of Chapter 9 and for large parts of other chapters. I am grateful to her for the prodding, inspiration, and work which helped make this book possible.

As the title suggests, this is not intended as a formal or definitive guidebook. It is neither encyclopedic in scope nor punctiliously systematic in arrangement. And this kind of book, more than most, is subject to the inevitable ravages of time. Restaurants and shops, art galleries and night clubs close, and new ones open. No writer can control the caprices and vagaries of a changing city.

BEN ADAMS

SAN FRANCISCO
An Informal Guide

ALSO BY BEN ADAMS

Alaska: The Big Land
Hawaii: The Aloha State
The Last Frontier: A Short History of Alaska

SAN FRANCISCO

An Informal Guide

by BEN ADAMS

Illustrations by CHARLES MATTOX

HILL AND WANG · NEW YORK

Manufactured in the United States of America by
the Colonial Press Inc., Clinton, Mass.

CONTENTS

Auto Tours
Tour by Water
A Gallery of Views

MAPS

SAN FRANCISCO
An Informal Guide

1: VIEW FROM THE TOP

When the Heart Beats Faster

STENDHAL, the French novelist, was once walking in Rome with a friend when they saw from one of the seven hills the great dome of St. Peter's.

"What purpose does that serve?" the friend asked in jest.

"It serves to make your heart beat faster when you see it from afar," Stendhal answered.

No one should ask what purpose a city serves. A city is prose in its workaday functions, not poetry or art. So it is with San Francisco—port city, financial capital of the West, headquarters for California's great agricultural empires, city of services and trades.

Look at it from a crowded street corner and it looms up in ungainly hodgepodge of utility: parking lots thrust into Bohemia by restless progress, pancake plate-glass modern skyscrapers rising from the old red-brick office buildings, a double-deck freeway choking the broad expanse of the Embarcadero.

Then look at San Francisco from a distance and you see a different city. Drabness and dissonance disappear. Buildings and streets and freeways, hills and fog and water blend in subtle harmony. Look at the city from any hill and your heart beats faster.

The city's central artery, Market Street, is a jumble of restaurants, honkytonk bars, and pinball parlors, of nondescript business buildings and stores and movie theaters.

But seen at night from Mount Olympus or Twin Peaks it becomes

1

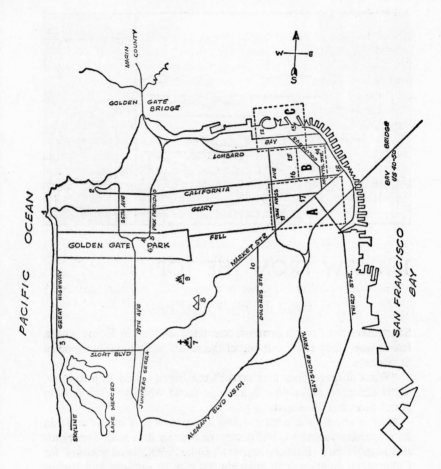

SAN FRANCISCO

A. Downtown Area map, page 16
B. Chinatown and North Beach map, page 57
C. Fisherman's Wharf and Aquatic Park map, 142

1. Cliff House and Playland
2. Palace of the Legion of Honor
3. Zoo
4. Japanese Tea Garden
5. De Young Museum
6. Aquarium and Hall of Science
7. Mount Davidson
8. Twin Peaks
9. Mount Sutro
10. Mission Dolores
11. Civic Center
12. Aquatic Park
13. Fisherman's Wharf
14. Telegraph Hill
15. Russian Hill
16. Nob Hill
17. Downtown area
18. Ferry Building

a soft diagonal of light bisecting the city. It joins imperceptibly the muted yellow arch of the San Francisco–Oakland Bay Bridge over the dark Bay which glows only intermittently with moon and neon and electric signs, then reaches out toward the night-sparkling hills of Berkeley and Oakland.

Look at San Francisco through a haze of fog and cloud from across the Golden Gate Bridge, from Vista Point, or from anywhere on the Sausalito waterfront. Even the dark skyscraper canyons assume an airy lightness. The glinting gray cubes of the buildings march up and down the hills, creating a modernist painting that generations of impressionist—and expressionist—artists have tried in vain to capture.

No matter how many times you look you will never see quite the same city. Viewing San Francisco from its hills or from across the Bay is like peering at it through a kaleidoscope. The city assumes new forms from each vantage point, reshaping with the changes of cloud and sun and moon.

Go in search of hills and views if you would feel San Francisco's magic. You will never penetrate to its source or see the city in all its aspects. But you will understand why San Franciscans look out the windows first when they inspect a new home or apartment, examining only later the mundane details of plumbing and kitchen equipment.

(For a listing of some of San Francisco's spectacular views see page 215.)

A City's Self-Image

San Francisco is the dream city of countless Miniver Cheevys in the hinterland, regretting their drab surroundings and yearning for a better time and place. It is an eternal El Dorado that draws artists and professionals of all kinds: newspapermen, painters, writers, artists, to say nothing of teachers, doctors, lawyers, social workers.

Praise of San Francisco unites the most diverse characters from the farthest corners of the earth; anthologies have been compiled of their tributes to the city. Rudyard Kipling sighed, "San Francisco has only one drawback—'tis hard to leave." Willie Britt, an old-time San Francisco boxer, exclaimed belligerently after the 1906 earthquake and fire, "I'd rather be a busted lamppost on Battery Street than the Waldorf-Astoria." Even Nikita Khrushchev was moved to say, "Of all the cities in the United States I have seen, San Francisco is the most beautiful."

San Franciscans admit the compliments are all true and concede that their city offers more beauty, pleasure, and enjoyment than any other in the United States—or anywhere else, for that matter. Fiercely divided along political and other lines, they agree on one thing. Their city is the greatest.

They have a surprisingly sharp and uncluttered image of themselves and their city. It is an image shared by the up-and-coming young business executive who works on Montgomery Street and has a fine suburban home in Marin and by the truck driver who lives in the blighted Fillmore area, now fast disappearing before the swinging power-driven steel balls that are the symbols of the urban redevelopment program. Both the truck driver and the businessman were recently asked by an inquiring newspaper reporter, "What is the biggest difference between Los Angeles and San Francisco?"

The truck driver said, "Los Angeles is just a big hick town. San Francisco is more metropolitan, like New York or Paris. And down south the people are small-minded and too involved in their personal lives. Here they're more broad-minded and more cultured." The businessman said, "Los Angeles isn't a city in the sense that it's a single unit like San Francisco. Los Angeles is just a conglomeration of small towns. San Francisco has a more cosmopolitan air, like the European cities."

Broad-minded, cultured, cosmopolitan—all part of the image San Franciscans have of their city. The adjective *sophisticated* should be added, and usually is.

San Franciscans feel that their city has a distinctive tone. It likes to be known as friendly and easygoing, but frowns on backslapping. It considers itself informal but draws a line against slacks for women and loud sport shirts for men in the downtown area.

One way to sense this tone is to pass some day during lunch time the Crown-Zellerbach office building (1 Bush Street at Market), a graceful twenty-story tower of glass and stone and aluminum, the city's proudest architectural jewel. Sitting on the ramps, against the stone slab at the center of the building and in the landscaped garden area are hundreds of young men in Brooks Brothers suits and young women in fashionable wool dresses calmly and leisurely eating their lunch. Paper bags are in their laps, sandwiches in hand, a container of milk or a bottle of Coke nearby. The scene suggests San Francisco's curious blend of formality and informality. It also suggests the widespread conviction that the city's beauties are to be enjoyed as well as seen. There are no keep-off-the-grass signs in San Francisco parks, no prohibitions against sitting or lounging in the shade of the city's finest office building.

San Francisco's atmosphere and character are as important to the truck driver as to the businessman, and he feels himself as much a part of the city. San Francisco is a union town, and every waitress wears a union button on her crisp uniform. The city's working people are relatively well paid—a fact that accounts for the higher price of some goods and services. Labor is a major factor in San Francisco, with union representatives on city commissions and most civic organizations and drives.

Many San Franciscans enjoy having friends and acquaintances from a diverse cross section of the city's population. Although the housing shortage is driving young middle-income families into the suburbs, San Francisco is not yet a city of the very rich and the very poor. Ethnic, social, and class groupings are not yet stratified to the point of no communication and no understanding.

San Franciscans are proud of the variety of their city, of the multitude of its nationalities with their differing foods, customs, and traditions; the Chamber of Commerce understandably makes quite a point of this. San Francisco is a city in which diversity is encouraged. It imposes no crushing conformity in morals or opinions or way of life.

When San Franciscans reflect on their city's finest moment, a good many recall the founding of the United Nations in 1945, when the flags of fifty countries fluttered from the stage of the Opera House. They brighten when visiting Japanese or Russian or Italian or Burmese dignitaries exclaim, as they often do, that this is the city in which they feel most at home. They like to feel that theirs is a world city, and they aren't far wrong.

Types, Stereotypes . . .

Newspaper writers enjoy searching for the typical San Franciscan and often conjure up the image of a suave, sophisticated woman, trim, lovely, and beautifully dressed to her white gloves and her smart hat. This stereotype, although more flattering than that of the harried, brusque New Yorker hanging onto a subway strap with one hand and reading an elaborately folded newspaper with the other, is no more accurate.

Alas for the image, hats and white gloves are fast disappearing as part of the ensemble of the smartly dressed San Francisco woman. Or maybe, as some commentators on the city's mores lament, there are now fewer smartly dressed San Francisco women. In any case, San Franciscans won't fit into any common mold.

The Pacific Heights society matron, patron of the fine arts who never misses an opening night at the Opera House and helps run rummage sales to support the Symphony, is a San Francisco type. So is the longshoreman with his white cap and black jeans, cocky, well paid, and respected. So is the North Beach Bohemian who works in an office or in a warehouse all day and comes down to the City Lights Bookshop in the evening to read his poetry. So is the Chinatown doctor who speaks flawless Harvard English with his Caucasian friends but can easily shift to fluent Cantonese or Mandarin. There are many San Francisco types—but no typical San Franciscan.

. . . and Characters

San Francisco prides itself more on its characters than on its types. It has always had a soft spot for mavericks and nonconformists, whether wise men or fools, good or deliciously wicked. San Francisco characters don't *have* to be eccentrics. But they do have to be a little different. The city is sufficiently tolerant to appreciate them, and sufficiently small that they don't get lost in anonymous vastness. Its current taste in characters is catholic enough to encompass a tycoon, a labor leader, and a former madam.

Cigar-smoking, hard-boiled Louis Lurie had to overcome the handicap of a painfully banal success story. Lurie used to sell newspapers in front of the Chicago skyscraper he subsequently bought along with choice bits of San Francisco real estate. Asked for the secret of his rags-to-riches epic, he mutters only, "Never give them change." Lurie has been saved from the mediocrity of the typical multimillionaire Horatio Alger hero by one endearing vice. He is stagestruck, always gambling heavily on theatrical productions and making a point of having a Broadway celebrity or two at the table in Jack's Restaurant where he has had his lunch for the past forty years or so. When he turned seventy-two, the government made a public ceremony of awarding him the first of the monthly social security checks due him. Nobody squawked.

Considered a wild man and a firebrand in the East, Harry Bridges is frequently praised in San Francisco newspaper editorials as a constructive labor leader. One of the city's most enduring characters, Bridges has managed to be himself and get away with it. Of course, the local strength of his Longshoremen's & Warehousemen's Union (which is considerable) hasn't hurt him. A master at the bargaining table, Bridges is equally at home at the race track. An avowed radical, he is also a registered Republican. A union militant, he has always been immaculately dressed, even when a formidable labor rival affected white cap and zippered windbreaker. A public advocate of Marxian economics, he is generally credited by the city's press with stabilizing the decidedly capitalist waterfront industries. Several deportation trials have failed to undermine his influence. Bridges goes right on through the years praising Soviet Russia and winning spectacular gains for his longshoremen.

Survivor of a vanished age of glamorous wickedness is Mrs. Sally Stanford, once the town's most successful madam. Plying her profession openly when it was sanctioned by local custom and complaisant police, she refused to retire into mousy obscurity when it was prohibited. Mrs. Stanford was accepted by at least some of the city's more elite social circles and even married temporarily into the celebrated Gump family of San Francisco merchants, whose art and gift shop is the city's most exclusive and expensive. Public opinion rallied behind Sally a few years ago, when she opened a bar and restaurant on the Sausalito waterfront and was forced into guerrilla warfare with bluenosed authorities who questioned her moral character and tried to take away her liquor license. Plump, middle-aged, graciously bawdy, she still presides over the Valhalla in Sausalito, furnished with a raucous parrot, overstuffed furniture, and other trimmings that never fail to remind San Franciscans of the days when vice flourished in Victorian splendor. And she continues to display a heart of gold. Her Pacific Heights mansion is usually teeming with down-and-outers asking for a handout or a job, and Sally rarely says no.

Mayor George Christopher is a Horatio Alger type with a San Francisco flavor. His is the traditional immigrant epic, the poor boy brought over from Greece who rose to the top and became the owner of the successful dairy that bears his name. He didn't forget other poor little boys, and his dairy regularly gives out free football tickets to Kezar Stadium, a fact that didn't cost him any votes when he entered politics. Christopher's adherence to San Francisco tradition is more zealous than that of many descendants of the Argonauts of '49. When a lady in slacks invaded City Hall, it was Christopher who escorted her out with an invitation to return when more suitably attired. Christopher most enjoys his role of San Francisco's official greeter and ambassador-at-large, which has inadvertently made him an expert on U.S.–Soviet relations. When Soviet Premier Khrushchev's visit to the United States in 1959 seemed precariously near collapse after a chilly reception in Los Angeles, Christopher came to the rescue by invoking the city's reputation of being polite to all its guests, Communist or capitalist. After warming Khrushchev up with some jovial joshing on the limousine ride from the airport, Christopher quite won the Russian's heart with a gallant gesture. At the City Hall welcome, Mrs. Khrushchev was pushed to the rear by the crowd. "Tula," the mayor said to Mrs. Christopher, "will you please find Mrs. Khrushchev?"

Mrs. Christopher brought Mrs. Khrushchev forward and presented her a big bouquet of flowers. The premier beamed.

Beniamino Bufano, a tiny wisplike man whose heroic statues are among the city's most distinctive adornments, gets into the newspapers more frequently than most politicians and businessmen. Unfortunately, the occasion is usually the city's rejection of one of his statues. Bufano's striking figure of World Peace and his Sun Yat-sen are prominently displayed at International Airport. But his attempts to give the city a great massive figure of its patron saint, St. Francis, have been repeatedly and not always graciously turned down (see p. 127). He is tolerated rather than respected or honored. This may be because Bufano is a serious man who expects to be taken seriously, whereas San Francisco generally expects artists to live up to the role of flamboyant, devil-may-care Bohemians. It may also be because San Francisco, which makes a great point of loving art (and really does), is sometimes cruel to its artists.

Three Conundrums

Why can't a city, which is gracious host to the whole world, get along with its neighbors only a few miles away? It doesn't, and the only answer seems to be that San Francisco's vaunted cosmopolitanism is seasoned with a strong dash of chauvinism which is charming at times but can also be a decided nuisance.

In the early days of San Francisco there was an earthquake which hit the city hard but left Oakland untouched across the Bay. Bret Harte explained this phenomenon very simply. "There are some things," he said, "even the earth won't swallow." This attitude has not completely died out in the intervening century. The Oakland Chamber of Commerce retaliates by referring to its environs as "the Mainland," thus expressing contempt for the deplorable geologic and historic freak by which San Francisco was built on a peninsula of sand and rock instead of across the Bay where it should have been. San Francisco and Oakland have quarreled for years over such matters as the locale of another Bay bridge and the creation of a port authority with effective powers.

The cities and towns of the Bay Area, knit together by geography and self-interest, are engaged in almost constant internecine strife. They unite only occasionally for the larger civil war between Northern and Southern California, between San Francisco and Los Angeles. The practical result is that the Bay Area, which should be ranked one of the country's three or four great metropolitan areas, is plagued by an appalling lack of planning in smog control, transportation, and other problems which cut across local boundaries.

How explain the indisputable fact that year after year the Golden City of the West has one of the highest suicide and alcoholism rates in the country? The usual answer is that this is Land's End. Here come the seekers, the restless, the discontented, the misfits. If they fail here, they have no other refuge except in a bottle or in the Bay. A possibly irrelevant historic note is that during the city's gold-rush period a thousand disappointed gold-hunters killed themselves every year. But maybe the same thing happens with those who hunt the more elusive goals of happiness and fulfillment. They have no place farther to go. And maybe the city itself, in some obscure way, does let them down.

Why did Willie Mays find it difficult to buy a home in a city that applauds his home runs and its own lack of color or race prejudice? There is no answer to that one—except that San Francisco doesn't always live up to its professions or to its own image of itself.

Cool, Gray City

San Franciscans may generally be divided into three groups: those who turn to the financial pages when they open their newspapers, those who check the athletic fortunes of the Giants or the Forty-Niners, and those who look first for the weather report. The latter are by far the most numerous. San Franciscans wait impatiently every morning to read the almost identical communique: "Early morning fog near the ocean, clearing in the afternoon."

In most places the weather is only a conversational gambit. It is generally recognized that there is little one can do with it except close an awkward pause. In San Francisco the weather is a serious matter, to be discussed at length with family and close friends. Although wise men long ago said all there was to be said on the subject, San Franciscans keep trying.

Mark Twain once muttered, "The coldest winter I ever spent was a summer in San Francisco." Perhaps the definitive word was spoken by William's *Pacific Tourist* in 1877: "The climate of San Francisco is peculiar and cannot be described in a few words." Yet this early guidebook did offer some helpful suggestions, among them: "There are few days in San Francisco when it is safe to dispense with outer wrappings, and when a fire is not needed morning and evening."

San Franciscans stubbornly ignored this good advice. For generations they maintained that central heating was unnecessary in a city with such gentle climate. As a result, they generally shivered in the morning and evening. Furnaces, steam heat, and radiators, commonplace elsewhere, were considered contrary to nature and local custom. The only concession they would make to the facts was an occasional fireplace or gas heater. Only in relatively recent years has central heating been installed in new buildings. San Franciscans still defy the injunction to wear "outer wrappings," if by these are meant topcoats. Heavy overcoats are as unknown as the light summer suits misguided visitors bring along.

Accustomed to brisk year-round weather, San Franciscans begin to swelter when the thermometer hits 70. They wilt when it gets over 80. Anything over 85 is worth an afternoon-paper headline, while 90 or above is usually an all-time record-breaker still good for box-car type in the morning papers. San Franciscans, who take cold winds and fog with equanimity, melt in the presence of what people in other places consider an ordinary summer day.

Transplanted Easterners miss the seasons, the extremes of summer and winter. They complain of the sameness of the weather, missing the obvious fact that the more San Francisco's climate is the same, the more it changes. San Franciscans are weather-watchers because they never know what will happen next. A warm day in January or February is as likely or unlikely as one in July or August.

San Franciscans feed the myth of dull and routine weather by boasting of their natural air-contitioning plant, meaning that the surrounding water cools the summers and warms the winters. They sometimes refer to the Bay as a natural thermostat. All this suggests a flawless push-button machine, which is not quite the way it works. The city's weather apparatus of ocean and Bay, valleys and mountains, produces several sharply contrasting kinds of weather in the course of a normal day—or even within several square miles of city area. The weather can be quite different in neighborhoods separated by only a few blocks and a hill or two. And it is generally more orthodox in the suburbs on every side, a fact which may explain their popularity among Philistines.

One of the peculiarities of the city is that its working people early took over many of the warmer spots, while the wealthy showed a preference for the fog belts. The fine homes in the Sea Cliff and St. Francis Wood areas are shrouded in perpetual mist, but far more modest dwellings are located in what its boosters call "the sunny Mission" or "the warm belt," which might possibly illustrate the humble wisdom of the poor. Or it might point up the aristocratic tastes of the rich in appreciating the city's greatest glory.

Even more than weather-watchers, San Franciscans are fog-

watchers. It is sometimes said that there are only a few days a year
when the sun does not shine somewhere in San Francisco. It should
be added that the days are even fewer when there is no windswept
fog. Winter or summer, there is fog. The white summer fog rolls
through the Golden Gate and over the hills in the morning, retreats
before the sun, and rolls back in the afternoon. In winter the fog is
even heavier, thicker. Sometimes the capricious tule fog, which
forms in the tule marshes off the Bay, swirls over the city, covering
whole areas with an impenetrable blanket and leaving others untouched.

For San Franciscans the fog provides the variety of esthetic experience furnished elsewhere by the color display of leaves in
autumn or the white mantle of snow in winter. The fog hides the
blemishes of the city and clothes its drab buildings in a luminous
haze. It creates a symphony of foghorns. Almost daily it produces
a noiseless fireworks over the Golden Gate as it takes a multitude of
shapes and shades in combat with the retreating sun. George
Sterling long ago wrote a poem, "The Cool, Gray City of Love,"
which rendered the city's final judgment of the fog:

> Tho the dark be cold and blind,
> Yet her sea-fog's touch is kind. . . .

The IBM Machine and the Poet

The cult of bigness is so pervasive that San Francisco has been
reluctant to admit, even to itself, one of its most endearing features
—it is a relatively small city as cities go. But the electronic com-
puting machines used to tabulate the 1960 census figures flashed the
implacable figures. San Francisco had fallen below the 750,000
mark. It was surpassed (the humiliation of it!) by Houston.

The trend has been in the making for a long time. Anybody who
takes a good look from any hill will be able to figure out what is
happening. Bounded by ocean, Golden Gate, and Bay, San Francisco has no living space for a serious population explosion. It has
been beneficiary and victim of the suburban trend that has affected
almost every American city.

While San Francisco hasn't grown, the surrounding Bay Area
has—and very rapidly. Besides, San Francisco can't be confined to
its city and county limits. It is both a state of mind and an
indeterminate but extensive chunk of Northern California. It remains *the City* for suburbanites and exurbanites for fifty miles
around, for Stanford University professors in Palo Alto to the south
and for Petaluma chicken-ranchers to the north. When they and

the residents of scores of other towns and communities talk about going out for dinner and a show, they aren't talking about the nightspots of Palo Alto, Petaluma, San Rafael, or El Cerrito. San Francisco remains the heart of a vast metropolitan area.

All the same, it hurt that the city's population was long ago outstripped by Los Angeles and was now being overtaken by crude Texas oil towns. San Franciscans tried to comfort themselves with the thought that their city had shown some growth, especially during the war years. As the fateful 1960 census approached, Chamber of Commerce estimates suggested that the city's population would show a reassuring increase—nothing spectacular perhaps, but solid and respectable, at least an offering to the unchallenged gods of gigantism.

Then came the stunning announcement that San Francisco's population had unmistakably declined. The city immediately denounced an obvious statistical fraud which proved only that liars figure and that IBM machines can go on the blink. Good citizens stepped forward to reveal that they had not been counted and to expose the inefficiency of the census-takers. Wholesale omissions in certain neighborhoods were charged. A small army of volunteer checkers was summoned to confront the government bureaucrats with the truth.

But suddenly the checkers withdrew from the fray. The mayor and the Chamber of Commerce lapsed into pained silence. Sadly the city licked its wounds, the pain assuaged only slightly when the Census Bureau later softened its initial blow by adding the city's absentee sailors, travelers, and merchant seamen. The fact remained that San Francisco *had* lost about 30,000 population. The newspapers reported that it would forfeit millions in state and federal funds allocated on the basis of population. A loss of representation in the state legislature was inevitable.

Los Angeles' victory was so complete it did not even bother to exult. More galling were the pretensions of a hot, sleepy little town fifty miles to the south in the Santa Clara Valley; San Jose, the center of growing industries in what were only recently prune and apricot orchards, passed the 200,000 mark and announced that within two decades it would overtake San Francisco.

Drinking their lunch at Shanty Malone's bar or eating it heartily at Schroeder's, San Franciscans speculated moodily whether their city would in the next fifty years become another Carmel, a quaint village on the ocean, with shops, tourists, motels, and sailboats—while Los Angeles would explode inexorably northward across the mountains, toward the Oregon border, and perhaps into Canada.

Then Herb Caen, the city's poet laureate in prose—newspaper columnist, chronicler of the San Francisco characters, and one of them himself—thundered in prophetic rage at the faint of heart. The news from the IBM machines was a triumph rather than a disaster, Caen proclaimed. To those who had left the city, he said —good riddance! To those who remained, he said—rejoice! With Caen's help, the city discovered that its secret shame, once revealed, turned into blessing. San Franciscans realized that they enjoyed the advantage of a city without the curse of gigantism.

San Franciscans could still live in their city without being engulfed in its vastness. They could still get to work without cultivating the sinister techniques of the subway quarterback. They could still visit friends anywhere in the city or around it without driving fifty miles or making a lost week end out of a social call. They could, within thirty minutes to two hours' driving, get to any number of beaches and wooded parks for a Sunday picnic. They had within easy access an almost inexhaustible variety of restaurants, night clubs, art galleries, concert halls, and theaters.

Of course, they grumbled about parking, traffic, the public transportation system, the high cost of decent housing. And there was plenty to complain about. Bumper-to-bumper autos were turning downtown streets into an impassible morass. The parking lot and the freeway were encroaching on the city, cutting deep gashes in business and residential areas. Medium-rent housing was almost unobtainable. San Francisco had problems. But they were not yet out of control. They were not insoluble.

Quietly, San Franciscans began to concede that one of the things they liked most about the city was that it was not too big, too overcrowded, too overextended into an infinite space of tenements and suburbs. The IBM machine and the poet finally made it possible for the city to face the reality, to complete the image of itself. San Francisco is, in truth, a small city. The adjective is relative. The noun is not.

2: JOURNEY TO NOSTALGIA

A Passion for the Past

SAN FRANCISCO has a passion for history and tradition, for legends and mementos of the gold rush and of the Victorian splendor that followed, for the old and slightly weatherbeaten in architecture, furniture, and interior decoration. Visitors from Europe or even from New York and Boston are sometimes amused.

"What history?" a British lady author recently snorted. After all, San Francisco was just a village before 1849 and only a booming wild frontier town for years after that. Unabashed, San Franciscans go right on cherishing old gingerbread houses with pointed arches and battlements, restoring battered brick buildings erected by the Argonauts, turning sailing vessels into museums, and dotting the city with metal historical plaques.

San Francisco's attachment to the past may be in part the ostentation of the *nouveau riche*. Having acquired history so recently, San Francisco flaunts what it has. But there is really more to it than that. Quite a lot of history, all of it gaudy and some of it melodramatic, has been crammed into little more than a hundred years. Because it is so recent, much of it is within the ken of old-timers who experienced it themselves or heard of it from parents and grandparents who came around the Horn in clipper ships or across the Plains in covered wagons. It is still part of their lives.

Of course, San Francisco's penchant for crystal chandeliers and red damask drapes is also in part yearning for vanished glories and supposedly better times. But the city's history is more than a decoration for the drab present. Because it all happened within a century, San Francisco's history has shaped the character of the city.

The very crudity of the past is in part responsible for San Francisco's worldliness today. Because it remained a recurrent frontier for decades, with one mining and financial boom following another and with new pioneers constantly pouring in, San Francisco never got a chance to establish a fixed and premature orthodoxy; new ideas and panaceas always got a hearing.

The city's receptivity to culture may have started with the awe of the frontiersman and the new mining millionaire for the finer things in life and with their thirst for something beyond gold. Persecution of the Chinese in San Francisco and of Mexican and Chilean miners were the prelude to today's generally good race relations. Violent strikes and labor disputes for more than fifty years preceded San Francisco's development into a union stronghold where a more-or-less peaceful labor-management situation prevails. By the time the character of the city of today was formed the violence had been spent. San Francisco acquired sophistication without the weariness or boredom of old age.

Bittersweet Walk

One way to start a journey into San Francisco's past painlessly is with an afternoon cocktail at the **Happy Valley Bar** of the **Sheraton-Palace Hotel** (Market and New Montgomery streets). The name of the bar suggests the peaceful memories of a vanished past. Actually, it refers to the old name of the area at the southern end of Montgomery Street where there was a tent settlement of impoverished immigrants in 1849 and where later arose the splendor of the Palace.

Dark wood paneling and crystal chandeliers evoke San Francisco's golden era, the times of opulence when mining millionaires and their ladies drove their carriages into the great court of the old Palace, surrounded by seven tiers of galleries topped by a magnificent opaque glass dome. Around the bar you will see on the walls sketches of old ships and ornate mansions, playbills of a vanished era, photographs of the actors and the singers and other greats who came to San Francisco and, of course, stayed at the Palace. On the

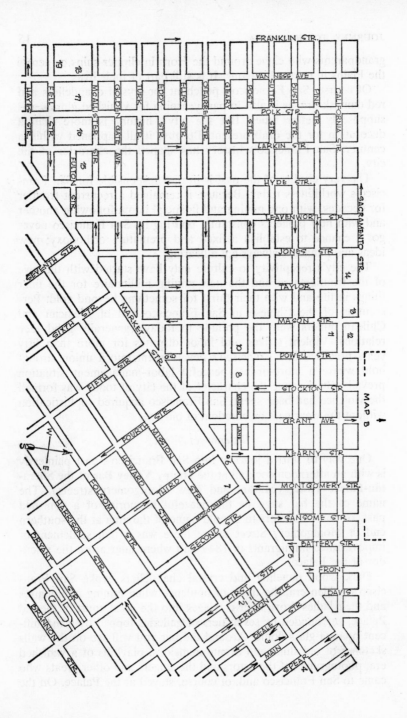

walls are also murals by Antonio Sotomayor, recalling the time
when the Cliff House on the beach was a place of faintly wicked
gaiety and when families would drive on Sundays to Woodward's
Garden near the old Mission, a private park with flowered terraces
and a lake, with a band platform and entertainment.

Dominating one of the murals is a painting of Emperor Norton,
San Francisco's favorite madman, complete with blue uniform, gold
epaulettes, and plumed beaver hat. The Emperor was born plain
Joshua Abraham Norton, a British Jew who was a rifleman in South
Africa and a trader in Brazil before he came to San Francisco in
1849 with a modest fortune. He invested his money in rice, operated the West's first rice mill, and prospered. But a few years later
he overreached himself by trying to corner the rice market, pushing
prices up from fifteen to sixty cents a pound. In the midst of his
speculation, three ships loaded with rice came into the harbor.
Prices plummeted and Norton was finished.

For several years he disappeared from San Francisco. When he
returned it was as an emperor. One day in September 1859 he
walked into the office of the *Evening Bulletin* and handed the editor
a document in which he did "declare and proclaim himself Emperor
of these United States" and summoned a convocation of the representatives of the states to "make such alterations in the existing
laws of the Union as may ameliorate the evils under which the
country is laboring." The whimsical editor published the proclamation, and as a reward the Emperor named the *Bulletin* his official
publication. Later it incurred his displeasure by burying one of his
state papers among the classified ads and he switched, first to the
Alta California and later to the *Examiner*.

For twenty-one years the city played along with Norton's grand
delusion that he ruled over the United States and Mexico. He paid
no fare on streetcars, ate free in sumptuous restaurants, ordered his
regal uniforms from the best tailors in town—he was very fussy

---

MAP A: DOWNTOWN AREA

 1. South Park
 2. Bay Bridge Terminal
 3. On-and-off ramps to freeway
 4. Rincon Annex Post Office
 5. Zellerbach Building
 6. Lotta's Fountain
 7. Palace Hotel
 8. Union Square
 9. Cable-car turntable
10. St. Francis Hotel.

11. Mark Hopkins Hotel
12. Fairmount Hotel
13. Huntington Park
14. Grace Cathedral
15. Main Library
16. Civic Center Plaza
17. City Hall
18. San Francisco Museum of Art
19. Opera House

about the royal attire, although he lived in a small room in a shabby boardinghouse. When he adopted two homeless mongrels, Bummer and Lazarus, the dogs received treatment almost as regal as his own. They sat in state with the Emperor at the royal box in the theater. Bummer's untimely death was commemorated by Mark Twain in an obituary for the Virginia City *Territorial Enterprise*. The Emperor issued currency with his signature and picture which was supplied by a friendly printer and accepted at its face value. Great financiers conferred solemnly with him and gave him a coin or two at the end. Some thirty thousand persons turned out for the Emperor's funeral in 1880 at the old Masonic Cemetery, and when his grave was moved to a new resting place in the 1930s there was another impressive ceremony. The municipal band played appropriate tunes and Mayor Angelo Rossi made a speech.

The Emperor was, of course, in part a creation of the newspapers, and the San Francisco *Chronicle* has continued the old tradition. It runs a promotional Emperor Norton treasure hunt each spring and thousands of San Franciscans dig up beaches and hills looking for one of the Emperor's medallions, which they can cash in for two thousand dollars. "In what other city," Robert Louis Stevenson once asked, "would a harmless madman who supposed himself emperor of the two Americas have been so fostered and encouraged?"

The story of the man who built the Palace Hotel is almost as fantastic as Norton's. There were always some people who questioned the Emperor's madness, suspecting that the old man had latched onto a good thing. But there was none who doubted the sanity of William C. Ralston. He was a solid man, but never stuffy; everybody called him Billy. He went far in a hurry after arriving in 1853 as an agent for a New York steamship company. He became treasurer of the Bank of California and San Francisco's leading financier. Since the bank controlled some of the richest properties in the Comstock Lode, it flourished with the great Nevada mining boom and so did its treasurer.

Billy Ralston was a big spender, but so were the other new millionaires. He built a $140,000 home on the fringes of Nob Hill and an even more expensive villa in suburban Belmont. He was brash and daring, something of a plunger who invested heavily in real estate operations that didn't always work out and in local industries that didn't always flourish. But this, too, was in the spirit of the times. He was a man with big ideas, and a lot of them had to do with building up San Francisco as well as Ralston.

In 1869 the Bank of California ran dangerously short of cash. If the story got out, the bank would be wiped out. Ralston appealed personally to President Grant to permit him to exchange the ample gold bullion in his bank for the gold coin in the San Francisco Subtreasury. The government turned him down; it was holding tight in the uneasy financial situation all over the country. In this crisis, Ralston acted. One September night in 1869, Ralston and three companions walked through the deserted financial district from his bank to the Subtreasury building. They staggered out with heavy bags of gold coin, returned with gold bullion. After several such trips, the Bank of California was amply stocked with gold coin. Depositors on hand for their money were quickly taken care of, and rumors about the bank subsided. Just how Ralston arranged to have doors and vaults of the Subtreasury conveniently opened was never explained.

A couple of years later two rough-looking miners came into Ralston's office with several large bags and a strange story. They had discovered a fabulous diamond mine. Ralston sent an emissary and later an engineer to examine this remarkable find. Both were fully satisfied; they saw diamonds, rubies, sapphires, and emeralds. Billy organized a company to exploit this unusual treasure-house, and many hard-headed businessmen invested. After he had paid over $300,000 to the two discoverers of the diamond bonanza, a curious scientist examined the mines and among other strange things found partially cut diamonds. The fraud was exposed. Ralston repaid all the investors. He lost a substantial fortune as a result of what has come to be known as "The Great Diamond Hoax." But his reputation remained solid.

Ralston became involved in building the Palace Hotel as the result of an unhappy real estate investment. He lost heavily on a scheme for extending Montgomery Street south to meet the Bay. After the street was cut through a sandhill for two blocks, local property owners refused to sell and blocked away further advance. New Montgomery Street stopped at Howard Street—and still stops there.

Undaunted, Billy Ralston decided to build one of the world's great hotels on his new street. Just why San Francisco needed a vast new hotel is somewhat unclear. The city had plenty of good hotels. Billy owned one of them, the Grand, across the street from the site of the new Palace.

As the foundation was laid and the mighty edifice began to rise, startling statistics were disclosed. The hotel would have eight hundred spacious rooms with fifteen-foot ceilings and cost no less than five million dollars. Billy made contracts with fifteen firms to get marble for 804 mantles, 900 washstands, and 40,000 square feet of pavement. He put in 755 noiseless water closets, arranged for 125 miles of wiring to connect new-fangled electric call buttons in each room. He ordered so much carpeting that W. & J. Sloane of New York opened a branch in San Francisco that has remained ever since. He supplied furniture from his own factory. He bought a ranch to supply oak flooring—but it turned out to have the wrong kind of oak.

A few weeks before the hotel was to open, the Bank of California crashed; its investments were overextended and it was too heavily involved in Nevada mining speculation. Billy Ralston went for his regular swim in the Bay from the Neptune Baths and never returned. But the Palace opened on schedule with a great banquet. Senator William Sharon, the Comstock mining millionaire who took over the ownership, stood on the second-floor balcony to address San Francisco's wealthiest and most prominent citizens and to pay tribute to "the proud and manly spirit of him who devised this magnificent structure."

It took years before the Palace paid off. Although many of its spacious rooms remained empty, the hotel became the city's showplace. Here were held the great banquets where new bonanza kings fumbled over their silverware and the fancy French menus. Here came King Pedro II of Brazil, King David Kalakaua of Hawaii, and assorted prizefighters, princes, and presidents. The Palace was still the city's great hotel when early in the morning of April 18, 1906, the guests, suddenly jolted out of their beds, dashed into the streets. Among them was Enrico Caruso, carrying a portrait of Theodore Roosevelt and wearing a towel around his throat. The elaborate fire-fighting system of the Palace failed to work. The hotel burned and was replaced in 1909 with the structure that still stands. Now it is called the Sheraton-Palace, part of a national chain, and it is no longer the biggest and most magnificent hotel in town. But it wears well the patina of past glories; its glass-roofed Palm Court and intricate iron balconies are still reminiscent of the old grandeur.

Pedestrians trying to make a green traffic light are not likely to linger over a tall, rather commonplace cast-iron fountain at the complex intersection of Market, Geary, and Kearny streets, one block west of the Sheraton-Palace. But to old-timers, **Lotta's Fountain,** set on a granite base with ornamented lion heads and weatherbeaten brass medallions depicting California scenes, evokes a flood of sentimental anecdotes and a torrent of great names.

The story begins in 1853 when the wicked city was titillated by the arrival of the notorious Lola Montez, the Spanish dancer and actress who had been the mistress of King Ludwig of Bavaria and was rewarded with the title of Countess of Landsfield. Wild applause greeted her famous spider dance, in which she vigorously shook whalebone and rubber spiders from her short dress and then just as vigorously stamped on them. Later that year Countess Lola received similar acclaim from the miners in the Grass Valley area.

There an eight-year-old miner's daughter, red-haired and black-eyed Lotta Crabtree, was introduced to the Countess. Lola was charmed by Lotta and taught her how to dance and sing. The young girl went on to become a sensational success. San Francisco was kind to her, showering her with gold as well as applause. To show her gratitude, Lotta donated this fountain to the city in 1875. She lived on long after that, to a ripe and comfortable old age supported by the income from real estate investments, while both she and her fountain faded into obscurity.

Then the old fountain became the locale in 1910 for the city's most sensational concert; a now timeworn bas-relief portrait of Luisa Tetrazzini was added to the cluttered base to commemorate the occasion.

The concert grew out of a clash of wills between the dazzling coloratura and Oscar Hammerstein, the all-powerful producer. Tetrazzini had made plans to sing in San Francisco on Christmas Eve. But Hammerstein announced she was under exclusive contract to sing for him and was due to perform in New York. He underestimated Tetrazzini, particularly when one of the great loves of her life—her romance with San Francisco—was at stake. This was the city that had first acclaimed her talent, and she would not let it down.

The two battled it out in the press. Hammerstein had prestige and some strong legal points. Tetrazzini had sentiment on her side. "I will sing in San Francisco if I have to sing there in the streets," she proclaimed in an angry statement, "for I know the streets of San Francisco are free. I never thought that I would be a street singer, but I want to do this for San Francisco, because this is the first place in the United States where I sang, and because I like San Francisco. San Francisco is my country."

So on Christmas Eve 1910 Luisa Tetrazzini appeared on a platform at Lotta's Fountain, wearing a trailing white gown, a broad-rimmed hat, white gloves, and carrying a white ostrich boa. A crowd estimated at between 100,000 and 250,000 thronged the busy streets in the early darkness while store windows glittered with ornaments and lights. She sang "I Would Linger in This Dream" and "The Last Rose of Summer." At the end tears were flowing freely while the crowd joined Tetrazzini in singing "Auld Lang Syne." On Christmas Eve 1960 several thousand sentimental San Franciscans turned out for a fiftieth-anniversary re-enactment of the scene with a young substitute Tetrazzini.

A longish four-block walk south from Lotta's Fountain will take you to **South Park** (off Third Street between Bryant and Brannan streets). It will take you through the fringes of Skid Row, past business buildings, pawn shops, run-down cafés, and a freeway exit to a quiet, oddly out-of-place wide street with a bedraggled patch of grassy park in the middle. Here are a couple of benches and a few sycamores and weeping willows. Both sides of the street are lined with battered old houses that somehow retain a frayed dignity, although they are only the modest successors to the great mansions that once stood there and must contend now with a scattering of small machine shops, hotels, and warehouses.

This street, once one of the most fashionable in young San Francisco, was the dream of George Gordon—who sometimes called himself Lord George, although he was the son of a middle-class Yorkshire family. In bawdy, brawling San Francisco he always played the role of the British gentleman. But he was quite able to take care of himself. Among other things, he was one of the city's smoothest talkers. He promoted his way to San Francisco by selling tickets to New Yorkers for a luxury voyage around Cape Horn to the gold fields. It is uncertain whether the battered old wreck he obtained for the would-be Argonauts ever got near San Francisco. Gordon made it overland with thirty thousand dollars he collected from his customers.

Lord George's first local project was building a two thousand-foot wharf into the Bay for Harry Meiggs, San Francisco's earliest big-time real estate operator. Honest Harry, as he was known, wound up owing eight hundred thousand dollars in bad debts and ran off one fine day to South America where he became a multimillionaire railroad builder. Unperturbed, Lord George went on to realize his scheme of erecting in San Francisco a fashionable London-type square surrounded by homes with marble steps and brass knockers, elegant homes with Sheraton furniture and Chinese vases, and English rose gardens.

The scheme worked. The houses were built, surrounded by iron grille fences. The Hearsts, the McAllisters, and other leading families moved there. Horsemen and horsewomen, properly attired,

cantered their silver-bridled steeds in the little park. Lord George
became rich. In due time, South Park declined first to a shabby
gentility and then in the end became a semi-slum area inhabited
mainly by Negro families. There the story would end, except for
one of those San Francisco legends which lingers around the names
of George Gordon and South Park and was later told in fictionalized
form by Gertrude Atherton, one of the city's romantic story-tellers.

The story starts before Lord George came to the United States
from England when he woke up one morning in bed with a pretty
but scheming Irish barmaid he had met in a Yorkshire pub. She
announced calmly that they had been married the night before while
the gentleman was in his cups. Gordon took his bride to San Francisco, regaling her on the way with tales of the wealth and luxury
they would find. There she discovered soon enough that the fabled
El Dorado was a rude mining camp with plank sidewalks and raucous saloons. She pleaded with Lord George to take her back to
Yorkshire. He refused. She announced that she was a secret alcoholic, and threatened to disgrace her husband with the fine society
folk with whom he consorted. He still refused, and went on making
money in real estate.

When a baby girl was born to the unhappy couple, Lord George
doted on his little Nellie. Mrs. Gordon was jealous, and took her
revenge. As one writer of San Franciscana put it, "Plotting and
scheming with the fiendish cunning of the mentally unbalanced,
she commenced to put drops of whiskey into the infant's food." By
the time Nellie Gordon was seventeen, she was a confirmed alcoholic. Lord George sent her to a boarding school. But the indomi-
table Mrs. Gordon smuggled bottles of whiskey to her inside bun-
dles of laundry. Nellie married a ship's surgeon who shared her
weakness. She died in her early twenties—San Francisco's first
born-and-bred alcoholic. Lord George achieved fame and fortune
in San Francisco, but never happiness. He died a few years later of
a broken heart.

If you are tired of the cloying sentimentality of some San Francisco legends, you can find an effective astringent in the **Refregier
Murals** (Rincon Annex Post Office, Mission Street between Spear
and Steuart). The Post Office stands on Rincon Hill, which was
partially leveled to make way for the approaches to the Bay Bridge.
Rincon Hill was once a fancy residential district rivaling George
Gordon's long-vanished project. You can get here in a brisk fifteen-
minute walk from South Park, north on Third Street to Mission

Street, then east on Mission to the Post Office. Or you can take in the murals while visiting the Embarcadero; it is only two blocks from the Ferry Building to the Post Office.

In any case, don't miss these bold, dramatic murals by Anton Refregier. They are eminently worth while both as art and history. In a distinctly individual modern style they present a broad sweep of San Francisco history, emphasizing much of the turbulence and turmoil. There is little sentiment in the Refregier murals, and no sentimentality. But there is plenty of excitement and drama.

Here are San Francisco Bay Indians, more slender and graceful as they paddle a canoe made out of tule leaves than we are accustomed to think from the early Spanish accounts, which describe them as slothful and lazy. Here is a cold, bearded conquistador with a calculating dream of empire in his eye and his hand on a globe of the world. Here are Portola's men looking down on the Bay, and here are lean padres and Indians working at the Mission Dolores. A bearded Russian with a gun on his knees sits on a rock near the stockade of Fort Ross, reliving the time when the Czar's empire extended within fifty miles of San Francisco.

The agony and the boisterousness of the gold-rush era is recaptured. A party of hungry men and women, treking over the snow by covered wagon to California, clusters around a man with an Indian arrow in his breast. Greedy, ragged, bearded prospectors, one with a villainous patch over his eye, exult over a nugget of gold at Sutter's Fort. Men and women arrive by steamship in San Francisco. Workingmen parade by torchlight; Chinese laborers move earth and stone to build the Central Pacific Railroad westward toward the ocean.

Here is James King, editor of the *Evening Bulletin,* being shot down by James Casey. In a corner of the same panel top-hatted vigilantes with guns watch one of the hangings that followed. The role of the vigilantes has been debated for a century; Refregier took the negative. Here are Union and Confederate sympathizers clashing in the streets during the turbulence of the late 1850s when San Francisco teetered between the two sides. Angry workingmen are shown rioting against the Chinese, agitated by demagogues to regard them as the source of unemployment and low wages. But Refregier notes the warning by an early labor leader that attacks on the Chinese are "antagonistic to the principles of American liberty."

In a panel devoted to San Francisco's golden days of art and culture, the celebrated Adah Isaacs Menken is shown lashed to a horse, riding across the stage in flesh-colored tights in her sensational role as the star of *Mazeppa*. The same panel depicts the better-remembered figures of Robert Louis Stevenson, Mark Twain, Frank Norris, Luther Burbank, and the young Jack London. In vivid contrast to the lightness of this scene are the somber subjects that follow—the earthquake, the fire, the reconstruction.

Here are some of the stormy San Francisco labor wars, scenes that helped create controversy around the murals for years. Here is a bitter portrayal of the story of Tom Mooney, shown being sentenced to jail by sinister-looking perjurers, one with his hand on a Bible. Here is a straw boss picking a longshoreman out of the shape-up with one hand, accepting a bribe with the other. A labor leader, strongly resembling Harry Bridges, is speaking to serried ranks of white-capped longshoremen standing at attention for their dead in the 1934 strike.

Against the slight pale figure of Joseph Baerman Strauss, the great designer of the Golden Gate Bridge, loom up the great girders of the bridges spanning the Bay. Then follow scenes of the war years, the big guns of the Allies defeating the Nazi mailed fist, helmeted welders with acetylene torches building ships, a family-of-nations group to represent the Four Freedoms, and finally the United Nations conference of 1945 in San Francisco.

It is little wonder that the murals stirred controversy. Refregier fully paid his respects to the seamy side of San Francisco history. Missing are San Francisco's Victorian splendors and all the romantic and whimsical tales it has cherished through the years. There are no Emperor Nortons here and no cable cars. This is serious art and serious, critical history. But out of it emerges a sense of the city's violent past, a feeling of its vitality and strength. The fact that the murals were retained, despite a massive campaign to remove them (see p. 126), is now also part of San Francisco history, indicating that the city has grown up some since the scenes depicted by Refregier.

Ride to the Top

A ride up to the vanished splendors of **Nob Hill** might wind up an afternoon's tour of the past. It will also give you a chance to ride the **California Street Cable Car** (walk north from the Rincon Annex Post Office to the terminal at Market, California, and Drumm streets).

This ride may not be quite so dramatic as the one up Powell Street. There aren't as many sharp turns, and since the car is two-ended there is no turntable you can help push. But the ride up the hill is spectacular enough, past the gleaming new Bethlehem Steel building at 100 California, where the Vigilance Committee of 1856 held sway in its battle with city officials at Fort Gunnybags, past the balconied and handsome John Hancock Insurance building, past the edge of the old produce market, through the financial district, through Chinatown while the cable car keeps climbing until you can look down on the Bay and the bridge.

After having clanged your way through the business district where the tycoons of old San Francisco once ruled, you can see the hill where their mansions vied with each other in exuberant display. Collis Huntington of the railroad Big Four used this cable car regularly. It was a very democratic way for the wily Huntington, who cajoled and bullied and bribed Central Pacific legislation through Congress, to reach the front door of his Italian-marble palace. Huntington's widow bequeathed the palace to the city. The mansion is long gone. But you can walk where it stood at **Huntington Park** (California, Taylor, and Sacramento streets), on gravel walks past neat shrubbery hedges.

You can't see Charles Crocker's mansion either. It was burned down by the fire of 1906 and the family gave the land to the Episcopal Church, and for decades there has slowly been brought to completion here the soaring edifice of **Grace Cathedral** (California, Taylor, Sacramento, and Jones).

Crocker, the hard-driving supervisor of Central Pacific's epic push to put the tracks east over the Sierras to Promontory Point, Utah, was determined to build the most palatial of all the Nob Hill palaces on this choice square bounded by four streets. But he ran into another determined man, an obscure Chinese known only as Mr. Yung, who owned a little house on a twenty-five-foot strip of the property on Sacramento Street and wouldn't sell for less than thirty thousand dollars. Crocker wouldn't buy at that price. He built his mansion anyway, but he surrounded the house of his distasteful neighbor on three sides with a forty-foot fence—which soon became known as the spite fence.

A favorite pastime of San Franciscans was to go up Nob Hill to look at Charley Crocker's fence and try to take home a piece as a souvenir. Dennis Kearney, the rabid anti-Chinese agitator of those times, on this occasion rallied to the defense of Mr. Yung. He led thousands of angry workingmen up Nob Hill to show their protest against this symbol of the arrogance of the railroad tycoon.

Only one of the old mansions survived the fire and still stands, the $1.5-million Connecticut-brownstone residence built by James G. Flood, of the Nevada mining Big Four. Flood had been one of the owners of the Auction Lunch and Saloon near the Stock Exchange. While the financiers of the day ate a delicious fish stew, Flood and his partner, W. S. O'Brien, picked up valuable stock-market tips. They invested in Comstock Lode stock and with two young miners, John W. Mackay and James G. Fair, rivaled the railroad Big Four in wealth. Jim Flood was no polished gentleman, but he aspired to gentility. He built a thirty-thousand-dollar brass fence around his mansion, and it is said that one servant had the sole job of keeping it shiny and bright at all times.

Flood would have been pleased that his old mansion has for many years been the headquarters of San Francisco's exclusive and aristo-cratic **Pacific Union Club** (northwest corner California and Mason streets). It is quiet and exceedingly respectable inside; you can oc-casionally see an elderly gentleman in a leather chair reading a newspaper. Of course, no women are admitted into this sanctum.

Two luxury hotels across the street from each other at California and Mason, the **Fairmont** and the **Mark Hopkins,** recall the names of other Nob Hill millionaires. Bonanza Jim Fair was going to build a mansion even more splendid than all the others. But he never got around to finishing it. On its foundations his daughter Tessie undertook the erection of a grand hotel to memorialize her father. The Fairmont was badly damaged by the fire; only the walls remained standing. But under the direction of Stanford White, the most celebrated architect of his time, the hotel was reconstructed and reopened in 1907. Crystal chandeliers, rich carpeting and draperies suggest the luxury of the nabobs. Mark Hopkins' widow presented his mansion to the San Francisco Art Association and here were held for years the extravagant Mardi Gras balls. When the hotel was put up in 1926, gold bathroom fixtures in some of the tower suites recalled the sybaritic taste in which the Hopkins mansion was furnished.

The nabobs were not always comfortable on Nob Hill, despite homes stuffed with the most expensive Victorian furniture and with antiques and *objets d'art* imported by the boatload from Europe. The mob brought up by Dennis Kearney in 1877 to pro-test Charley Crocker's spite fence was only one symptom of the resentment down below. Young publisher William Randolph Hearst, himself the son of a rather wealthy mining family, ran violent editorials in his *Examiner* denouncing the Big Four of the Central Pacific, later the Southern Pacific. Big front-page cartoons excoriated "The Octopus" of the railroad, its tentacles extending to gain control of the entire state. A young novelist named Frank Norris wrote a white-hot novel on the same theme. Only occasion-ally now does an echo of those days reverberate faintly.

When the Southern Pacific a few years ago put up a huge *SP* sign, which you can see from the top of the hill, editorials and letters to the editor blasted the railroad for arrogantly blocking the public's view of the Bay. But the Southern Pacific is just a railroad now, not a symbol of opulence and extravagance. The old mansions are gone, and the old resentments and protests which divided the city have long since cooled.

Friars, Dons, and Señoritas

There is an imposing monument to Capitan Don Luis Antonio Arguello, first governor of Northern California under Mexican rule, in the secluded garden cemetery adjoining the **Mission Dolores** (Dolores and 16th streets). Take J streetcar to 16th Street and walk one block east, or include as part of a driving tour of the city; see p. 213.

The name Arguello resounds in early San Francisco history, and there is an Arguello Boulevard running north and south through the Richmond district. But it is not Don Luis who is most remembered, or even his father, Comandante of the Presidio. It is rather Don Luis' sister, Maria Concepción Arguello, who has gone down in history as the heroine of the most enduring romantic legend of San Francisco's Spanish period. Concepción's story has been told by innumerable California writers, including Bret Harte, Gertrude Atherton, and Mrs. Fremont Older; some felt they knew her intimately enough to call her Concha.

Concepción was only fifteen, a dark-haired, dark-eyed Spanish beauty, when a Russian ship appeared in the Golden Gate under the guns of the Spaniards. The ship carried Nikolai Petrovich Rezánov, a high-placed nobleman and an emissary of the Czar. Rezánov's immediate mission was to establish trade with the Spaniards to get grain and food for the starving Russians at Sitka, Alaska, whose settlement had only recently been overrun by Indians. But the handsome, dashing ambassador had bigger ideas.

Rezánov was a principal advocate in St. Petersburg of Russian expansion into the Pacific all the way to North America, and he had pushed the Czar into making colonization of Alaska a government project. Now he had his eyes on California. The Spaniards were courteous to Rezánov, but cool and suspicious. He was getting nowhere with his effort to exchange Russian furs for Spanish food.

Suddenly love blossomed between the young Concepción and the forty-year-old Rezánov, a widower and a veteran of Russian court intrigue. They were separated by age, religion, language, and position in life; she was only the daughter of a minor Spanish offi-

cial. But love overcame all obstacles, including the opposition of
Spanish priests and Concepción's father. It was finally agreed that
Rezánov would return to Concepción as soon as he could win approval for the match in St. Petersburg and Rome. As Mrs. Older
tells the next episode in her *Love Stories of Old California:*

On the last day before his departure, Rezánov and Concha knelt
for an hour at Mission Dolores, their hands clasped in rapt ecstasy.
"This is marriage, Concha," her lover murmured.
"Forever," she vowed, while the sacred images looked down upon
them.

Rezánov's ship sailed out into the Pacific, bearing a cargo of
grain for Sitka, but he never returned. Concepción waited her
whole life, and eventually became California's first nun. Only many
years later did she hear that her lover had remained true, that he
died riding across Siberia to get permission for the marriage from
the Czar.

Chroniclers of this love story have usually omitted the one authentic document in the case, a businesslike report from Rezánov
to the Czar. He gave a rather unflattering view of his betrothed as
having "an unlimited and overweening desire for rank and honors,"
which explained her infatuation with an older but distinguished
man. He also noted that the romance was "not begun in hot passion, which is not becoming at my age," but "under the pressure
of conditions—remoteness, duties, responsibilities." He carefully
cited the advantages that might accrue from his connection with
the Arguello family, the profits of trade and the possibility that
"even without any great sacrifice on the part of the treasury, all
this country could be made a corporeal part of the Russian Empire."

In the mission garden there is a statue of Padre Junipero Serra,
walking with his hands folded behind his back. If any one man can
be credited with starting the Spanish colony on San Francisco Bay,
it is Padre Junipero. He was the ascetic, hard-driving father superior of the Franciscan missionaries in California, and he was in-
sistent on the founding of a new mission dedicated to the patron
saint of his order. Legend has it that the Spanish viceroy retorted
to the good father, "If St. Francis wants a mission, let him show us
his port and we will found one."

This was a wry reference to the unsuccessful efforts of the Spaniards for more than two hundred years to find a good harbor on the
Northern California coast. They had a name for the harbor already
picked—the Bay of St. Francis. But they weren't quite sure where

it was, and for a long time there was confusion between San Francisco Bay and Drake's Bay, discovered by Sir Francis Drake in 1579. Anybody who has seen the fog pouring through the Golden Gate can readily sympathize with the difficulty faced by the Spaniards in finding the Bay.

In any case, Padre Junipero Serra kept pressing for action. A land party led by Captain Gaspar de Portola sighted the real San Francisco Bay by land in 1769, and six years later a Spanish ship finally anchored inside the Golden Gate off Fort Point. The padre got his wish when in 1776 the first *Te Deum* was chanted at the Mission San Francisco de Assis; the mission acquired its present name later.

The Franciscan friar energetically converted the natives, enlisting them for labor in the mission fields and workshops. The Indians did most of the work on the cool, dark chapel we still see at the Mission Dolores, which was built with four-foot-thick adobe walls and a roof of redwood timbers lashed together with rawhide. The friars preferred Moorish and classic styles, but evidences of the Indian craftsmanship are still visible in many details, among them the red-and-white triangular designs in vegetable colors between the redwood beams over the ceiling.

The monument of a proud Indian maiden, Tekakwith, Lily of the Mohawks, stands in the mission garden; it is engraved in "prayerful memory of our faithful Indians." There are also buried at the mission some fifty-five hundred Indians, a statistic that suggests they did not flourish under the rule of the padres. The mission was the center of Spanish life; here were consecrated birth, marriage, death. All the dignitaries of the Spanish, and later the Mexican, government were buried here. For a time under American rule the mission was neglected and the cemetery desecrated. Duels were fought and bull and bear fights were held on the grounds. But it was restored to the Roman Catholic diocese, and after a break of a few years the mission cemetery continues the chronicle of San Francisco life and death. Here there is a memorial to Thomas Murphy, who served faithfully the Columbian Engine Company until his death in 1855, and there are headstones sacred to the memory of Charles Cora and James Casey, hanged by the Vigilance Committee of 1856.

Beneath the Hallowed Ground

Portsmouth Plaza   Kearny Street between Clay and Washington streets. Take the No. 30 bus at Market and Third streets to Kearny and Clay, or include this on a Grant Avenue walking tour (see Chapter 4, p. 51). This is a grandiloquent name for what has long been merely a hilly little square of green worn thin by generations of Chinese youngsters, running up and down the slope while their elders sat on the benches and read the intricate scrollwork of Chinese newspapers published a few blocks away. The only adornments have been a flagpole in the northwest corner and a monument to Robert Louis Stevenson topped by a bronze galleon set to sail away for Treasure Island. The setting is hardly imposing; there are Chinese restaurants on all sides except for the grimy old police-department headquarters and jail on Kearny Street. But for thousands of San Franciscans this is hallowed ground—which is now being desecrated.

The little park was once the central plaza of a sleepy village called Yerba Buena; it was close to a rounded cove with the same name—derived from the "good herb," mint, that grew everywhere. Occasional foreign ships entered the harbor and a few British sailors and American merchants settled nearby, but little was done to build up the port. The Spanish dons and their descendants were more interested in their great ranchos sprawling over the hills and valleys in every direction than in vulgar trade. Finally, in the 1830s the Mexican government, which had taken over California, opened the port for commerce. They laid out a plaza and built an adobe custom house there; nearby clustered a village with perhaps thirty families.

In 1846 life began to quicken around the plaza. Up the slope marched sailors and Marines from the USS *Portsmouth* and planted the American flag; the flagpole in the park marks the spot. That was how the little Mexican plaza became Portsmouth Square and later Portsmouth Plaza. The main business of overthrowing the weak Mexican regime with headquarters about fifty miles away in Sonoma had been accomplished a few days earlier. A so-called surveying party, led by a young officer named John C. Frémont, was behind the revolution which set up the short-lived Bear Flag Republic. Supporting Frémont were a few merchants and adventurers from Yerba Buena who had a vision of great things to come when the port was under American rule.

One of these was a handsome dark-skinned businessman, William Alexander Leidesdorff, whose home and store were across the street from the plaza. San Francisco's first promoter, he managed to make a fortune before the gold rush. Leidesdorff was among other things a real estate man, a shipowner, a lumber agent. He was also probably the little city's most prominent citizen. He gave a glittering ball for Commodore Stockton, who commanded the *Portsmouth*. And he read the Declaration of Independence from a platform on Portsmouth Square a few days later, July 4, 1846. When Yerba Buena became San Francisco the next year, Leidesdorff was elected *alcalde* (mayor), and before that he had been United States vice-consul in Yerba Buena. Despite these offices, he was never a United States citizen.

Leidesdorff was warm and friendly, but he was also an enigma even to his intimates. He never married, and he never talked about his early years. It was known that he was the son of a Danish trader and a West Indian woman. A popular legend has it that he lived for a time in New Orleans and there became betrothed to a beautiful and wealthy girl. He considered it the course of honor to tell her he was Negro on his mother's side. The girl said her father would never approve and she broke the engagement. A few months later young Leidesdorff was walking through the streets when he saw a funeral procession. He inquired whose it was and learned that it was that of a young girl who had died of a broken heart. He asked her name; it was his sweetheart. Whatever the truth of the story, he did leave New Orleans to go wandering up and down the Pacific in a small schooner. Finally, he settled in Yerba Buena in 1841. He had seven prosperous, active years. He died suddenly of brain fever when he was thirty-eight and was buried under the floor of the Mission Dolores. A small, narrow alley in the financial district bears the name of the Negro who was one of San Francisco's founders.

To another of the city's pioneers the coming of American rule was a considerable disappointment. This was Sam Brannan, the unlikely shepherd of a flock of more than two hundred Mormons seeking to escape the persecution they had encountered in the United States. The boisterous, loud-mouthed Brannan had hoped to turn California into a Mormon refuge. But he arrived too late, a few days after the flag-raising at the plaza.

Disgruntled by the turn of events, he left town and set up store at Sutter's Fort, where gold was found in 1848. Brannan was said to have gone around among the early miners collecting a tithe for the church, which soon disowned him. When Brigham Young protested, Sam replied, "You can go back and tell Brigham that I'll give up the Lord's money when he gives me a receipt signed by the Lord, and no sooner."

In any case, Brannan turned up at Portsmouth Plaza running up and down the streets with a whiskey bottle full of glittering dust, shouting, "Gold, gold from the American River." That did it. Everybody left for the gold fields, while thousands more started pouring into the no-longer-sleepy town with the new name of San

Francisco. The square swarmed with serape-draped Mexicans, Chileans, Peruvians, Malays, Chinese, Hawaiians, Americans from every state. On every surrounding street sprang up hotels, gambling joints, and saloons. Harlots arrived from Latin America, later from Paris. Eggs sold for a dollar apiece, and stores with twenty-foot frontage on the square rented for $3500 a month.

Into the town poured the riffraff of every country, including our own. The town boomed and so did crime. A gang of ex-soldiers, who volunteered for the Mexican War too late to fight, did the next best thing by marching around with fiddle, fife, and drum, hunting Mexicans and others of dark skin. The Hounds, as these would-be military men were called, soon were robbing and murdering lighter-hued citizens as well. Active in similar pursuits were the Sydney Ducks, a choice collection of Australian cutthroats who were blamed for the repeated fires which swept the town's ramshackle buildings.

In the wake of the fires and the mounting crime wave, Sam Brannan mounted a box at Portsmouth Plaza, surrounded by a mob of four thousand. "The laws and courts never yet hung a man," Sam declaimed. "I want no technicalities. Such things are devised to shield the guilty." When the Vigilance Committee of 1851 was formed, Sam Brannan became president. "Mr. Sam Brannan, the lion-hearted, a man always in love with shedding the blood of the wicked," he was called by Josiah Royce (who chronicled those days in California before he became a Harvard philosopher). Two days after Sam organized the vigilantes, John Jenkins, one of the Sydney Ducks caught stealing a safe, swung in the moonlight from a beam of the adobe customs house, now the City Hall. "Every lover of liberty and good order lay hold the rope," Sam shouted. Brannan was active again in the Vigilance Committee of 1856, although this time less flamboyant characters were in the forefront. Sam was also busy at other pursuits, becoming the richest man in town, sprucing himself up with handsomely groomed chinwhiskers and a diamond stickpin.

In 1858 the body of United States Senator David C. Broderick lay in state in the Union Hotel off the square. Broderick, a supporter of the Union, fell in a duel with David S. Terry, fiery chief justice of the state supreme court, a man with a most injudicious temperament who narrowly escaped hanging by the vigilantes. One old man touched Broderick's body and murmured, "California has lost her noblest son." The next day thirty thousand gathered at the plaza, now furnished with a grandstand for speakers, to hear Colonel Edward D. Baker, the town's most expensive lawyer and its most eloquent antislavery orator, declare, "As in life, no other voice among us so rung its trumpet blast upon the ear of freedom, so in death its echoes will reverberate amid our mountains and valleys until truth and valor cease to appeal to the human heart."

Fifteen years later a crowd gathered at the plaza to watch a strange new contrivance called a cable car climb up and down Clay Street from Leavenworth to its terminal at Kearny, where it was swung around on a turntable. The crowd was skeptical when inventor Andrew Hallidie took the controls, after signaling for the power to go on and the cable to start moving beneath the slotted street. But the thing worked, and nearly a hundred spectators jammed a car and trailer built to hold twenty-five, a situation which has since become familiar to San Franciscans.

In 1906 terrified Chinese ran around the plaza beating drums to ward off the fire devils, a method which proved no less effective than some of the others attempted. Shallow graves were dug in the grass to hold the dead, and homeless San Franciscans camped there during the reconstruction.

In 1927 the San Francisco Board of Supervisors officially gave Portsmouth Square the old Spanish designation of *plaza*. San Franciscans kept on calling it *square*.

Late in 1960 a big fence was put around the square. Bulldozers and power shovels began digging up the little park that was destined to be honeycombed by an underground parking garage. For months the city seethed with protest. The landscape architect retained to restore the square quit in protest, claiming that the promoters of the garage were interfering with his plans. But the bulldozers kept working. A strange new Portsmouth Plaza replaced the old.

(History buffs will find the story of the waterfront and Fisherman's Wharf in Chapter 3, background on the Chinese and other national groups in Chapter 4, and information about San Francisco's literary and artistic past in Chapter 7.)

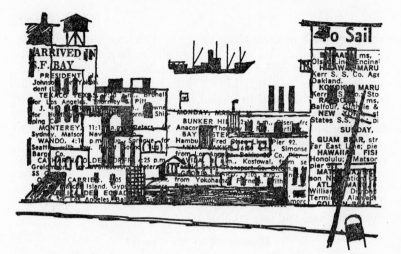

3: THE PORT CITY

Down to the Embarcadero

FOR MANY SAN FRANCISCANS the city's main street is not Market, and its heart is neither in the downtown area nor in North Beach Bohemia. For them the main drag is the two-hundred-foot-wide Embarcadero, and the heart of the city is the port. On their days off longshoremen, sailors, and other waterfront workers return to the Embarcadero from which they had been hoping to get away all week. They loiter on the docks, sit at the edge of piers, talk to friends, drop in for a beer at a nearby saloon, and reminisce about the old days.

When a double-deck freeway was built along the Embarcadero, blocking the view of the Ferry Building and docks, indignant letters of protest poured in on the newspapers and angry editorials blistered the dunderheads in Sacramento who sacificed the romance of the waterfront to the concrete mammon now taking over our cities. The Embarcadero Freeway never did become popular as either a structure or a means of transportation. In the end an abutment of one of the decks was closed off for sightseers to watch the port and the Bay—the function that should have been given priority in the first place.

The Freeway and its sightseeing deck to the contrary notwithstanding, the best way to see the Embarcadero is just to go down

there and walk or drive along slowly or try a combination of both.
You can feel the wind and the spray off the Bay, smell the spices
and the roasting coffee in nearby plants, hear the humming diesel
engines of the little Belt Line Railroad along the docks and the
creaking winches used to unload the great coffee sacks and other
cargo, watch the goods from all over the world being hauled in
lively fork-lift jitneys and then loaded on trucks, including some
survivors of the 1920s with small motors and low-slung beds.

(*Bon voyage* note: One way of going down to the Embarcadero
and acting as if you have important business there is to join the
crowds seeing passengers off on the big Matson and American
President Line luxury passenger ships. Check the newspaper for
departure time and pier number.)

Monument to the Ferries

The old **Ferry Building** (any Market Street bus will get you
there) serves as a guide to the Embarcadero. To the north are the
odd-numbered piers and street numbers in ascending order; to the
south even-numbered piers and street numbers. It also serves as a
guide through time, changing with the decades. Once this was the
gateway to the city and it remains a monument to nostalgia, to the
ferries that are no more. But part of the building has been modernized to fit the needs of a bustling import-and-export mart, and more
reconstruction is being planned.

When it was built in 1898, modeled in the then-current Spanish
vogue after the Giralda Tower of the Cathedral of Seville, the
Ferry Building was hailed as the most durable and solid structure
in California; it was intended to last through the ages. For a year
after the 1906 earthquake, the great hands on the clock tower
pointed to 5:17, the exact time that morning of April 18 when the
San Andreas Fault shifted and the city on top of it trembled. The
building survived, only its sandstone facing shaken off.

The ferries were to San Francisco what railroads, buses, planes,
and autos are today, and through the Ferry Building passed as
many as fifty million passengers a year. Generations of San Franciscans met visiting cousins, aunts, and uncles at the flower stand.
Hundreds of thousands of commuters from the East Bay and
Marin County converged on the Ferry Building every day from a
half-dozen terminals to the north and east. The ferries regulated
life no less rigidly than the commuter trains of the East, but they
were amiable tyrants. Making the ferry schedule might be a chore,
but crossing the Bay opened sleepy eyes in the morning and soothed
troubled spirits in the evening. Regulars played cards together on

the ferries. There were coffee clubs on the old paddle-wheelers, and sharp-tongued debaters argued the great issues of the times through the sound of the foghorns. Passengers on one of the Oakland ferries endured a volunteer barbershop chorus. The San Francisco *Chronicle* ran a column of ferry gossip and lore.

With the coming of the Golden Gate Bridge in 1936 and the Oakland–San Francisco Bay Bridge the following year, the ferries were doomed. For a time the Southern Pacific Railroad ran two ferries between Oakland and San Francisco for the convenience of train passengers, but even these were abandoned in favor of buses a few years ago. The ferries succumbed before the hard facts of transportation economics, and now there is not a single one left on the Bay. Some businessmen have contrived to use them for restaurants and shops. But no merchant of nostalgia has found the old vessels profitable as ferries or cruise boats, not even on week ends or long summer evenings. Here the New Yorker with his Staten Island Ferry is one up on the San Franciscan.

Alfa Romeos and Sacred Fungi

The north wing of the Ferry Building has been refurbished with chrome, aluminum and marble, more reminiscent of the Brussels International Fair than the Cathedral of Seville, to house the **World Trade Center** (open Monday through Friday, 9 A.M. to 5 P.M.). Here the San Francisco World Trade Association has set up a global shopping center where more than a hundred importers and exporters display their wares in discreet dignity amid restrained modern office furnishings. Along the terazzo ramps are attractive Covarrubias murals portraying in a colorful and sympathetic way the native dwellings, the economy, and the peoples as well as the flora and fauna of the Pacific. On the third floor is a picture-window cocktail and dining club with one of the best views of the city, for members of the association.

You can make a round-the-world shopping tour here through displays of Alfa Romeo autos, Japanese bicycles, Rhine wines, canned delicacies, oriental art objects and furnishings, Swedish tools, Indonesian wood carvings. Many of the firms sell at retail, and this is a good place to buy imported oddities and gifts.

Wander into the Asia House, which is a museum as much as a merchandise mart. There are precious old statues with careful explanations alongside. Note the figure of the eight Taoist immortals —especially the charming one of Ho Hsien-Ku, a seventh-century daughter of a shopkeeper who, having eaten of the sacred peach, became a fairy and lives on powdered mother-of-pearl and moonbeams. She wanders about picking sacred fungi and is revered as a Protector of House Holders and Recluses.

Of course, most of the emphasis at the World Trade Center is on business opportunities rather than on sacred fungi. An International Bulletin available at the center lists such offers as that of Lun Cheong in Hong Kong to buy secondhand air-conditioners and of Glorious Traders in Kobe to sell an assortment of coral products.

San Francisco's shipping fraternity is world-oriented. It has little alternative. The railroads have all but taken over the once-flourishing intercoastal trade, and they have cut deeply into coastwise trade up and down the Pacific. San Francisco's billion-dollar-a-year foreign trade in exports and imports is now the mainstay of the port.

Off the docks on both sides of the Ferry Building come all the assorted odds and ends of world trade—toy animals and little transistor radios from Japan, Madras cloth from India, jam from South Africa, glassware from Finland, clothing from Hong Kong. Foreign automobiles are a substantial item, too—Volkswagens, Simcas, Renaults, Austins, Hillmans, Volvos. Every once in a while you see on the docks, carefully masked against damage, a gray fleet of Rolls Royces. The bulk of imports through the harbor are more prosaic—coffee, raw wool, nonferrous ores, copra, newsprint, jute and burlap, and fresh and canned fish. Out of the port go raw cotton, machinery, petroleum products, dried and canned fruit from the San Joaquin and Santa Clara valleys, rice from the Sacramento area, grains, iron and steel, automobiles and iron ore.

San Francisco is a major coffee port, and here are unloaded coffee sacks from Brazil, Colombia, Mexico, Guatemala and, recently, Ghana. The sacks are taken off the docks on fork lifts, loaded into trucks, and taken to the coffee-processing plants close to the Embarcadero, where the beans are stored and then roasted. Sample sacks are tested as they move on a belt into the plant, then emptied mechanically, and the coffee beans slide along chutes, coffee from one chute automatically blended with coffee from another, until at the end the cans are sealed and packed by machine. Only the tasting is left to the human hand and palate. The principal San Francisco coffee-processors—Hills Brothers, Folgers, and MJB —encourage group tours through their plants. But they zealously guard from visitors, as if it were a precious military secret, their instant-coffee process. At roasting time the smell of coffee is heavy and pungent along the Embarcadero.

Into a narrow channel of the Embarcadero come the banana ships of the United Fruit Company. Great stalks of green bananas are put on belt lines that carry them to the dock. Lifting the stalks is still considered one of the more backbreaking jobs on an increasingly mechanized waterfront. Nearby is the copra dock, where crushed coconut comes in from the South Pacific and is processed in plants on the dock.

In and out of the harbor move an average of thirty ships a day, some half of them under foreign flags. In a typical month recently there arrived ships from twenty-one nations—old British freighters, sleek Norwegian and Dutch ships, freighters of every vintage and description from Japan. There are few ships from Communist countries, and none from Red China. San Francisco shippers eye with envy Canada's business with the Chinese mainland and recall nostalgically the flourishing China trade of old.

The foreign ships at the docks are strange, self-contained little worlds. The sailors maintain a little England or Japan or Denmark in their quarters below deck, eating their own foods and drinking their own beer, venturing out only occasionally to the night spots in North Beach or to a Market Street bar. There is little along what was once the wicked San Francisco waterfront to entice them into sin or separate them from their modest earnings.

Of Mother Bronson and Shanghai Kelly

Old-time sailors and longshoremen like to talk about the variety of ships that have sailed in and out of San Francisco harbor, the white-sailed clipper ships that brought the Argonauts to the city of gold more than a century ago, the steam side-wheelers, the steel-hull square-riggers, John Masefield's "dirty British coaster with salt-caked smokestacks." There are still some who reminisce about the legendary sailors and sea captains of a bygone day, about Captain William Matson, the Swedish skipper who started a far-flung shipping empire when he sent a two-hundred-ton schooner to Hawaii and came back with a cargo of sugar; about Scottish-born Robert Dollar, who was a humble lumber worker in his youth and later founded a great steamship line.

But not even the most sentimental old-timer will wax nostalgic about the life of a sailor in those romantic days of the schooners and square-riggers. In a world full of rough ports, San Francisco was probably the worst. The term *shanghaiing,* also known as *crimping,* originated in San Francisco, deriving perhaps from the practice of sending a helpless victim off on a long slow voyage to Shanghai or some other equally distant port. In all the streets running off the waterfront were the dens of the Barbary Coast, where sailors ventured at their peril and where crimps did a business running into millions of dollars a year.

Most enterprising of the crimps was Shanghai Kelly, who presided over a three-story establishment at 33 Pacific Street. Sailors were enticed to Kelly's crimp parlor by runners bearing fabulous tales of the wine and women they would find there. Whiskey was poured unstintingly, but it was usually doped. The rare sailor who could resist the liquor would succumb to one of Kelly's opium cigars. Victims would be maneuvered over a trapdoor, and waiting boats would take unconscious sailors out to ships waiting in the harbor.

In 1875 Shanghai Kelly managed the seemingly impossible job of finding sailors for three notorious hell wagons on which no sane seamen would ship. He spread the word along the Barbary Coast that it was his birthday and that he wanted all his special friends to join him for an excursion on the Bay. The riffraff of the waterfront gathered on the *Goliath,* an old paddle-wheel steamer Kelly chartered specially for this purpose. On board, the genial host poured the doped whiskey freely. When all the guests were reduced to a stupor, the *Goliath* pulled up to the three ships waiting outside the Golden Gate and Kelly delivered up some ninety denizens of the Barbary Coast. A fortunate accident helped the crimp-master make a triumphal return to the city. While he was cruising around wondering how he would explain the absence of his friends, the *Goliath* came upon the wreck of the ship *Yankee Blade* off Point Concepcion. Kelly brought the survivors back to San Francisco and was hailed as a hero.

The story is also told how another crimp, Calico Jim, shanghaied one after another six policemen sent to arrest him. Jim, sensibly enough, left immediately for his home town of Callao, Chile. When the shanghaied policemen returned to San Francisco they drew lots to decide which would have the privilege of going after Calico Jim. One of the policemen is said to have hunted him down on the streets of Callao and shot him six times—once for each of his victims.

Mother Bronson, a gentle lady six feet tall with hands like hams, operated an establishment on Steuart Street, a block off the Embarcadero. Mother's competitor was Miss Piggott on Davis Street, who served a special cocktail made with gin, whiskey, brandy, and dope. After this, a gentle tap on the head with a wooden mallet usually made a sailor amenable to a long, long trip. Miss Piggott's runner was a gnarled little Laplander known only as Nikko. Among other talents, he was also a master dummy-maker. Nikko would fashion straw figures with a covering of clothes which he unloaded on skippers as unconscious sailors.

This was a less risky practice than shipping corpses out to sea. In either case the crimp would collect a fee of fifty or a hundred dollars for a sailor. When the deception was discovered it was usually too late for the captain to do anything about it. There were hundreds of unsolved murder mysteries along the waterfront in San Francisco's early days, most of them attributed to the crimps or their agents.

While the passage of time has made these antics seem mildly comic, San Francisco sailors were not amused by the crimps or by the sadistic skippers about whom Jack London used to write. The Sailors Union of the Pacific, organized in 1891, published *The Red Record,* a compilation of sixty-three cases of unpunished brutality aboard ship. The book was bound in a blood-red cover showing a hand gripping the belaying pin which was to seamen the symbol of corporal punishment aboard ship.

It took a long time to eliminate the crimps and the tortures visited on sailors at sea. It also took a tireless, seemingly endless crusade by Andrew Furuseth, who led the Sailors Union for forty years. Furuseth was a strange, irascible man who brooked no contradiction from his union members and seemed himself to belong to the era of the sailing ships. But he had to his credit the passage by Congress in 1904 of An Act to Prohibit Shanghaiing in the United States as well as the Seaman's Act of 1915, which protected sailors against peonage aboard ship.

All Quiet on the Front

It is all bustle on the Embarcadero now, and all quiet on the side streets where once there were crimp parlors, whorehouses, and raucous saloons. An old-timer will point to a decrepit red-brick building and say it used to be the busiest bordello on the front, but it is just a rundown old hotel now. A block off the Ferry Building is Drumm Street, once notorious for its dens of iniquity. At 116 Drumm is now the eminently respectable Scandinavian Seamen's Home and in the basement is Steve's Scientific Aviary, where the chirping of hundreds of canaries has replaced the sounds of revelry.

If echoes of the wicked past keep you away from the Embarcadero, you ought to hear the complaints from bartenders and other shoreside entrepreneurs about how times have changed. Whether the changes are all for the worse depends on one's point of view. Certainly no visitor to the Embarcadero need fear any longer that he will be shanghaied or rolled or have his pockets picked.

"The Front is dead now," says Eddie Sammon, who has done business for years on the Embarcadero. "You should have seen this place in the old days." Small and dapper in crisp white jacket with green lapels, Eddie officiates at the **58 Club** (58 Embarcadero, a block south of the Ferry Building), across a 140-foot bar said to be the longest in town. For all his complaining, there isn't an empty stool at the bar at lunchtime as the longshoremen come in for a shot or a beer and for a hearty, inexpensive lunch at the far end.

Every once in a while Eddie counts out a few bills and hands them to a customer, then writes down the amount in a big old-fashioned account book. Like other barmen up and down the waterfront, Eddie has been the banker of sailors and longshoremen for decades. While this banking business has declined substantially, it still continues. Some of the Embarcadero financiers used to take their customers and perhaps still do; others, like Eddie, continue to make substantial loans without interest and are kindly remembered by waterfront characters who once needed this service. Of course, even the most generous lenders get their money back in trade.

Longshoremen used to have numbered brass checks which served as identification. On payday they were supposed to present the brass checks at the company office where they would be paid in cash. But many would turn over their brass to a favorite bartender in return for drinks, and the bartender would cash in the token on payday. Now longshoremen are paid by check twice a month at a central office. The longshoremen's wife is usually the ultimate recipient of the check, a fact that helps account for the decline of waterfront bars. Many sailors are now young career men with families, another cause for regret by some Embarcadero entrepreneurs.

A visitor can now walk along the Embarcadero at will and quite safely, savoring the sights and sounds and smells of a great port. You can drop in for coffee and a sandwich at **Pier Seven,** a quiet coffee shop overlooking the Bay that is frequented by longshoremen. Or tour the Embarcadero at night when lights play on the harbor and the ships sway gently at their moorings. Drop in week ends at **On the Levee** (987 Embarcadero, near Filbert) for genuine New Orleans jazz. Or you can take in **Pier 23** across the street, where a jazz trio and piano alternate.

The Bustling Wharf

Fisherman's Wharf   End of Taylor Street. Take Powell Street cable car at Market and Powell to last stop. Or take a No. 32 bus anywhere on the Embarcadero. Old-timers on the wharf have mixed feelings about the flashy prosperity that has come to the narrow

strip of streets surrounding the old fishing harbor at the end of the
Embarcadero. "Of course, the wharf isn't what it used to be," says
Nunzio Alioto as he parks your car at Taylor and North Point.
"But how can I complain?" Nunzio, usually dressed in a brown
business suit, likes to refer to himself as the world's richest parking
attendant, and he probably is. At fifty-eight, he doesn't have to
work. "But I enjoy coming down to the wharf every day, talking to
people, keeping an eye on things."

Nunzio's wealth comes from the crab-fishing business, and he
has invested his profits in real estate and other wharf enterprises.
He owns **Pete Alioto's Hofbrau,** a few steps away (2737 Taylor).
His mainstay is the **N. Alioto Fish Co.** (167 Jefferson), now operated by his son Frank—who drives a Cadillac with a gold crab on
the hood, symbol of the prosperity that has come to the second and
third generations of San Francisco's Italian fishermen.

If you drop in for some seafood at **A. Sabella's Capri Room**
(2770 Taylor) you may notice Mrs. Isabel Sabella, a chic, slender
matriarch with smartly groomed hair, bustling around, keeping a
sharp eye on the service and the quality of the food, exchanging
greetings with a uniformed scoutmaster in with a troop from Stockton or with a table of visiting businessmen or old customers. "The
wharf is too crowded now," says Mrs. Sabella. "The old flavor is
gone. Too many gift shops." But she shrugs her shoulders and adds
with a smile, "I just opened up a gift shop myself the other day."
Mrs. Sabella's son Luciano is now the active head of the business.
Her ancient father-in-law of the same name, the fisherman who
started it all, was still coming around occasionally in 1961.

As early as the 1850s, Italian fishermen sailed the waters of the
Bay and out the Golden Gate in feluccas, small boats with triangle-
shaped sails similar to the fishing boats of Genoa and Naples. By
the 1870s an even older type of craft was seen in the Bay—high-
prowed Chinese junks with square sails, built in San Francisco.
The Chinese took over much of the shrimp industry, operating to
the north in San Pablo Bay and to the south at Hunters Point. But
they were kept out of the present Fisherman's Wharf area, which
remained the territory of the Italian and Portuguese fishermen. The
wharf dates back to 1900, when the state took over the area and
developed harbor facilities for fishing boats.

Just who started the first restaurant on the wharf is a matter of
some dispute. The Castagnola family claims the credit. But Pete
Alioto contends that the first restaurant was the **Harbor Grill,** on
the site of his present **Hofbrau.** Fishermen used to sell part of their
catch directly to housewives. Then some unknown genius got the

idea of cooking up and selling clam chowder on the spot. Tom Castagnola seems to have been the first to put in tables; he also concocted a dish called Crab Louie by mixing crab with Thousand Island dressing.

In the 1920s San Franciscans started discovering that Fisherman's Wharf was *the* place to get fresh seafood. The wharf was lined with great iron pots where the live crabs were cooked, often after the customer made his selection from an ample display. "We started the first drive-ins here," says Nunzio Alioto. "People from uptown used to drive in and eat some seafood off a tray in their cars. Competition was fierce in those days. We used to pull in people off the streets. I was like a barker, yelling, 'Get a nice crab cocktail,'" Pete Alioto recalls. "Wood for the crab pots was so precious that we used to lock it up at night to keep competitors from stealing it."

By the 1930s there were several going restaurants on the wharf. But the big boom started in the 1940s and is still continuing. Now the wharf is lined on every side with gaudy restaurants, gift shops, and sideshows with assorted sea monsters. There is even a plush sukiyaki house on the wharf. But most of the restaurants still favor names of old San Francisco Italian families like the Sabellas, the Aliotos, and the DiMaggios (they had a kid called Joe who didn't like fishing and wasted his time throwing a ball around on a lot behind the wharf). When two Irishmen started a fish restaurant a few years ago they tactfully named it **Tarantino's** (206 Jefferson Street). There are still a few old crab pots around the wharf. But they are heated with gas now, not wood.

While the restaurants and other assorted businesses have flourished, the San Francisco fishing industry has gradually but steadily declined. The old oyster beds in the Bay long ago disappeared. Salmon and cod fishing declined. Not so long ago the wharf was lined with tall-masted seventy-foot sardine trawlers, and there were sardine canning and processing plants up and down the Bay. But the little fish suddenly and mysteriously disappeared in 1949. Now crab fishing is the mainstay of the port. But the local fishermen can no longer keep up with the demand, and many San Francisco restaurants have to supplement their supply of local crab with shipments from Seattle and Alaska.

Most of the fishermen are now older men; the youngsters prefer going into business or the professions. On week-end mornings the crab fishermen can still be seen mending their nets or tinkering with the motors of their boats, usually one- or two-man, thirty-five-foot affairs. Many of the fishermen still speak Italian among themselves, and you can often see them after a day's fishing at **Andy's Lookout** (Pier 47) on a corner of the boardwalk off the main bustle of the wharf. This is not a fish place; the fishermen usually order hamburgers.

For all the lamentations of old fishermen about how times have changed for the worse, the wharf is still a good place to get a solid seafood meal (see p. 104) or just to stand around and watch the boats sway at their lines. It is also one of the best places in San Francisco to get the feel of the port city—if you're willing to wander around and look beyond the restaurants and the gift shops. You can relish the bittersweet smell from the old red-brick buildings of the **D. Ghiradelli and Company** chocolate plant (800 North Point Street), or inspect bargains from all over the world at **Cost Plus** (see p. 182), or revel in the past glories of vanished sailing ships at the **Balclutha** and the **Maritime Museum** (see pp. 47–50). At Fisherman's Wharf you can take a harbor tour around the Bay, a must for tourists and San Franciscans alike (see p. 214). If you really want to enjoy the wharf and its attractions, stay away Sunday afternoons and week-end evenings and come down during the week when it is less crowded.

The Magic Tote Board

A longshore union official who was a devotee of the race track was once watching the odds flashing on and off the tote board at Bay Meadows. Suddenly it occurred to him that the union could use the same kind of system to dispatch longshoremen to their jobs. The idea was adapted, and you can watch it operate every morning and evening at the **Longshoremen's Hall** (301 North Point Street, near Fisherman's Wharf).

In their distinctly modernistic copper-dome building the longshoremen group around an elaborate electrical board and attentively watch the flashing numbers. *H95,* for example, is intended for men who work in the hold of the ship. The magic number tells them they are eligible for the next hold job if they had ninety-five hours or less during the current work period. They then proceed to little glass-encased cages up front, where dispatchers assign them to their ships and docks.

The tote board is the symbol of equality in work opportunity through what is called rotary hiring. It is also the symbol of the new era of labor-management cooperation on the waterfront. But the turbulent old times are not wholly forgotten. Once a year on July 5 old-time longshoremen place a wreath at the corner of Mission and Steuart streets, where two of their number were killed in the bloody 1934 strike. Perhaps more significant than this commemoration of the past is the fact that longshore employers now pay half the cost of operating the modern hiring hall at Fisherman's Wharf. Most shipowners prefer the new order to the payolas, kickbacks, and rackets that once flourished on the waterfront.

Pilfering used to be an organized business, much as it was on the New York waterfront, particularly during the reign of King Joe Ryan. Men still tell stories about the time, years ago, when thirty grand pianos were stolen from a freight car off the front. Mostly they exchange tales about would-be pilferers who outwitted themselves.

There is a story about the longshoreman who was intrigued by a shipment of fancy ladies' underwear. He put on a dozen pair underneath his hickory jeans. As fate would have it, this was the day he fell off a ladder and broke his leg. Astonished doctors and nurses cut through layers of lace before they got to his leg. "I wished I was dead," he told his gang later. Another longshoreman was unable to resist the lure of frozen Australian butter and just before getting off the night shift wrapped twelve pounds of butter under his shirt. But the walking boss called the gang back to work overtime. The longshoreman worked for hours under the hot sun, while butter melted through his shirt, down his jeans, and all over the ship. Pilfering is now negligible, but occasional cases of Scotch whisky retain a curious tendency to break open around Christmastime.

Once the most casual and underpaid of workers, the longshoreman is now one of San Francisco's labor aristocrats. He is well paid, earning on the average seven thousand to eight thousand dollars a year. His working conditions are good, although longshoring is still hard and often hazardous work. Most of all, the longshoreman values his independence and security. He has no fear of being fired, and a new employer-financed fund protects him against layoffs. If he feels like taking off a few days to go fishing, he can do so and report for work on his return. When he retires, he receives a pension and lifetime medical care.

A favorite waterfront legend concerns the longshoreman who has a forty-thousand-dollar split-level home in an exclusive peninsula suburb. Every morning he dresses in a gray flannel suit, drives off in his Cadillac to the Embarcadero, where he changes into work clothes at the YMCA. In the evening he dons his gray flannel uniform again and drives home to suburbia. He has informed his neighbors that he works "in transportation." The story, even if true, is far from typical, and not only for the obvious reason that it exaggerates longshore wages. Most longshoremen would never dream of denying their trade.

Prosperity has failed to turn the longshoreman into a conformist, not even in the union to which he has a fanatical devotion. Longshoremen vote for Harry Bridges as president of their international union, and as often as not elect so-called right-wingers critical of Bridges to head their San Francisco local.

Even in these days of union security, characters are still drawn to the waterfront. There are still sailors who when on the beach read obscure poetry in dimly lighted San Francisco cellars. The longshoremen's union, while still a rather boisterous, rowdy brotherhood, has a fair quota of former writers, teachers, lawyers, newspapermen, and other professionals. Some of them are attracted by the good steady pay, others by the romance and glamor of the Embarcadero—even in a benighted time when cargo is loaded in vans and hoisted by monstrous cranes.

Still working regularly as a longshoreman is Eric Hoffer, the chubby, pink-faced author. Hoffer achieved unusual prominence some years ago when it was revealed that former President Eisenhower, until then regarded as an exclusive devotee of Westerns, kept Hoffer's *The True Believer* on his nightstand. Hoffer continues working on the front and continues writing in a dingy rooming house his angry aphorisms directed against the fanaticism and hysteria he regards as endemic in mass movements. He is the prototype of the self-educated worker, and there are still some of them around on the waterfront. Hoffer discovered Montaigne while on Los Angeles' skid row. He is a typical longshoreman in one respect. A critic of Bridges' political and social views, he supports his union leadership.

Square-Riggers and Clippers

Balclutha   Pier 43; Jefferson and Mason streets near Fisherman's Wharf. Open 10 A.M. to 11 P.M. Adults fifty cents; children under twelve twenty-five cents, under six free. Men along the waterfront used to shake their heads sadly about the fate of the square-riggers. These steel-hull sailing vessels were so fast and durable that they survived into the early years of the twentieth century. But now they were rotting and disintegrating, and soon not a single one of the great old ships that sailed around Cape Horn would be left.

Karl Kortum, a maritime historian and the director of the San Francisco Maritime Museum, decided that something should be done about preserving one of the square-riggers; he had a passion for the old ships and had himself sailed around the Cape in one of them early in World War II. The inevitable choice was the old *Balclutha,* last of the square-riggers to carry the American flag and still sound enough to be saved.

The *Balclutha's* history was long and honorable. Built in Glasgow in 1886, she had sailed around the Cape seventeen times. She had been a fast grain racer out of San Francisco and a jute-carrier out of Calcutta. She had carried lumber across the Pacific, then was drafted for the Alaska Packer's Fleet under the name *Star of Alaska.* She survived shipwreck off the Alaska coast in 1904 and continued in the Alaska trade until 1930. After that she was used as a movie prop and for twenty years was a rather decrepit and unsuccessful exhibition ship along the West Coast under the name *Pacific Queen.*

Buying the *Balclutha* was easy; the asking price was only $25,-000. But the $250,000 cost of restoring the old relic seemed prohibitive. Then waterfront business firms made their services available without charge and skilled workmen from fourteen unions contributed thousands of hours of labor. So did amateur yachtsmen, retired sailors, and navy men. Finally, the *Balclutha* was towed across the Bay from Oakland where she had been refitted and berthed near Fisherman's Wharf.

The *Balclutha* now looks ready to sail at a moment's notice—except, alas, that her spars have no canvas. There she stands, all neat and trim and gleaming with new paint and her rigging in perfect order. Volunteers help keep her that way, and you can see earnest young Sea Scouts polishing the brass. You can climb into the foc's'le, where neatly lettered explanations on wooden boards assure you sailors never went to sea sober if they could help it. There are chanties posted all over the place:

> Oh, the work was hard
>   And the wages low;
> Leave her, Johnny, leave her.
> We'll pack our bag and ashore we'll go;
>   It's time for us to leave her.

The old ship has authentic atmosphere, including an ancient duffle bag and trunk, a complete carpenter's shop, a shining galley, and the steward's pantry—also known as "the slop chest." Youngsters go crazy on the *Balclutha.* They climb all over the place, and you can see them standing at the compass or the wheel pretending they're the master of the ship. You can see the red settee where the captain took cat naps and the velvet plush room where his wife kept the sewing machine. There is a little book and souvenir shop, and something of a museum below where all sorts of sea lore is displayed, including mementos of the Barbary Coast and the exploits of Shanghai Kelly.

San Francisco Maritime Museum   Aquatic Park at Beach and Polk. Open daily except Monday 10:20 A.M.–5:30 P.M.; Saturdays, Sundays, and holidays 10 A.M.–6 P.M. Free. The Maritime Museum stands in the midst of a miniature muscle beach on the Bay where many San Franciscans come to sun themselves on the sand or on the steps of an otherwise unused stadium. During the 1930s the WPA cleaned up the beach and built an elaborate bathing casino in the shape of a triple-deck ship. The casino has fine views of the Bay from the decks and is handsomely decorated inside with murals of deep-sea life by Hilaire Hiler. But the Bay is not one of the world's cleanest or safest bathing beaches—and the casino turned out to be a white elephant. Finally, the Maritime Museum took over in 1951 and gave the building a distinctive and eminently useful function.

Under the driving and energetic Karl Kortum, the museum has recaptured something of the feel of the old ships that sailed in and out of the port. There is an eight-foot model of the *Preussen,* the only five-masted full-rigged ship ever built. There are mementos of Yankee clippers, Columbia River gillnetters, downeasters from Maine, early Pacific steamers, Cape Horners, the old Bay ferryboats, and lumber-carrying steam schooners. Nameplates of historic West Coast ships are suspended from the ceiling. On the walls are some proud wooden maidens, once the figureheads of old ships, and a rather quizzical British empire-builder, Clive of India, resplendent in a red coat, looks out from the prow of the *Star of Peru.*

The anchor of the old *Constitution* stands in massive splendor. Harpoons and toggle irons used by the whalers who sailed out of the port are on display. A scrimshaw exhibit shows off the carvings made by sailors out of whalebone with saw file and jackknife. A big attention-getter is the exhibit of shipwrecks in and around the Golden Gate. The photographic collection of old ships is considered one of the best anywhere. Particularly striking is the historic photo of five hundred ships beached on the Bay in 1851. It catches the spirit of that hectic time when ships were hastily deserted as passengers and crews made for the gold fields with cries of "There's plenty of gold so I've been told, on the banks of the Sacramento."

But the real pride of the museum is not in models and photographs so much as in the real thing—in saving and preserving old vessels like the *Balclutha*. With the help of state funds the Hyde Street pier adjoining Aquatic Park will become a living museum with restored vessels like the steam schooner *Wapama,* the side-wheel ferry *Eureka,* and the lumber schooner *C. A. Thayer.* Before too long San Franciscans will have a whole gallery of historic ships to revive their memories of the old days at sea.

The Marina

On Sunday afternoons San Franciscans like to walk in **Marina Park** (Marina Boulevard between Webster Street and Yacht Harbor), a broad expanse of green along the waterfront facing the substantial and relatively new homes on Marina Boulevard. Here they resume their enjoyment of the port city, which is interrupted briefly by Fort Mason, the Army transportation center on the Bay. People walk their dogs or lie on the grass and sun themselves, and children play ball or fly kites. The Marina is in one of the city's warm belts, a fact which adds to its popularity.

At the end of the park is **Yacht Harbor** (Marina Boulevard between Scott and Lyon streets), where hundreds of small craft bob up and down in municipally owned berths. This is where San Francisco's boating enthusiasts descend on week ends, sailing their small craft on the Bay or daringly past the Golden Gate into the ocean. Sheltering the harbor is a fifteen-hundred-foot breakwater; you can walk out on it until you feel you are right in the middle of the Bay.

Just off the Marina (at Lyon Street) is the faded glory of the **Palace of Fine Arts,** the only surviving structure from the multi-million-dollar display of the Panama–Pacific International Exposition of 1915. The semicircular building was designed by Bernard Maybeck, San Francisco's great architect in the early years of the century, to recall a Roman ruin. Built on a lagoon and surrounded with greenery, it was intended to transport San Franciscans back into a contemplative and quiet past. For a few years the Palace housed the collection of the San Francisco Art Commission, then was allowed to fall into disrepair. The great rotunda and the Co-rinthian columns and the statuary and the friezes began to resemble a ruin far more realistically than Maybeck had planned. With a combination of public and private funds, a $5.8-million program to restore the Palace was launched in 1961.

(For a map of the Aquatic Park and Fisherman's Wharf area, see page 142.)

4:
SAN
FRANCISCO
INTERNATIONAL

Around the World on Grant Avenue

GRANT AVENUE is only about a mile and a half long from where it starts in the downtown heart of the city to its end in abrupt descent to the Bay. But in its short span it is successively a street of smart sophisticated shops, the main street of Chinatown, the broadway of Bohemia, and a street of old Italian homes and stores and pasta factories. In a walk of a couple of hours, which includes time for brief detours on other streets, you can wander through several Grant Avenues, through several of San Francisco's many worlds.

Grant Avenue begins off Market Street with a typical dash of San Franciscana, flower stands jauntily gay against massive competition a few steps away from the Podesta Baldocchi shop which flaunts ornate window displays of waxlike antheriums and rare orchids and glistening white camelias. You walk past department stores, women's specialty shops, exclusive and expensive, past a tiny indentation in the street called Tillman Place (with a candle shop, a bookstore, and an art gallery), past the discreet luxury of silver and gold and diamonds in the window of Shreve and Company, where San Franciscans have bought jewels and expensive silverware for more than a century.

Pause for a moment when you reach Bush Street. On the northwest corner you may notice the Lot-A-Burger stand, which serves a square meal on a bun, and across the street the Grant Café, which offers Coca-Cola, hamburgers, and Chinese-American dishes. You may also notice the ornate lampposts topped by Chinese-style lanterns. This is the gateway to Chinatown.

Of East and West

The transition is not entirely abrupt. A pseudo-rustic tavern offers *cappucino,* an "Italian" hot-brandy-and-chocolate drink. Up a flight of stairs there is a Greek café. But gradually Chinese stores, mainly featuring Japanese wares, begin to predominate.

A strange miscellany clutters the store windows. Jade Buddhas and aloof Chinese patriarchs on faded scrolls rub elbows with modern novelties. The **Peking Bazaar** (458 Grant) displays teak-wood furniture; ornate tables and chests with brass handles are in the window along with a little illustrated lesson on the origin, value, and durability of teak. The **Golden Dragon** (425 Grant) sells abacuses in various sizes and woods; it also sells tiny Japanese cameras and appropriately inscribed souvenir panties for retarded Occidentals.

At almost every corner there is an open stand displaying big jars of penny candy, chewing gum, pistachio and lichee nuts, candied melon, ginger and coconut—an Oriental approximation of the fast-disappearing old-fashioned candy store. Stores with ancient Chinese kitchen wares have installed electric pony rides outside to entice the adults to shop while the kids ride. Amid modern shops and restaurants there are still, on Grant Avenue and on the adjacent side streets, sweatshops out of a supposedly vanished era where Chinese women work until late at night for substandard wages while their young romp among the sewing machines.

You see young westernized Chinese in sport jackets and old men, thin, wrinkled, slightly hunched, strolling leisurely or stopping to chat with cronies. You see smartly dressed young Chinese women with children in tow, and older women in slit-skirt black dresses shopping at the markets, examining the chicken and ducks in the butcher stores and arguing about how fresh they are. That is, you see them if you walk along Grant Avenue in the daytime, before the street swarms with Caucasians looking wistfully for an exotic Chinatown of opium dens and gambling parlors.

Once past Bush Street you are in a world of pagoda-style buildings lit up with neon signs, of modern storefronts flaunting intricate Chinese characters, of Chinese shops offering Japanese wares, of slum tenements concealed behind the glittering attractions offered the ever-curious tourist crowds. You are in a world that is both phony and real, both Chinese and Western and yet not quite either. Chinatown is often described as a bit of China jammed into a few square blocks of San Francisco, the largest Chinese community outside Asia. But it is separated by geography, history, and politics from China—and it was long rejected by the city that surrounds it on every side. Chinatown is part of the flesh and bone of San Francisco, yet isolated from it.

Sun Yat-sen and the General

Walk a few steps off Grant Avenue to 520 Pine Street and you see an old brick building with a pagoda front and tiled roof characteristic of Chinatown architecture. This is the **Kong Chow Temple,** dedicated in 1857 to Kwan Ti, a general who flourished around 400 B.C. and was deified as a symbol of courage, patron of soldiers, explorers, miners, and laborers.

The latter two categories of Chinese in San Francisco particularly needed the old general's help. There were thousands of them even in those early days in the city they called Old Gold Mountain. They had been brought over, mostly from outlying peasant districts near Canton in Kwangtung Province, to do the menial work in the mines and in San Francisco. They were needed—but they were not wanted. From the first they were taunted and exploited.

So a group of Chinese from the Kong Chow district of their old province, seeking some refuge of their own in the strange new world, built a shrine to the general. They also formed the Kong Chow Benevolent Association, the first of the district organizations which have remained ever since a potent influence in Chinatown. The original temple burned down in 1906, but Kwan Ti's statue miraculously survived and a new shrine was built here on Pine Street.

Mount the steps and enter through bright red doors into a bare corridor that ends in a blank wall. This is the passageway of peace, offering protection against evil spirits, which travel in straight lines. From a courtyard you walk up to a third-floor shrine. The general still looks fierce and courageous as he sits on an altar surrounded by silk hangings and old wood carvings. Only a few elderly Chinese come here now, lighting joss sticks and bringing offerings of food and money.

If you want to consider the Kong Chow temple a symbol of the old, superstitious, ancestor-worshiping China from which hungry peasants came a hundred years ago to seek humble labor, there are symbols of quite a different sort across the street at **St. Mary's Square** (right off Grant between Pine and California). A striking twelve-foot statue pays tribute to Sun Yat-sen, the father of modern China, who came many times to get help and money from San Francisco Chinese and who plotted the 1911 revolution against the Manchu dynasty from an office in the old Montgomery Block. Sculptor Beniamino Bufano has portrayed a benign figure with face and hands of rose-colored granite, draped in austere robes of stainless steel. There is also a tablet to the Chinese-Americans who fought in World War II.

Although a massive garage now honeycombs beneath the park, it is still a little oasis in the city. Clerks from nearby glass-encased office buildings come here to munch their sandwiches in peace and quiet.

Sweet Mystery

Across California Street from the park, its Gothic tower somehow quite at home among the pagodas and the tile roofs, is **Old St. Mary's Church** (Grant and California streets), a San Francisco landmark since 1854, when it was built of brick from New England and granite from China hoisted into place by Chinese workmen using wooden derricks. Once the seat of the Roman Catholic diocese on the West Coast, this is now the parish church of the Paulist fathers, to whom, incidentally, the park owes its existence in a rather roundabout way.

For decades the church stood near the bagnios and opium dens on Dupont Street, as Grant Avenue was called before the earthquake, when it was known as one of the wickedest streets in San Francisco. There were high-class and high-priced bordellos toward Market Street and less exclusive Chinese houses farther up Grant Avenue and along the dark alleys. Chinatown was notorious for its varied institutions of commercialized vice, patronized not only by the Chinese men who had been brought over to San Francisco without wives and families but also by Caucasians intrigued by the sweet mystery of Chinese womanhood.

In any event, the quite unconcealed prostitution on Dupont Street outraged the good women of San Francisco, who demanded that the bordellos be put decently out of sight behind the houses and tenements. So many of the most notorious joints were moved to what is now St. Mary's Square. This soothed public sensibilities but outraged the Paulist fathers, who were then subjected to the raucous cries of prostitutes hawking their ware and to the noisy brawls of seamen.

For years the fathers crusaded for a public park there, and for years city officials managed to spend otherwise funds set aside for this purpose. Finally, the fire of 1906 wiped out the red-light district. The park was finally established, and, in a desperate effort at a new start, Dupont Street was renamed Grant Avenue. The street changed.

But San Francisco historians and old-timers still like to tell anecdotes about Ah Toy and Selina, the golden courtesans of the early days or about Little Pete, the Tong chieftain who terrorized Chinatown. And there is still a reference to the temptations of the past in the inscription below the clock on Old St. Mary's tower, *Observe the time, son, and flee from evil.*

White Men Only

A visitor, observing the proliferation of stores, businesses, and restaurants in Chinatown, may conclude sagely that the Chinese are a commerical people who don't like to work with their hands. On the evidence of old shrines and exotic food stores, he may decide that they are a clannish, stick-in-the-mud people who resist change.

But the history of Chinatown suggests contrary conclusions. San Francisco's Chinese came to this country as malleable as any other immigrants. They came as manual laborers who were extremely dexterous with their hands. In fact, they were victims of their excessive adaptability, of the amazing speed which they acquired new trades and skills.

The first Chinese—who came at the time of the gold rush—showed they were good workers, and they were imported later by the tens of thousands to build the railroad across the Sierra Nevada Mountains. When the railroad was finished, the laborers flocked to San Francisco, swelling the already substantial number of Chinese. They worked hard; they were ingenious. They started doing just about everything. They became fishermen, shoemakers, cigarmakers, mechanics. Henry George, who shared the prejudice of his time against the Chinese, wrote in 1869, "Beside the stall where the Chinese butcher carves his varnished hog, or makes mince meat out of stewed fowl, you will see Chinamen running sewing machines, rolling cigars, working up tin with the latest Yankee appliances."

When hard times came, the Chinese were the obvious target. White craftsmen, hard-pressed for jobs, banded together against the Chinese. The union label dates back to those unhappy days. The Cigar Makers' Association put printed announcements on their boxes that the contents had been manufactured by WHITE MEN. A demagogue named Dennis Kearney denounced the Chinese at great mass meetings attended by as many as twenty thousand working-men. Brass-knuckled bravos known as Hoodlums (that was how the word entered the language) descended on Chinatown, beating people up, setting fire to laundries and stores. To harass Chinese laundrymen, the San Francisco Board of Supervisors solemnly prohibited the carrying of baskets suspended from poles across the shoulders. Other local ordinances were aimed at the wearing of queues and the shipment of the Chinese dead for burial in China. On a national scale stringent Chinese-exclusion legislation was en-acted.

The Chinese in San Francisco were compelled to create a little world of their own, based on the customs and even the geographic divisions of the small area near Canton from which most of them came. The anti-Chinese agitation forced the immigrants from Kwangtung Province inward on themselves in an overcrowded slum ghetto. It made it difficult for Chinese to bring their families to America, encouraged vice, limited economic opportunity; until 1941 Chinese who weren't born here were barred from owning property, and many Chinatown stores were owned by Japanese and others fortunate enough to have been born in the U.S. The hostility of the outside world delayed Americanization and created a distance between Chinese and Caucasians in San Francisco that has taken decades to narrow.

Six Companies with No Business

A glazed blue building with extending balconies and red-tiled roof recalls the more somber aspects of Chinatown's past. This is the headquarters of the **Six Companies** (843 Stockton Street, one block west of Grant Avenue), which doesn't do any business. It is made up not of affiliated companies but of the associations formed by the Chinese, when they first came to San Francisco, on the basis of the districts in Kwangtung Province where they were born.

In the old chaotic days, traditional district, family, and benevo-lent organizations transplanted from China were important in es-tablishing some order in a Chinatown attacked by demagogues from without and undermined from within by vice and corruption. City officials generally preferred it that way, leaving it to Chinese organizations and leaders to run Chinatown. The arrangement worked, but the effect was to turn Chinatown into an autonomous city within the city.

The Six Companies has for generations been Chinatown's un-official government, adjudicating differences, settling business quar-rels and family disputes, raising funds for the Chinese hospital and

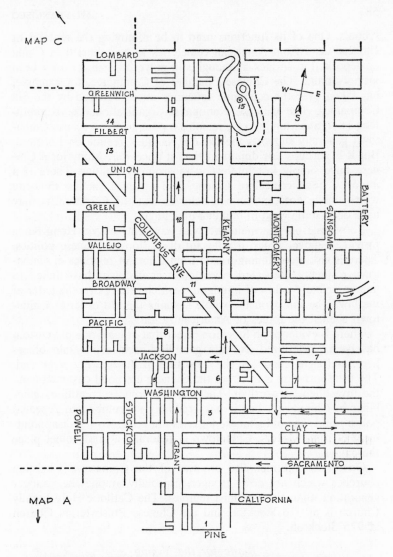

MAP B: CHINATOWN AND NORTH BEACH

1. St. Mary's Square
2. Commercial Street
3. Portsmouth Plaza
4. Merchant Street
5. Ross Alley
6. Bella Union Theater
7. Jackson Square
8. Ping Yuen Housing Project
9. Entrance to Embarcadero freeway
10. Adler Street
11. Broadway and Columbus—center of night life
12. Upper Grant Avenue
13. Washington Square
14. Church of St. Peter and St. Paul
15. Coit Tower and Telegraph Hill Park

schools. One of its functions used to be removing the remains of Chinese dead from American cemeteries to be reburied in China or deposited in shrines. Although still powerful, it has slowly been losing ground. The Chinese Chamber of Commerce, for example, has taken over the economic functions once exercised by the Six Companies. The Chinese Nationalist organization, the **Kuomintang** (846 Stockton Street), remains a potent force because Chinatown generally supports the Chiang Kai-shek regime on Formosa. But it is perhaps less dominant than it once was. Many local Chinese have simply lost interest in old-country politics. There is a minority trend critical of Chiang, and an even smaller minority which, while not Communist, believes that the Communists may have done some good in building up China.

Refugees from the mainland who have entered via Hong Kong provide a ginger group heating up discussion of Chinese politics. There is also a continuing trickle from China of relatives of Chinatown residents. Repeated government crackdowns have failed to halt completely a flow of immigrants which often skirts the letter of the law. The influx on the whole sustains the old order in Chinatown against the forces of Americanization.

There is evidence on Stockton Street that at least one old custom has been modernized. Nevada gambling casinos maintain offices here, and signs announce the departure of buses every week end. The transportation is free, but the Chinese are good customers and the investment is worth it. There is still some surreptitious gambling in Chinatown, but it has gradually succumbed to repeated police raids. The old Chinese lotteries are gone. To the disappointment of some visitors, Chinatown is generally a pretty quiet place these days.

On Stockton Street also are two of the Chinatown Christian churches which are now stronger, especially among the younger generation, than the Buddhist temples. The Catholic Holy Family Church is at 916 Stockton and the Chinese Presbyterian Church at 925 Stockton.

Battle for the Young

A few steps off Grant Avenue is the stone building of the **Nom Ku School** (755 Sacramento), designed in traditional Chinese courthouse style. Stone lions guard the set-back upper story, roofed with bright glazed tiles. Here about two hundred Chinese children between the ages of six and fifteen go in the afternoon after public schools are let out to study Chinese language, calligraphy, history, and Confucian philosophy. There are seven such schools in Chinatown. While Chinese youngsters have attended unquestioningly for decades, there is now increasing grousing from the younger generation, especially the teen-agers, who feel little need to study Chinese and would prefer to spend their time more entertainingly.

You enter the **Chinese YMCA** (855 Sacramento) through a traditional Chinese gate. But inside Chinese children are playing ping-pong or splashing around in the pool, usually joined by several Caucasians. The Y is one of the many influences gradually pulling Chinese youth toward closer identification with their contemporaries of all races and away from the insularity of Chinatown. The public schools, of course, exercise an even stronger pull. Chinese pupils are good students and active in extracurricular activities. In several junior highs and high schools, Chinese have been elected to student government offices. They are popular with other students and often make close friendships with them.

On your way back toward Grant you will notice, on the north side of the street, the Chinese Children's Playground in three tiers on the Sacramento Street hill. A small pagodalike building serves as a clubhouse for the playground that is busy through the afternoon and is often brightly lighted at night for evening activities. You can usually watch some fast tennis being played on a concrete court, and San Francisco's Chinese Baseball Team, which has toured the Far East, got its start here.

The playground's upper tier fronts a tiny alley, one of the many that flit darkly through Chinatown, called Pagoda Place. This one is dominated by a huge arrow pointing to the **Hang-Ah Tea Room** (Pagoda Place, corner of Sacramento), specializing in Dim Sun, the delightful Chinese tea lunch (see p. 84).

Sweets and Spices

Chinatown remains a battleground between old and new, between tradition and the inroads of commerce. Across the street from Old St. Mary's Church is the **Cathay House** (728 California Street) where up a flight of stairs and under an awning you enter one of the many restaurants where Chinese cuisine has been adapted to American food tastes. United Press International tickers whir noisily in the windows of the Chinese-language newspapers.

Stores and restaurants jostle each other on Grant Avenue. Neon signs become flashier. Stylish storefronts feature stylish women's clothing in Americanized-Chinese designs and distinctly Ivy League men's suits and sport coats. But many stores continue to favor traditional housewares and foods, leaning on Japan, Hong Kong, and Formosa for the supplies which once came from China.

You can buy sweet noodle puffs for ten cents each at **Fong-Fong Bakery** (824 Grant). There are also other Chinese delicacies and pastries such as lotus, black soybean, yellow bean, and melon cakes; also wife cakes, which are stuffed with winter melon. These pastries have a flaky crust and are not quite so sweet as their American counterparts. They make a good munch-while-you-walk dessert after a Chinese lunch or dinner. But the Chinese teen-agers who have made this bakery a hangout for years generally prefer lemonade, orangeade, hamburgers, and pies. A specialty of the house is ginger ice cream; small pieces of candied ginger cut the sweetness of the ice cream and give it a spicy, piquant taste.

Displayed in open shelves on the street at **Shing Chong Company** (800 Grant) are many of the exotic delicacies of Chinese cooking. Salted duck eggs sell at two for twenty-five cents. Here are bitter melons; they look like big wrinkled cucumbers and are delicious in the soups you can get in most Chinese restaurants, and they add a pungent taste to many meat dishes and to cakes and pastries. Here are elongated crisp heads of Chinese cabbage, almost endlessly long string beans, angle squash, so called for their sharp angular ridges, young green pea pods. Inside are dried mushrooms, barrels of dried fish, pieces of ginger root, herbs and spices. There are also broiled chicken, long sausages, and other cooked delicacies. Like many Chinese markets, Shing Chong also runs a catering business serving Chinatown families and organizations. Except for a few bottles of American whiskey on the shelves, there are no concessions to modernity in this musty store. It has been at the same location for fifty years, and Lu-ye, the withered patriarch who founded it, still comes around to look things over.

Smack in the middle of Chinatown is the **Italian Meat Market** (966 Grant), where Chinese butchers wrap up chickens and ducks prepared Chinese style in shopping bags proclaiming in Chinese characters the Italian origin of the market.

Across the street at the **Chong Kee Jan Company** (957 Grant) you can rummage among the sights and smells of a Chinatown slowly disappearing before the advance of the new stores and the modernized decor. This is a combination grocery, hardware, and novelty store. In little waxed-paper packets on racks are dried plums—quite sour and salty to Western tastes—dried shrimp, preserved kumquats, preserved olives, and licorice-flavored sliced ginger. Here too are Chinese cooking implements, ferocious-looking meat cleavers, great steel bowls, and Chinese ornamental pickling jars, ivory and wooden back-scratchers, native spears from

Formosa at $3.75 each, traditional Chinese two-string fiddles and other musical instruments.

Of all Chinatown merchants the herbalists have been hardest hit by the ban on trade with Communist China; some of them were prosecuted a few years ago under the trading-with-the-enemy act. Their influence used to be sufficient to trouble Chinatown doctors, graduates of modern medical schools who frown on the old-country remedies. But as the source of supply has been cut off, business has declined sharply. The herbalists are still around and they display some wondrous medicines—including Korean Ginseng Tea, supposedly a male rejuvenator. But they are increasingly being forced into new sidelines and now sell the toy guns, dolls, and other cheap novelties from Japan so much in evidence in Chinatown.

The Gradual Exodus

When you get to Pacific Avenue you will notice the long rows of handsome apartment buildings. This is the **Ping Yuen** (Tranquil Gardens) public-housing project where about four hundred Chinese families live. Imaginative details subdue and almost conceal the usual drab, antiseptic public-housing architecture. The name of the project is spelled out in giant Chinese characters. There are Oriental balconies fronting the apartments, and a gate at the main entrance is a replica of the gate of the Marble Pagoda in Peking's Yellow Monastery.

This project is the first overt hint that people really live in Chinatown. Although you see hundreds of Chinese on Grant Avenue and all the adjoining streets, there are few indications of homes and apartments. But more than twenty thousand of San Francisco's thirty-six thousand Chinese actually live in the few square blocks of Chinatown in overcrowded tenements behind the storefronts and above the restaurants. The rents are staggering, sanitary conditions poor, privacy nil, the tuberculosis rate high. The Chinese stayed in Chinatown partly because they had nowhere else to go, partly because they preferred their own dingy quarter to the alienation and hostility they would have to face on the outside.

In the last few years the exodus from Chinatown has begun. It has been gradual rather than spectacular, a response to the equally gradual breaking down of the restrictions on housing and employment and of anti-Oriental prejudice. But it continues steadily, and at an increasing rate. The Chinese have spilled over into the surrounding streets beyond Chinatown, into North Beach, up the slopes of Telegraph and Russian hills, intermingling with Italian and other families. Many have moved far from Chinatown into the Richmond and Haight–Ashbury residential districts. It is still hard for Orientals to rent apartments in San Francisco. But Chinese with money, and there are many of them, have been buying homes throughout the city since the outlawing of restrictive covenants. There are also now scores of Chinese stores and markets outside Chinatown.

Few Chinese think the exodus portends the eventual disappearance of Chinatown, and fewer still would like this to happen. Even for those who have left, Chinatown remains a meeting place and a center of social life. But many Chinese businessmen and professionals in their thirties and fourties think the move outside does portend greater integration of the Chinese in San Francisco and a shaking up of the old order in Chinatown, an end sooner or later of Chinatown's secluded isolation.

North Beach Medley

Chinese Grant Avenue ends in a sudden intersecting and crisscrossing of several different worlds where it meets Broadway and Columbus Avenue. Here Grant Avenue becomes part of North Beach, which is simultaneously the heart of San Francisco's large Italian community, the center of the city's night life, the locale of many of its best restaurants, a fortress of Bohemia and—particularly along the slopes of Telegraph Hill—an expensive residential area.

Broadway is an ersatz Neapolitan café world competing with a dissonant medley of other café worlds. You can find every kind of entertainment here, Italian arias sung in softly lighted bars while you sip a "Venetian coffee" (coffee and brandy topped with whipped cream), female impersonators holding forth at **Finnocchio's** (508 Broadway), gay-nineties variety shows, jazz combos. Restaurants line both sides of the street: tourist traps as well as modest, inexpensive places with good home cooking; Italian, and also French, Spanish, and Mexican eating places, remnants of the national groups once clustered here. There is a Chinese teahouse on one Broadway corner and on another a drugstore with signs in *three* languages—*Botica Española, Pharmace Française,* and *Pharmacia Italiana.* You can wander around the never-never land of San Francisco's Broadway or save it for a night on the town (see Chapter 6).

Columbus Avenue has its quota of night clubs and restaurants, but it is considerably more sedate. It is primarily the main street of Italian North Beach, with banks, businesses, travel agencies, with wonderful bakeries and aromatic food stores and delicatessens. But before exploring its sights and smells, you might first continue up Grant Avenue past Broadway and Columbus.

Upper Grant Avenue

Upper Grant Avenue is a hodgepodge of old Italian business establishments, Bohemian bars, tourist traps full of assorted bric-a-brac, fine arts-and-crafts shops, and Chinese garment factories. It is a battleground of conflicting influences, and the outcome is not yet in sight.

Only a few years ago this was a quiet Italian neighborhood street, with some artists and Bohemians in the little alleys up the hill. Many fishermen and their families used to live in the flats over the grocery stores. The wives ran the small shops while the men fished. Then came the influx of sad-eyed, restless young men and women who became known as *beatniks* (see page 131 for background). After them followed a massive tourist invasion, with smart entrepreneurs at hand to cash in.

There are still bearded youths and their sandaled girl friends around on Grant Avenue. But the beatnik phase has receded into myth and memory and faded newspaper headlines. Empty storefronts stare vacantly where only recently were jumping bars and bistros.

Gone now is the Co-Existence Bagel Shop which for six years flanked a ravioli factory on Grant Avenue. Opened as a fourth-rate Jewish delicatessen which actually served bagels, it soon turned into a dark, smoke-filled bistro which attracted a motley and disparate crowd. Here came young people seeking they knew not what, artists and pseudo-artists, organization men trying to escape the gray flannel suit for a week end, and leather-jacketed boys on motorcycles looking for noise, excitement, and a fist fight.

The results were sensational enough to fill newspaper columns on dull Monday mornings. For years the Bagel Shop fought a guerrilla war with Patrolman William Bigarani, who was assigned the upper Grant Avenue beat. He frequently arrested its denizens, and they in turn lampooned him in lurid pictures and violent verse. Bigarani was eventually transferred, but it was a Pyrrhic victory. The Bagel Shop succumbed soon afterward. It never paid its way. The beat bartenders who worked there gave away oceans of beer and tons of potato salad. Too many customers nursed one cup of coffee too long, and too many tourists came to look without spending any money. In its place there opened the Bugle Shop, an off-beat novelty store featuring such items as sandals for dogs.

The **Coffee Gallery** (1358 Grant), which was only slightly less stormy than the Bagel Shop at its heyday, closed down for a while at the end of 1960 and then reopened under new management in a pallid, scarcely recognizable reincarnation. Once "Orgies of Poetry" were held here and local poets read their works, drawing crowds that lined up for more than a block. Now only occasional tourists and sailors wander in to watch a few young amateurs in clumsy imitations of Elaine May–Mike Nichols skits.

While some Italian establishments were displaced by novelty shops, beat hangouts, and art galleries, two *pasta* companies hung on grimly in the shadow of the Bagel Shop. One is the **Panama Exposition Ravioli Factory** 1336 Grant), the other the **Panama Canal Ravioli Factory** (1358 Grant). How did Panama get mixed up with the *ravioli?* A clerk who has been at the Panama Canal place for seventeen years didn't know. But obviously the name dates back to the Panama–Pacific Exposition of 1915 in San Francisco.

Middle-aged North Beach residents and their parents before them have been shopping at the two pasta emporiums for as long as they can remember. These are just old stores with beat-up wooden fixtures; the *pasta*-making machinery is in the back. Each has ardent partisans who will never venture into the other, and both make every conceivable kind of *pasta*. At the Panama Canal, ask for their "special" *ravioli* if you must buy the store kind. What Italian housewives prefer is to make their own filling and bring it into the store, where the *pasta* is stuffed and cut. The Panama Canal also specializes in the sale of *pasta* by the yard. Housewives buy the sheets of *pasta* and then cut them up to suit themselves, filling them with a ham-and-cheese mixture and covering them with sauce to make a wonderful concoction called *cannelloni.*

The **Trieste Caffe Espresso** (501 Vallejo at Grant) outlasted its more spectacular neighbors like the Bagel Shop and retains something of the atmosphere of a European coffee house. The smell of freshly ground coffee permeates the place. Italian men sit around, unhurriedly reading their newspapers, impervious to the few young people in the unmistakable beat uniform who occasionally drop in. When the place was started a few years ago, a handsome white-haired Italian was brought over from Milan to officiate in style over the gleaming *espresso* machines. The maestro is gone and the performance is less dramatic. But the *espresso,* the chocolate, and the pastries are still excellent.

La Pantera (1234 Grant) still offers family-style Italian dinners for less than $2.50. You sit down at long tables next to whoever happens to be there and help yourself from great tureens of minestrone, heaping platters of pasta, baked fish with Italian sauce, chicken or veal or whatever the entree is that night.

As upper Grant Avenue became crowded with tourists looking for the fabled beatniks, smart businessmen moved in. **Street Fair** (1300 Grant) displays artists at work in the window and offers watercolors of San Francisco at $1.50 each. These are not bargain prices. **Things, Unlimited** (1309 Grant) is pretty much what the name sounds like, with a somewhat better-selected miscellany than some of its competitors and a good stock of Mexican imports.

House of Nile (1441Grant) offers custom-made skirts and tunics in an African decor. The long tunics are designed to conceal anything the wearer has in common with Marilyn Monroe but seem to be popular with the Bohemian set. Dorothy, the proprietress, does all the sewing herself, while her longshoreman husband designs sandals in off hours. You can pick up a good leather belt or a shrunken head, neither outrageously priced. The **Black Knight** (1435 Grant) offers bizarre styles in men's clothing.

There are a number of serious craftsmen with headquarters on upper Grant Avenue, some old-timers on the street, some newcomers in search of tourist dollars (see p. 186). **Designer Craftsmen of California,** a guild representing about fifty artist-craftsmen, is now at 1507 Grant Avenue. Several avant-garde art galleries are also located in this area; one of the more interesting is **The Scene** (1420 Grant), where two local artists show their work.

Gradually, at around Union Street, the Grant Avenue tourist attractions begin to thin out. The slope of Telegraph Hill becomes steeper and the streets assume the quiet flavor of what North Beach was like when an older generation of Bohemians lived cheek by jowl with an older generation of Italians. You can see Coit Tower above and the ships at their docks below. Here are the little streets where artists and writers once used to live in apartments renting at ten dollars a month; Gerkee Alley and Edith Lane, Whiting Street and Pfeifer Street. Old flats have been modernized and new contemporary apartments have popped up at fancy rents. In fitting homage to its Italian ancestry, Grant Avenue comes to a full stop at the Roma Macaroni Factory at Francisco Street. From there a steep flight of stairs takes you down to the Embarcadero.

Little Italy

If upper Grant Avenue represents the exposed and infiltrated flank of Italian North Beach, retrace your steps to Columbus Avenue to find the main stronghold of fifty-five thousand San Franciscans of Italian extraction, by far the largest of the city's national groups and one of the longest entrenched. There were a few Italians here in the 1840s when San Francisco was a village, and a couple of decades later Italian fishermen were sailing their feluccas through the Golden Gate. The major influx came in the latter part of the century, from every part of Italy—Romans, Neapolitans, Genoese, Tuscans, Sicilians, Venetians. Many became ranchers and dispersed throughout Northern California. But most of them settled in the northeast corner of the city, in the North Beach area—which really used to be a beach before the Bay was filled. The area surrounding Telegraph Hill and the inland sea below somehow reminded them of home. There were also less sentimental reasons. Land and rents were cheap, and fishermen could hardly find a more convenient location.

Soon the Italians far outnumbered the Irish, Mexicans, and other nationalities in the area. They stayed, and many of them prospered—some modestly like the children and grandchildren of many of the fishermen, others spectacularly. The city's mightiest financier was Amadeo Giannini. San Francisco's mayor in the 1930s was Angelo Rossi; its folk hero was Joe DiMaggio. Although most Italians clustered around North Beach, it was not a ghetto. San Francisco Italians built their own community there, moved away when they wanted to.

At the outset of the Italian part of Columbus, before it has shaken off the night-club and tourist atmosphere of Broadway, **Thomas Cara Ltd.** (306 Columbus) presents a gleaming showcase of the wares required for Italian and continental gourmet cooking. The store flaunts an aloof, sophisticated atmosphere, appealing more to the outlander than to the home folks in North Beach. But the broad-bearded Thomas Cara gets a gleam in his eyes when he shows off the casseroles of every size (which come with free veal *scallopini* recipes), apothecary and spice jars, chafing dishes, glasses of all sizes, fine Italian bottles. He is fully equipped to take care of the current *caffè espresso* craze, offering glistening copper and steel machines in every size, from frighteningly expensive monsters to simple little gadgets easy to operate on your own kitchen stove. You can also find whimsical, skinny-as-a-rail *espresso* cups in brilliant colors.

Many old North Beach residents buy their espresso equipment and their machines for making and cutting *pasta* at home at **Biordi's** (412 Columbus). There is nothing streamlined about this store cluttered with flowered majolica ware, plates and bowls with gay patterns, Venetian lanterns for electric lights or candles, Murano glassware with an odd stippled effect. Glassware and pottery here tend to the colorful and the ornate rather than stripped-down modern. Biordi's has good spaghetti bowls and oil and vinegar bottles, also *cannoli* tubes for those who know how to make that luscious, cream-filled Italian pastry.

There are now some fancy delicatessens in North Beach, with modern decorations and fixtures. But **Molinari's** (373 Columbus) stubbornly clings to old fixtures and decor. Here you will find all sorts of imported goodies—wines, cookies, cheeses, *antipasti, panettone* from Milan, dried codfish called *bacala*. Famous for sausages made on the premises, this is the only place in San Francisco where gourmet chefs can get the finest Italian sweet sausages and the hot Sicilian sausages called for in many Roman and Bolognese dishes. Giant *provolone* cheeses and salamis hang from the ceilings. Here are *prosciutto,* the thin Italian ham, and *mortadella,* a sausage of veal and pork cut in huge round slices. On top of the counter are layers of *fogaccia,* the flat luscious breads flavored with onions and other seasonings.

Columbus Avenue is lined with wonderful bakeries where you can buy crunchy bread sticks, aromatic rum cakes, and delicious *cannoli,* Napoleons, and chocolate pastries. North Beach bakeries are the best in the city. Although prices have gone up over the years, they are still astoundingly reasonable for the quality. Favorite of many of the old-timers is the **Columbus Pastry Company** (507 Columbus). Specialties of the house are the St. Honoré cake, a dreamlike concoction of tiny puffs filled with rum-flavored Italian cream, a delight to look at and to eat, Napoleon pastries, and cakes made with scores of layers of flaky light dough interspersed with Italian cream. There are also displays of luscious cookies, of sweet, round *panettone* larded with glacé fruit, and of imported Italian candies. A perennial treat is to buy some of the pastries and walk over to nearby Washington Square and eat them without waiting to get home.

One of San Francisco's greatest glories is the sourdough French bread that originated in this area, although the biggest and most successful of the bread bakeries have moved elsewhere in the city. San Franciscans believe there is nothing quite like their French bread anywhere in the world. It is, of course, influenced by French and Italian prototypes, but is somehow quite different. The crust is crunchy but not hard, the inside soft, the flavor indescribable. When you eat in a new Italian restaurant, you can tell from the start whether the food will be good. The French bread is the tipoff. Expatriate San Franciscans sometimes have it shipped in by plane to wherever they may be, and it has been described as San Francisco's secret weapon in its never-ending battle for bigger federal appropriations. Mayor Christopher was having a hard time in 1960 getting $500,000 from the federal government to extend the runways of the city's airport. He was almost in despair until, according to newspaper reports, he heard that the official entrusted with making the decision had a passion for San Francisco's French bread. The mayor had six loaves of sourdough French bread flown to Washington by jet and capped a dinner for the recalcitrant official with this finest of the city's gourmet foods. The inevitable result was a more enlightened attitude toward the runways.

Lucchesi's (543 Columbus Avenue) is remembered by North Beach residents as Lippi's, the name it had for many years. Except for the name, this vegetable and grocery market hasn't changed. The storefront and the interior are as unprepossessing as ever, with the goods apparently just thrown around at random. There are no plastic wrappers here. You can feel the vegetables, pick them up and smell them. But to gourmets all over the city this is almost a shrine. They come here to buy the herbs called for in many Italian and French recipes—fresh tarragon, oregano, basil, bay leaves. The owners will go to the produce markets for old customers to buy hard-to-get items. Fresh artichoke hearts, tiny but green and perfectly formed, are a specialty here. So are the yellow squash blossoms Italian families fry in hot olive oil.

Many Italian families do their general food shopping at **Buon Gusto** (480 Columbus) and **Rossi's** (627 Vallejo near Columbus). Moving from department to department, they can buy in either store little artichokes and long green *zucchini,* thin slices of veal for veal *scallopini,* Italian sausages, and dry romano and parmesan cheese. A scandal in one of these markets a few years back rocked North Beach when, as a result of business rivalry, brother informed on brother to the immigration authorities, alleging illegal entry to the United States. The community was split into rival factions, but the informer had by far the worst of it. North Beach was also shaken by the marriage of Joe DiMaggio and Marilyn Monroe. Middle-aged matrons said sadly that Joe had married the wrong girl and professed not to be surprised at the subsequent divorce. North Beach is still a small town in the midst of the big city.

The town square is **Washington Square** (Columbus Avenue and Union Street), a rather unlovely little park not much improved by the digging and landscaping that went on there for years and by singularly inappropriate statuary. A bronze statue of Benjamin Franklin, bequeathed by an elderly eccentric, is the square's main adornment. The park was also the beneficiary of Lillie Hitchcock Coit, the unquenchable lover of fire engines, who left it a monument to the volunteer firemen of San Francisco's early days. There is no statue to Christopher Columbus, a North Beach hero even more durable than Joe DiMaggio. A massive Columbus stands, instead, atop Telegraph Hill facing the Golden Gate he never saw and the harbor he never entered. Quite oblivious of the park's esthetic deficiencies, generations of North Beach oldsters have sat on the benches and philosophized with their cronies and countless North Beach children have played there on the grass.

Rising high above the square are the two spires of the **Church of Saint Peter and Saint Paul** (660 Filbert Street). This church is less than forty years old; even newer are the mosaics in the doorway of Dante working on his *Paradiso* and of Columbus discovering America. But it has become a center of many North Beach activities. Opposite the church is the reviewing stand for the annual Columbus Day parade, a major spectacle complete with elaborate floats and reenactment of Columbus' feat, in which thousands of San Francisco Italians participate. From this church starts the procession to Fisherman's Wharf for the blessing of the crab fleet on the first Sunday of October. Two blocks away is **St. Francis Church** (620 Vallejo Street off Columbus), by far the oldest church in North Beach and one of the oldest in the city; the present building dates from 1859. In front of the church stood for some years a massively gentle and peaceful St. Francis by Beniamino Bufano (see p. 127).

Some old-timers lament the vanished past in North Beach, the good little restaurants where you once could get a first-class meal and real Italian wine for fifty cents, the familiar markets and stores that are no more, the decline of old-fashioned quality in others, the dilution of the old-country Italian atmosphere. They note as a sign of the times that the queen of one recent Columbus Day parade was a girl from suburban Kentfield who didn't even know her way around North Beach. But much of this is just another manifestation of the nostalgia common to San Franciscans.

North Beach has survived repeated invasions by the Bohemian hordes, and will probably continue to do so. It has probably even gained something in the process. Its residents, as well as other San Francisco Italians, have endured the fires of the melting pot without altogether losing their identity. They are San Franciscans and Americans, but with a definite Italian flavor that has enriched both them and their city. North Beach has also been little affected by the exodus of the thousands of Italians who now live all over the city and in the suburbs. They all come back to shop or for family occasions and celebrations. The story is told of one wealthy resident who decided to spend his declining years on the Italian Riviera. Before very long he was back in North Beach. He said that he preferred to die at home. North Beach is still home to Northern California Italians. It is also a continuing delight to other San Franciscans.

From Bataan to Kearny Street

On the fringes of North Beach and Chinatown along Kearny Street are a few dingy hotels and restaurants which serve as headquarters for San Francisco's still underprivileged Filipino community. Hundreds of Filipinos came long ago as agricultural workers, domestic servants, culinary workers. A few worked their way up and became businessmen and professionals, but not many. Then after World War II there was a new influx, survivors of the famed Philippine Scouts, the twelve thousand men who had fought under General MacArthur in the early stages of the war. Many of the Scouts had records of twenty to thirty-five years in the U.S. Army, and a grateful government gave them U.S. citizenship as a reward for their service. So the Filipinos started coming to San Francisco and other West Coast cities in order to retain their newly gained citizenship and to find jobs. Their hope was to make enough to bring their families here.

But the government that had acclaimed their war record allowed them only half the retired pay awarded other enlisted men of equal rank. It also denied them back pay for the period of the Japanese occupation of the Philippines. The discriminatory treatment was disillusioning. Besides, they were destitute and handicapped by their advanced age and a formidable language barrier. So they clustered together in cheap flophouses like the **International Hotel** (848 Kearny Street). The basement of this old brick building has been handsomely redecorated and now houses the **hungry i,** one of the city's sophisticated night clubs. But the lobby and the rooms upstairs are as bare and rundown as before. Filipinos also hang out at the **Bataan Lunch** (836 Kearny Street) which looks like a dive but serves excellent, inexpensive Filipino dishes. Aided by social-work agencies, the Philippine Scouts and other immigrants from the islands have begun to find their way into useful employment. Their situation has improved from the low point of the early postwar years, but San Francisco's twelve thousand Filipinos still have a long way to go.

By no means all of San Francisco's many worlds are to be found in the Chinatown–North Beach sector within easy access of a walking tour. Others are scattered through the city's neighborhoods in the Western Addition, in the Richmond district, in the Mission district, and on Potrero Hill. These areas aren't as colorful as Grant Avenue or Columbus Avenue. But they do have attractions worth visiting, and the nationalities that live there are an important part of San Francisco's fantastic diversity.

Japanesetown

Around Post and Buchanan streets in the Western Addition (a Fillmore 22 bus will take you within a block) you will notice Japanese grocery stores, restaurants, and shops poised on the brink of chaos, next to the gaping scars and cavernous excavations created by wrecking crews with bulldozers and steel balls operated from giant cranes. San Francisco's Japanesetown is smack in the middle of the giant redevelopment program dedicated to demolishing the old stores and the rundown sprawling masterpieces of Carpenters' Gothic in what is called the Western Addition.

While Japanese imports have flooded stores throughout the city, you can get good buys and some hard-to-get items in the modest shops in this area. There seems to be some sort of affinity between American plumbing fixtures and Japanese *objets d'art*. Hardware stores display pottery, vases, and antiques, lower-priced than in the downtown stores, along with wrenches and toilet seats. **Soko Hardware** (1698 Post) offers the best buys in rice bowls, teapots, and planters. Similar assortments are offered by **Seiki Brothers** (1640 Post) and **Taiyo** (1656 Post). In addition to miscellaneous bric-a-brac, the **Japanese Trading Company** (1600 Post) has a good selection of attractive *zabutons* (floor cushions, to the uninitiated) at reasonable prices.

If you prefer looking at Japanese folk art in more esthetic surroundings, stop in at **Honnami Taieido** (1709 Buchanan), which displays gift items minus the hardware. You will see a large variety of *origami*—birds and animals created by the Japanese paper-folding art. Caucasians, children and adults, might enjoy trying their hands at this, although they shouldn't expect to equal the work displayed here. This store also has heavy stoneware pottery in muted shades of gray and brown. There are books in English about Japanese children and an assortment of the latest magazines and paperbacks from Japan. The cover girls look disconcertingly like those on our own movie magazines and paperbacks.

In this neighborhood there are several small restaurants with simple, good Japanese food. Try chicken teriyaki, crisp like Southern fried chicken but tantalizingly different with the Japanese sauce, at the **Matsuya Restaurant** (1729 Buchanan Street; see p. 91). Every Friday, Saturday, and Sunday from 6:30 P.M. on, Japanese movies are shown at **Kimnon Hall** (Bush and Buchanan streets). While the art houses show some Japanese films, this is where you can see Japanese swordplay thrillers about the samurai, quite similar to our own Westerns, or an occasional sleeper which is really good.

Many Japanese families and some stores have moved out of the Post–Buchanan sector, and more will probably do so under the impact of the redevelopment program. Others will shift headquarters into a modern Japanese shopping and restaurant center projected for the area. But in one form or another, San Francisco's Japanese will adjust to the change in this area. They have taken, within our time at least, the worst beating of any group in San Francisco, and they have come back strong.

In the 1920s and 1930s, many of the shops on Grant Avenue in Chinatown were owned by Japanese. They were also solidly established in the Western Addition, gradually having settled there after the 1906 fire. In addition to homes and businesses, they had newspapers and a community life of their own. The younger people generally clustered around the Japanese YMCA and YWCA. The Japanese were probably on the whole more Americanized than the Chinese.

World War II suddenly changed all this. The school children began to be ostracized and were called "Japs." The Japanese Tea Garden in Golden Gate Park, one of the city's abiding glories created by skilled Japanese gardeners, was renamed the Oriental Tea Garden. In 1942 the gardeners and several thousand other San Francisco Japanese, most of them native-born American citizens, were rounded up and put into so-called relocation centers, actually semiconcentration camps in the most desolate areas of the West. The Japanese lost their homes, their businesses, their possessions. The wholesale uprooting of a hundred thousand Japanese throughout the West Coast was described as an urgent measure for military security. It is now generally considered the outstanding idiocy resulting from World War II hysteria.

Japanese-Americans, born here, educated here, and without the slightest division in their loyalty, somehow maintained their sanity when they were treated as dangerous enemy aliens. Many enlisted and fought and died at Anzio and elsewhere. In the relocation camps they kept themselves busy with hobbies and art work. They also kept their dreams alive. Although some of their old area was taken over by the wartime influx of Negroes, they re-established themselves, building up a community of some ten thousand Japanese-Americans. With little capital, they again started stores and businesses. Gradually but persistently they broke down residential and employment barriers. Today Japanese secretaries are in great demand in business offices; employers have discovered they are efficient and hard-working. Japanese business people have bought homes where they please in residential areas. Japanese school children are popular with their fellows. The bitterness of the relocation period isn't all gone, but its main reflection is a quiet determination not to take any nonsense in the future.

Japanese decor is much in vogue in San Francisco. *Shoji* screens and *zabutons* are now standard in many Caucasian homes. Chinese and Japanese foods are great favorites. But, surprisingly, San Francisco does not provide the same link with Asia that New York maintains with Europe; it is not particularly attuned to the conditions and problems of the Far East. Constant wars and political turmoil in the Far East for a generation probably have something to do with limiting development of stronger ties. Oriental influence in the city was also curtailed by the old discriminations against the Chinese and Japanese. Recent efforts to change this situation include plans for a Japanese cultural center in the Western Addition. Perhaps in the future San Francisco will be able to enlarge its scope as a gateway between Asia and America, helping each to know and understand the other.

Upheaval in the Fillmore

Many of San Francisco's Negroes are intermingled with the Japanese in the Western Addition—the Fillmore district, as it is more often called. **Bop City**'s sign at Post and Buchanan is a quiet reminder of the Negro strongholds in the heart of Japanesetown. It is quiet, that is, until 2 A.M. when this after-hours night club opens. Then, when the other night spots are all closed, both Negro and white musicians come here to relax or sometimes to play a set or two. Most of the jazz greats have performed here with the house band, and aspiring young beginners hang around to get a chance to hear one of the big names in action (see p. 117).

The Fillmore is still a center of Negro social and business life. Negroes still shop here, and they still eat authentic Southern barbecued meats and delectable sweet-potato pies at **Leonard's Hickory Pit** (1423 Fillmore) and **Kansas City Hickory Pit** (1355 Fillmore).

They still come down here to go to church, and the hotels and night spots are still crowded on week-end nights with Negro men and women in evening clothes.

But increasingly Negroes have been moving out of the Fillmore. They have been pushed out by the redevelopment program, which is erecting modern, expensive apartments in place of the old flats that once stood here. Redevelopment shook up a new Negro community none too firmly rooted and just beginning to find its own leadership and common aims in improving living conditions, job opportunities, educational levels. It left San Francisco Negroes without a single focus and aggravated existing problems.

Before the war there was a small, well-established Negro community of perhaps five thousand. Negroes were not without housing or job difficulties. But they felt at home and shared the prevailing chauvinism that exalts San Francisco above all other cities. Then Negroes came in the thousands from the South to work in shipyards and other war industries, expanding throughout the area and moving into the homes of the evacuated Japanese. The influx continued after the war, resulting in an explosive burgeoning of the Negro population to seventy-four thousand in the 1960 census—more than 10 per cent of the total population.

When the war was over and the good jobs at good pay disappeared, Negroes found themselves with serious problems of social adjustment. They didn't find in San Francisco the extremes of bias to which they had been exposed in the South. But they did find it hard to get work, although San Francisco was the first California city to pass a fair-employment law. They also found it hard to get decent housing, and often paid exorbitant rent for substandard flats. To be forced out of the dingy flats and the painfully purchased old houses they called home was a difficult blow.

As the old Fillmore district has been demolished by the wrecking crews, rival centers of Negro population have developed. Negroes have moved south to the Oceanview or Ingleside district, into the neat little houses of a middle-class residential area. The white population quickly moved out, leaving behind a developing Negro ghetto with the familiar problems of ghettos everywhere—juvenile delinquency, gang fights, unstable family life.

Negro leaders see more hopeful signs in the Bayshore district in the extreme southeast, near Candlestick Park. Negroes have long owned small homes here among Italian and other white families. Although more Negroes have moved in, few white families have moved out. Real estate values have not declined. Negro and white neighbors generally get along, belong to the same community improvement clubs and P-TAs. Interestingly enough, the social problems found in areas of more concentrated Negro population are largely absent.

The Jewish Community

The pungent smells of Jewish foods begin to infiltrate Fillmore Street where it meets McAllister Street, south of the major Japanese and Negro communities. At **Shenson's Delicatessen** (1171 McAllister) you can get green sour tomatoes and kosher pickles, pastrami, salami, delectable smoked salmon, buying food to take home or sitting down at the counter for a sandwich if you can't wait. The **Ukraine Bakery** (1100 McAllister) has wonderful onion rolls, crisp salt sticks and fresh bagel, excellent cakes and pastries. But it is best known for its black Russian soldier bread, which it now sells to restaurants and stores throughout the Bay Area. This is real bread, in substantial loaves, not the neatly presliced, prepackaged, tasteless white mush that passes for bread these days.

Only remnants are left of what was once a substantial Jewish population in the Fillmore. But the stores have remained and are patronized by Jews (and non-Jews) from all over the city.

San Francisco's forty thousand Jews have no special area of concentration. They live where they please and have never been subjected to discrimination, not even the customary subtle exclusion from the higher levels of society. They came, mainly from Germany at first, in the early gold-rush days and helped build the city. Adolph Sutro was once mayor of San Francisco; his tunnel under the Comstock Lode made him a millionaire and enriched countless investors in Nevada mining stock. The Fleishhackers, the Zellerbachs, and the Slosses have been big names in San Francisco business and civic life for generations. Jews have been congressmen, millionaires, founders of the California Society of Pioneers. They have also been rogues like Boss Abe Ruef, who turned City Hall into a gravy bowl of graft during the early years of the century, and lunatics like Emperor Norton.

Immigrants from Eastern Europe who came after the early settlers found that Jews were accepted without question as part of the city. Probably the largest single Jewish community is in the Richmond district north of Golden Gate Park. Here are some of the impressive temples and synagogues of San Francisco Jews. On the fringe of this area is the **Jewish Community Center** (California and Presidio), which is a focus of social, recreational, and educational activity.

South of the Slot

On St. Patrick's Day it seems that San Francisco is an over-whelmingly Irish city. The shamrock is drowned in innumerable bars. Green ties and ribbons are seen everywhere in the streets. The St. Patrick's Day parade on Market Street is a massive affair, and the post of grand marshal is a conspicuous plum. The Irish pre-dominate in politics, especially Democratic politics. The roster of the city's Democratic Central Committee reads like a list of digni-taries at the annual Robert Emmet Day observance in Golden Gate Park: Hagerty, Sullivan, Reilly, O'Brien, Maloney. An Irish name is a major asset in any election. But appearances are deceiving. The influence of San Francisco's Irish has little relation to their num-bers; there are fewer than forty thousand. The undoubted political flair of the Irish has something to do with their prominence in city affairs. But more than organized national group or political power house, the Irish are a San Francisco tradition.

There were many Irish prospectors among the Forty-Niners. There were Irish millionaires, like William S. O'Brien of the Com-stock Lode Big Four. But most of the Irish were the teamsters, the carpenters, the longshoremen, the men who worked in the railroad roundhouse. They were the city's hewers of wood and drawers of water, and they were the most articulate spokesmen for popular resentment against the snobs on Nob Hill. The names of San Fran-cisco's early labor leaders were almost exclusively Irish. The Irish were liberally sprinkled among the crowds that gathered on the sandlots to protest inequity and injustice, and the speakers were almost invariably Irish.

The Irish lived south of Market Street on the wrong side of the tracks, literally south of the slot. The designation referred to the iron slot in the middle of the cable-car tracks on Market Street; it divided not only the street but also the city. This part of town was also called the Mission district for the old mission on Dolores Street and for the main street that wound erratically through the south-of-Market area. There were others besides Irish in the old Mission district along the little alleys like Jessie, Clementina, and Minna (named after the city's pioneer prostitutes) and farther south along the hills and valleys of the area. There were Slavs, Scandinavians, Poles, Dutch, Russians, Jews, almost all workingmen and their families who felt they, and not the swells north of Market, were the city's real people, the people who did the work and had built San Francisco. It was the feeling expressed in a ballad by an old south-of-Market boy:

Whether you know your location or not,
The heart of the city is South O' the Slot!
That is the spot
True to the dot—
The heart of the city is South O' the Slot!

It was the feeling expressed with a more conscious class angle, but also with delightful humor, by Jack London in a story called "South of the Slot." The story is about the Dr. Jekyll-and-Mr. Hyde conflict between the worlds on both sides of the slot that rages inside a sociology professor called Freddie Drummond. To facilitate his research work on a massive tome about Unskilled Labor, the professor lived and worked for a few months south of the slot and assumed the name of Bill Totts. As book followed book, the professor returned repeatedly for more research. On campus, Freddie Drummond was a dry-as-dust pedant. As Bill Totts, he was a hard-drinking, two-fisted union militant. A complication ensued in the person of a dark-eyed Irish girl, a vivacious little organizer for the Glove Makers Union. Bill Totts was getting too involved south of the slot. So Freddie Drummond decided to end the double life and go back to the campus for good. He was even going to marry the daughter of the head of the philosophy department. It was all set when one day he went driving with his betrothed down Market Street and ran into a savage battle between police and striking teamsters. Freddie Drummond watched impassively for a while. Then suddenly Bill Totts took over and, single-handed, routed the cossacks. The strikers cheered their hero who walked off, his arm around the little organizer. He married the girl, of course, and became a union leader himself. Freddie Drummond never did get back to the campus. He stayed south of the slot.

The iron slot is long gone. Perhaps half the city is now south of Market Street from the Bay to the ocean. All kinds of people live in the Mission district in all kinds of houses in all kinds of neighborhoods, including squalid semislum streets and delightful hilltop retreats. Many Irish are still there. Many more have scattered through the city and have, of course, gone up in business, politics, and the professions. But there still clings to the San Francisco Irish an earthy flavor, a suggestion of the old vigor and the old times when they were the underdogs and the champions of the underdogs; this is part of their heritage and perhaps it is their political secret. There is also a remnant of the past on downtown Mission Street now ugly with warehouses, furniture stores, decrepit headquarters of light industries. The shrubbery still grows green around **St. Patrick's Church** (Mission Street between Third and Fourth streets). This is probably the most Irish church in the United States, with stained-glass windows depicting the visions of St. Patrick and ancient Irish myths; the Irish have worshiped here for more than a century.

Farther out Mission Street, once the main thoroughfare of the Irish, the flavor is now predominantly Latin-American. Here have moved thousands of new immigrants from Mexico, Nicaragua, and El Salvador. The streets are dotted with stores that have *Se habla Español* signs, and there are churches, restaurants, and movie theaters catering to the Spanish-speaking population. There is nothing quaint about most of these places, and some of the proprietors take a dim view of Anglos who ask for Mexican foods but can't pronounce the names. Better write out *canned mollé powder* than risk a dirty look after trying to pronounce it.

Most interesting of these Mission-district establishments is the **Sanchez Spanish Book and Music Store** (2130 Mission Street). Shopping here is like a bit of Mexico City. None of the regular customers bother to speak English, and most of the merchandise is Mexican or Spanish. There is a wide selection of Spanish-language records, paperback books, and periodicals. There are also soaps, goatskin wine jugs, church goods, and fancy jewelry imported from Spain. Sanchez has a colorful display of *piñatas*—crêpe-paper-decorated clay jugs which are filled with candy and broken by blindfolded children at Christmas. But the beautiful donkeys, parrots, and what have you are on display at Sanchez the year round.

The Potrero Hill Russians

Tenants in the new three-story, glass-walled apartments on Potrero Hill often watch on Saturday afternoons to see the smoke rising in the yards back of the old frame houses where their Russian neighbors live. Literally scores of the yards contain bathhouses replete with fireboxes covered with stones. After the stones have heated up to just the right point, whole families troop through the back yards for the weekly steam baths.

To many San Franciscans Russian Hill isn't the hill where the artists and writers lived and which is now one of the most exclusive residential areas in town. It is Potrero Hill, southeast of the business section of town where there really are Russians. They came shortly after the turn of the century when the hill was still sparsely settled and the few residents kept goats and chickens and cows. The Russians were mostly Protestants who fled Czarist Russia to escape conscription in the Russo-Japanese war. Today they and their descendants make up a large portion of the residents and on Sunday the Molokan and Russian Baptist churches are filled with bearded patriarchs and their shawl-draped wives.

Up through the end of World War II Potrero Hill, although close to the center of town, was still semirural. In fact, the last of the hill's "goat ladies" continued her long legal battle with the city health department into the 1950s before she was finally routed. She had previously fought the city to a compromise whereby she was permitted to retain one goat. The city had complained there was no way of preventing the development of a flock if she had two. Now the goat ladies are gone. So are the old sailors who retired here to watch the ships below.

Long-neglected Potrero Hill, which enjoys the best weather in the city and some of the best views of the Bay, has at last been discovered by artists and Bohemians and by the real estate developers who have been hot on their trail. The shacks of the goat ladies have been turned into studios. The portholes of the sailors have been draped with fishnet curtains. Land values have risen astronomically, and multistory apartment houses now overshadow the traditional single-family house.

The Russians on the hill are now a slowly dwindling minority, and other areas in town have become more important as centers of Russian life. Russians coming into San Francisco in the last few years, many of them refugees, displaced persons who had wandered all over Europe and Asia, have settled in the Richmond district. It is in this area that you now find some wonderful, unpretentious Russian delicatessens, bakeries, and restaurants (see pp. 99–100).

San Francisco International

San Francisco's international atmosphere derives partly from the fact that the city was not shaped by peoples of any one or even two or three national backgrounds. There are at least a dozen major groups that have influenced the city.

If the Italians have a slight edge numerically, the Germans are not far behind. The impact of two world wars has caused them to subdue many of their cultural and German-language activities. But there is still a German weekly paper, and there are literally scores of German athletic, hiking, and singing societies, most of them with headquarters in what used to be known as Deutsches Haus and is now more discreetly called **California Hall** (Polk and Turk streets). There is an excellent rathskeller downstairs; here you can get old-fashioned sauerbraten and other German delicacies.

The French are outnumbered by the Irish, the Chinese, the Latin-

Americans, and the Russians. But they were among the city's pioneer storekeepers and financiers and have been an important factor ever since. Back in 1850, Felix Verdier, a wealthy republican refugee from France, put up his sign *La Ville de Paris* on a jerry-built store which has since grown into the City of Paris department store. Skilled French laundresses came over to wash the dirty clothes of the Forty-Niners who had been sending their laundry as far away as Honolulu and Canton. And there is still an active French community in San Francisco, which turns out en masse every year to Golden Gate Park to celebrate Bastille Day.

San Francisco has substantial colonies of English and Welsh, Scandinavians, Yugoslavs, Czechs, and Hungarians. It also has small but cohesive groups of Maltese and Samoans and Pakistanis. And there is a growing number of American Indians, who have recently left reservations. There are at least sixty different national groups in San Francisco. Church services are performed regularly in twenty-three different tongues. There are twenty-five newspapers published in fourteen languages, including Chinese, Japanese, Russian, and Italian dailies. There are several radio stations specializing in foreign-language broadcasts. And the city's varied peoples all celebrate their national holidays, giving the city a continuing sense of festivity and diversity.

Chinese New Year is a major event, as brass bands blare, drum majorettes of all nationalities twirl their batons, and a papier-mâché lion prances through Chinatown. For the Chinese as for the Irish, green is the color for luck, and the local merchants hope for the best by pinning up dollar bills and strips of lettuce on their storefronts. The former are picked up by the lion and turned over to Chinese Hospital on Jackson Street.

Bay Area Italians rally for a weekend of Columbus Day celebrations—complete with a champagne Coronation Ball at the Italian consulate-general, where the Columbus Day Queen is picked, a parade from Market Street to North Beach, and a re-enactment at Aquatic Park of the landing of Columbus, usually an event fraught with mishaps and saved from disaster only by the ever-alert Coast Guard.

The more faithful of the Irish celebrate not only St. Patrick's Day but also Robert Emmet's birthday, gathering at the martyr's statue in Golden Gate Park, where Irish ballads are sung and Emmet's defiant "Speech of the Dock" is solemnly recited. The Scots have their Robert Burns Day, the Poles their Pulaski Day. The Finns regularly observe the appearance in book form of the *Kalevala,* their ancient sagas. The Greeks commemorate Greek Independence

Day, and the Welsh celebrate St. David's Day with a banquet and with songs and dances in their ancient Cymric tongue. At the Japanese Bonn Festival every August, even some Americanized Nisei participate in traditional dances while the old folk honor the dead with offerings of incense and flowers in the temples.

One factor which keeps alive old national customs is a continuing trickle of immigration. Into San Francisco every year comes an average of four thousand immigrants, a surprising number at a time of rigid quotas and restrictions. There come Chinese from Hong Kong; Russians, Japanese brides of American soldiers, Hungarians, Latin-Americans. In 1959 the new arrivals were from eighty-four different countries and came in about equal proportions from Asia, Europe, and Latin America. A substantial service agency, the **International Institute of San Francisco** (2209 Van Ness Avenue) welcomes the immigrants with a "New Arrivals Party" the third Friday of every month at its headquarters in a sedate old mansion near the Western Addition. The Institute also runs a variety of social, cultural, and educational activities to help the immigrants become acclimated.

There must be something about San Francisco which draws people from all over the world. While San Francisco's record as a family of nations is far from perfect, men and women of diverse races and nationalities have probably felt more at home here than in most other American cities. There has been on the whole an appreciation for differing ways of life and an absence of forced or synthetic integration. Most San Franciscans of foreign ancestry and various racial and ethnic stocks are a part of the city and of the larger community of their fellow citizens. But few national groups are so assimilated that they do not preserve at least some vestige of old-country tradition or language or customs. The result adds to San Francisco the verve and color and variety that are among its most delightful aspects.

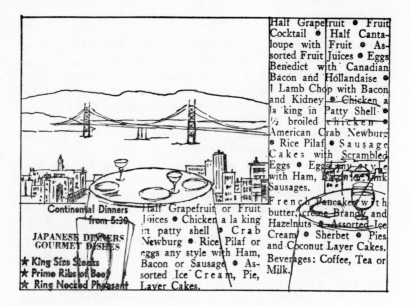

5: EATING OUT

THE HIGHLIGHT of San Francisco eating out is the infinite variety of restaurants offering good—and sometimes great—food at inexpensive or moderate prices. The city has several high-priced and well-known eating places that regularly win magazine awards as among the nation's best, and no doubt they deserve them. A couple of these are listed in the obviously incomplete chronicle that follows. Personal predilections naturally enter, but we have intentionally put emphasis on restaurants that will appeal to the working gourmet who doesn't happen to be unusually affluent, on those temples of gastronomy where food rather than decor or swank is the thing, on restaurants offering delicacies from all over the world at prices most people can afford, at least occasionally.

Don't forget the wine! Wine is pretty much *de rigueur* in most San Francisco French, Italian, and other European-style restaurants. It is a pleasant custom and will not boost the price of your meal excessively. A good California wine will usually cost less than a French or German wine of similar quality. You can't go wrong if you stick to wines from the Napa Valley, the best wine-growing district in the state, and perhaps in the country. Charles Krug, Inglenook, Beaulieu, and Louis Martini wines are all highly recommended. Extremely inexpensive and surprisingly good Napa Valley wines (about $1.25 a half-gallon at retail) are produced by Montebello. A number of restaurants use Montebello as their house wine. House wines are ordinarily cheaper than brand names, and are often quite adequate.

Rosé wines have become increasingly popular in San Francisco since they will go with almost any kind of food. In ordering white wines, you might vary the usual sauterne by trying the more delicate and lighter Chablis (actually a white Burgundy) or a tart Riesling. You might also try a light claret (it may be labeled cabernet or zinfandel) instead of a Burgundy when ordering red wine. The tart, full-bodied Italian wines, usually known as *Grignolino, Barbera,* and Chianti, are also extremely popular in San Francisco.

Except for the Chinese and some of the smaller Russian restaurants, virtually all the eating places listed serve wines. The larger Japanese restaurants serve saki. Most of the larger places listed, including the Chinese and Japanese, have bars.

Some San Francisco restaurants are given, or have given themselves, the label *continental*. This refers usually to Italian restaurants which also carry some French dishes, although it can cover almost anything from Armenian *sarma* to Swedish smorgasbord. Because of the vagueness of the label, it isn't used here. A restaurant that is primarily Italian or French or Armenian is so listed, even if it has some other national specialties on its menu.

Unless otherwise specified, restaurants listed are open seven days a week and serve both lunch and dinner at the usual hours.

Warning. Addresses, prices, and hours change, so check by phone before going to a particular restaurant.

Chinese

If you have time or money for only a few restaurant meals in San Francisco, at least a couple should be Chinese. And if a tight schedule limits you to only one, it should be a tea lunch, what the Chinese call Tiny Heart or *Dim Sun*. This is a unique delight of San Francisco restaurant eating, something you are unlikely to encounter in any other American city, except on a more limited scale in New York. Even in cosmopolitan San Francisco, only a relatively few Caucasians are familiar with *Dim Sun,* which makes a spectacular and inexpensive lunch or Sunday brunch.

Dim Sun consists mainly of various kinds of pastries, generally not sweet; the dough is stuffed chock-full of meat or fish and finely chopped vegetables, then boiled, steamed, baked, or fried. The delicacies include buns stuffed with roast pork (*char-shew bow*), rice-flour dumplings with shrimp, pork meat balls, mushrooms stuffed with fish, and custard egg tart pastries (which *are* sweet). The tea-lunch houses also serve delightful noodle dishes: soft, pan-fried noodles with vegetables and pork or beef.

In most of the restaurants—there are now about a dozen offering this specialty—the clientele is primarily Chinese. The waiters may not know English, and there are often no menus. But there is no real problem about ordering. Just ask for a tea lunch, or say *Dim Sun,* and the waiter will bring a tray loaded with all sorts of delicacies. Pick the dishes that look most delectable to you, and the waiter will take the rest back. You can always get refills. When you are through eating, the waiter counts up the little dishes and figures out your check. No matter how well you have scraped the plate, he can always tell what was in it. If there is a party of three or four, the bill will come to about a dollar each for an ample lunch, perhaps a little higher if you are alone and want to sample a variety of dishes.

Hang Ah Tea Room   1 Pagoda Place, off Sacramento between Grant and Stockton. 11 A.M. to 3 P.M. Closed Sunday. YU 2-5686. The little alley on which this teahouse is located isn't easy to find, but it is worth looking for. It is directly opposite the three-tiered Chinese playground on Sacramento Street, and a huge arrow painted on a wall shows you the spot. There is nothing fancy about this place. It is a big, bare room with plain tables, decorated only by Chinese lanterns. The only one of the teahouses to be discovered as yet by a substantial Caucasian clientele, it maintains an excellent cuisine in the face of some pretty stiff competition from newcomers to this field.

Yank Sing Tea House   1357 Powell Street, corner of Broadway. 10 A.M. to 5 P.M. Closed Friday. SU 1-1111. You may have to stand in line to get into this one, unless you miss the peak lunch hours. It is a small place, quite devoid of atmosphere and Chinese lanterns. Its success is a tribute to the adaptability of George Chang, a refugee from mainland China who started it a couple of years ago. Chang, a university graduate and one-time government official with Chiang Kai-shek, picked up the culinary art while traveling all over China. Starting a restaurant seemed the only way he could earn a living in this country when he finally got here after a few years in Hong Kong. This is strictly a family enterprise; Mr. and Mrs. Chang do the cooking; during summers and week ends their two lovely schoolgirl daughters are the waitresses. The delicately flavored *ha-gow,* shrimp rolls, are probably the best to be obtained outside

China. The custard egg tarts are another specialty. The bill of fare
includes a North China delicacy called *tza jiang mien;* this is sort
of a Chinese variant on spaghetti (or probably vice versa), a
noodle dish with a pork sauce which is a real treat for serious gourmets. If you want to be daring, ask for *suan la jie tsi,* sweet-sourish
and pickled mustard greens. Yank Sing is considered Number 1 in
the teahouse line by knowledgeable San Francisco Chinese.

   Eden Cafe   531 Jackson Street at Columbus Avenue. 9:30 A.M.
to 5:30 P.M. YU 2-1708. Mr. K. C. Wu runs one of the newer and
better tea-lunch restaurants in town. Mr. Wu has traveled widely
over China and has decided ideas about Chinese food. He believes
that the ingredients and the cooking methods have a lot to do with
preventing disease, that a Chinese diet will protect you against
cancer and other calamities. He also has a wide repertory of dishes
and offers a number of Northern Chinese delicacies. The specialty
of the house is Roasted Peking Cake, which looks like a big round
cookie; it is covered with sesame seeds and has a delicious meat-
and-vegetable filling. If you'd rather not pick and choose, you can
just ask for the tea lunch—and you will get an excellent and complete meal for seventy-five cents.

   Modern Restaurant   735 Jackson Street. Tea lunch served 10
A.M. to 3 P.M.; dinners in the evening. SU 1-9730. A special
delicacy here is curried beef in a flaky pastry dough. The food belies
the nondescript name of the restaurant and the big *Chop Suey* sign
over the door. Ignore the plain marble-top tables and the drab
interior—and the menu which lists familiar Chinese dinner dishes.
If you ask for the tea lunch, you will get one of the best in town for
the same seventy-five cents to a dollar as at the other teahouses.
While you eat, an old Chinese at a nearby table may be filling thin
pats of dough with pork. In another booth a young Chinese, dressed
in a sport jacket, may be reading *Time* or *Newsweek*.

   Songhay Tea House   650 Jackson Street. Tea lunch 10 A.M. to
6. P.M.; dinners to 10 P.M. YU 2-3344. A large plain dining room
favored by Chinese businessmen and residents. Turn to the back of
the menu for a list of tea-lunch delicacies, including lotus bean with
egg-yolk buns, shrimp with bamboo shoots, birdnest and pork,
sweet rice roll with pork sausage—all very inexpensive indeed. You
can also get a substantial dinner, including occasional specialties
such as abalone with black mushrooms, for about a dollar per
person.

   While Chinatown dinner restaurants depend more heavily on
tourist trade than the tea-lunch houses, the patronage of local

Chinese is an important factor for all and decisive for many. San Francisco Chinese are big eaters-out; family groups celebrate birthdays and other occasions in restaurants. And they are serious and discriminating about their food. They are loyal to the quality of the food rather than to the restaurant. If a chef leaves one restaurant for another, his clientele will often follow. In closely knit Chinatown, word-of-mouth advertising determines the fate of an eating house; it can doom an establishment that lets its standards slip or make a smashing success of one which features new and entrancing delicacies.

The Chinese community is the conscience of the Chinatown restaurants, a barrier against backsliding into the morass of greasy-spoon cafés, the phony Americanized Orientalism which has been the fate of so many Chinese eating houses throughout the country. Chinatown restaurateurs boast of the freshness of their ingredients and offer statistics on the number of chickens (more than 5000) and ducks (more than 1200) slaughtered daily, on the lightness of fried foods unmarred by excessive grease, on the crispness of their vegetables and the delicacy of their seasonings and sauces. It would be an exaggeration to say that Chinatown restaurants are just a bit of old China plunked down in San Francisco. They modernize their decor, Americanize their cuisine, even make the grudging concession to Occidental gaucherie of adding chow mein and chop suey to their menus. But the better ones keep alive an authentic core of the Chinese culinary art, making it possible for San Franciscans and visitors to the city to dabble in the wonderful (and delightfully inexpensive) mysteries of Chinese cooking.

Price is not a problem in Chinatown eating out. It is difficult to spend more than five dollars per person even in the most lavishly decorated Chinatown restaurant appealing chiefly to the tourist trade, and it is relatively simple to find a good meal for less than half that amount. What to order can be a more serious matter; most people don't know, and the menu isn't always enlightening. The decision involved here is whether you are willing to experiment with the unknown or whether your food tastes are conservative and fixed. At least a little experimentation is recommended.

Most Chinatown restaurants offer family dinners at $1.50 per person and up. If you are a novice and want to start off easy, this is one thing you can do. You will miss the fine points of Chinese cuisine, and experts and old China hands will raise their eyebrows, but it is one way to start.

A slightly more advanced alternative, and sometimes cheaper, is to order à la carte but to stick to familiar Cantonese dishes which are the tried-and-true favorites of Caucasians in Chinatown. Although the Chinese usually eat their soup at the end of the meal, you can start off with *won ton* soup, a delicious chicken broth served with filled dumplings and garnished with slices of pork. You can follow with such dishes as sweet-and-sour pork, oyster beef (thin slices of beef served with a pungent oyster sauce), prawns with peas, crab with lobster sauce, lobster with black bean sauce, almond chicken or chicken in paper (chicken cooked in a cellophane wrapping), fried *won ton* (crisp, deep-fried dumplings with a sweet-and-sour sauce), crisp and delectable pressed duck. You should also include a *chow yuk*, a vegetable dish cooked with meat; green pea *chow yuk*, made with crisp green pea pods, is almost invariably excellent.

Real experimentation requires hurdling the language barrier. Some of the best dishes in Chinatown restaurants aren't even included on the English menu. If they are listed at all, these are tucked away in the Chinese-language part of the menu. One solution is to ask for the *wo tsoi*—harmonized dishes. This is simply the equivalent of the family dinner offered on the Chinese menus. This is the way a Chinese family or group orders; the food you get is different, better, and less expensive. A more direct approach is to note what a nearby table of Chinese is eating and tell the waiter in your best English, pointing all the time, "We want that!" One inexpensive little experiment on your own is to ask for *lap chong*, the tangy Chinese sausage.

A real gourmet treat, and one that even rank beginners will enjoy, is **Peking Duck.** Old China hands tell us that the preparation of this dish is a high art, beginning with the breeding and feeding of just the right kind of plump, delectable duck. (The Long Island duck is said to be a descendant of the Peking duck, brought from China by a New England sea captain.) The ducks chosen for banquet treatment are put in a small box and force-fed the last few weeks of their brief lives until they are virtually square, filling the box on every side. The crackling-crisp skin of ducks so nurtured is said to be beyond description. The ducks are cooked for twenty-four hours and served with appropriate ceremony. The skin is eaten first, sandwich style, in a steamed bun with a pungent plum or bean sauce. Several Chinatown restaurants will prepare Peking Duck if you phone them twenty-four hours in advance. China experts maintain that the resulting product is only a faint approximation of what they have exulted over in Shanghai or Peking. They claim that the ducks available here are not properly fattened and that the Cantonese chefs in Chinatown don't have the know-how to prepare this North

Chinese delicacy. To this, defenders of Chinatown cuisine reply that the ducks used in the local restaurants are carefully fed in advance on a duck farm in South San Francisco and that several chefs in the city have mastered the difficult art of preparing Peking Duck. Whether the dish available in Chinatown is fully authentic Chinese cooking or not, it is authentic good eating. The usual price for a good-sized duck is about $7.50, including buns and condiments. There is enough duck for four to six people; only two or three more dishes (say a soup and a *chow yuk*) are really needed for an adequate and unusual meal.

The case of the Peking Duck suggests the major criticisms leveled at Chinatown restaurants by serious students of Chinese food. They point out that Chinatown, where chefs and residents alike come almost exclusively from the Canton area, specializes in Cantonese food and that the hot and fiery dishes of Szechuan and Hunan provinces and the delights of Peking and Shanghai cooking are unavailable. They find the cuisine too limited. But to most Americans the variety will seem infinite and bewildering.

Several restaurants, moderate-priced by any general standard but relatively high-priced in Chinatown, offer excellent versions of the Cantonese dishes mentioned earlier. They all have many Chinese customers, but they have adapted their English menus to American tastes. Depending on what you order, dinner will total two to four dollars per person.

Tao Tao   675 Jackson Street. Closed Thursday. YU 2-6125. Traditional Cantonese cooking offered in somewhat more traditional surroundings than most Chinese restaurants. An interesting feature is the permanent exhibit of thirty pre-1906 Chinatown photographs by Arnold Genthe. The vivid shots of men with pigtails and women with bound feet and black silk trousers communicate a sense of the vanished Chinatown that was a city within a city.

Nam Yuen   740 Washington Street. Closed Monday. SU 1-5636. Ginger beef and bitter melon soup served in the shell are among the specialties, but most dishes are excellent here.

Sun Hung Heung   744 Washington Street. Closed Tuesday. YU 2-2319. A modest Chinese family restaurant with white-top tables only a few years ago, this has become one of the most popular and crowded places in Chinatown. The new Chinese-moderne decor has been no improvement, but prices are still reasonable and the quality of the food has for the most part been maintained. The *won ton* soup here is probably the best in town.

Kuo Wah   950 Grant Avenue. YU 2-3706. This one may run

just a bit higher than the three restaurants above and caters chiefly to a non-Chinese clientele. The quality of its Cantonese dishes is excellent. Lobster Cantonese is a specialty. Kuo Wah will prepare Peking Duck if you phone at least a day in advance. A tea lunch is also available, 11 A.M. to 2 P.M. daily.

For the more venturesome there are a number of lower-priced restaurants frequented almost entirely by Chinese where a family of four can eat for a total of five to six dollars. You can have the same kinds of dish here as at the fancier restaurants above. These are good places to experiment with unfamiliar dishes if you are so inclined.

Sun Tai Sam Yuen   622 Jackson Street. 11 A.M. to 9:30 P.M. YU 2-2844. An unpretentious Chinese eating house with regular dinners and all the tried-and-true Chinatown dishes. But you can also get here some delicious and unusual specialties—Chinese sausage, salted vegetable with pork, and Chinese red cheese and pork.

Kay Kay Garden   835 Washington Street. 5 P.M. to 2:30 A.M. YU 2-0702. This extremely inexpensive and modest eating house, we are told, is the closest thing in appearance to a typical Chinese restaurant. It has such traditional hallmarks as a long flight of stairs going up, round tables, and a spittoon in the corner of each booth. Especially recommended are water chestnuts and pork as well as a *won ton* soup with a curry flavor.

For many years San Francisco had no restaurants offering Northern Chinese food. Recently two eating places have moved into this gap:

Four Seas   731 Grant Avenue. EX 7-5577. The name of the restaurant is taken from Confucius: "Within Four Seas all men are brothers." The motto on matchbooks and advertisements is "Food from all the provinces of China." And Four Seas does offer an unusual variety of dishes and Chinese culinary styles—with lots of atmosphere and at rather high prices. The decor is subdued and tasteful Chinese modern. The waiters are dressed in red aprons. Count on spending at least three dollars per person—and up to five or six if you want to order some of the interesting specialties, or what is described as the "special gourmet dinner." But the food is good, and you can get here dishes unavailable elsewhere in Chinatown. Barbecued Mongolian Lamb, thick slices of marinated lamb barbecued with Chinese parsley, is an unusual and genuine treat. Or try Bamboo Shoots Szechuen sautééd with mustard greens. You can get Peking Duck here at eight dollars if you order it in advance; also Szechuan duck, steamed whole and deep-fried to produce a wonderful crisp skin.

Golden City   939 Kearny Street. EX 7-3543. San Francisco's relatively few Northern Chinese hang out in this modest and inexpensive restaurant featuring Shanghai-style cooking, which is more highly seasoned than Cantonese. The place looks like a dive, and the quality of the cooking is sometimes erratic. But you can experiment here with such delicacies as Peking-style fried meat dumplings (*gwo tiar*), Szechuan-style pickled vegetables, and Shanghai-style pan-fried soft noodles; the latter are called *chow mein* but otherwise have no similarity to the Americanized dish. A specialty is ginger beef, thin slices of beef sautéed with ginger.

Many Chinese restaurants keep late hours. This is to serve the midnight snacks which are a specialty of a number of Chinese eating houses. A bowl of *won ton* soup is a treat after the theater. You might try **Sam Woh** (813 Washington Street; YU 2-0596) for a traditional late snack—rice gruel over slices of pork, beef, or duck.

Japanese

Yamoto Sukiyaki House   717 California (near Grant). Closed Monday. Dinner $3–$4. EX 7-3456. The oldest Japanese restaurant on the West Coast, and one of the most elegant. It has the restrained decor and muted color that fans of Japanese movies will expect. You sit cross-legged on *zabutons* (cushions) at low tables in small, tastefully furnished rooms. Soft-voiced waitresses in traditional costume cook your *sukiyaki* at the table on a *hibachi*, quickly blending together tender strips of beef, green vegetables, bean sprouts, soy sauce, and other condiments. All the familiar specialties are served; the broiled filet of beef with spicy soy sauce called steak *teriyaki;* the shrimp *tempura,* like abstractionist butterflies in their light batter. The *oyaka donburi,* scrambled eggs and chicken, is delicious over rice.

Mingei-Ya   2033 Union Street. Closed Monday. Dinners about $4. JO 7-2553. This is supposed to be Japanese country-style dining, as contrasted with the greater formality of Yamoto; *mingei* is the Japanese word for folk art and is intended to suggest simplicity and spontaneity. Miyo Rudzinki, the attractive owner, has gone to considerables pains to insure authenticity. You are served not on shimmering lacquerware but on heavy deep-glazed pottery. And on warm days you can eat outdoors in a

Japanese-style courtyard. It seems hard to believe that they do things quite so luxuriously back on the farm in Japan. There is some city slickness and soft selling—including little throwaways and post cards—mixed up with the country atmosphere. But the result in any case is an exceptionally charming and relaxing restaurant with first-class food. Be sure to make reservations, especially on week ends, and be prepared for a long, leisurely meal. If you order tempura, you get all sorts of delightful and oddly shaped delicacies, long slivers of fish and fresh vegetables as well as prawns. The specialty of the house, *O-Mizu-Tak,* is something like *sukiyaki* but with a cream-base sauce. It's interesting, but rather rich. Conservative tastes will prefer the *sukiyaki* and tempura. Saki is available with the meal, and you can order some bold and unusual drinks from an imaginatively furnished little bar. One of San Francisco's most delightful eating places. In an adjoining shop you can buy the same beautiful pottery you are served on.

Matsuya Restaurant   1729 Buchanan Street. Dinner $1–1.50. JO 7-7600. No Japanese decor. No atmosphere, except the contemporary Japanese Tin Pan Alley songs on the juke box. Just good, simple cooking and exceptionally reasonable prices. This is where many Japanese who live in the Buchanan–Post Street neighborhood go to eat out. The food is authentic, and fish dishes are the dominant note. The *suimono* (clear broth) has a strong fish flavor. The shrimp *tempura* compares favorably with that offered in the more expensive Japanese restaurants. The *nabe Yakudon* (noodles with mushrooms and vegetables) appeals to the Western palate, but the *chiri nabe* (fresh vegetables cooked with sliced fish and seaweed) may be too exotic. The *sunomono* (salad) with shrimp is cold and crisp. The *tsukomono* (pickles) in little side dishes are tangy and good. If you want a good, inexpensive Japanese restaurant, this is the place to go. In case you want to experiment on your own, there are half a dozen similar restaurants serving the Japanese community close by.

Indian

The Curry Bowl   4221 Geary Boulevard. Dinners about $3. Open only Friday and Saturday, 6–11 P.M. SK 2-2636. It is typical of San Francisco that some of the best Indian food in town is served by Tom Lee, a tall, affable Eurasian who lived most of his life in China. Magnificent in his tall white chef's hat, Mr. Lee likes nothing better when his cooking's done than to sit down with his guests and tell about his travels all over the Far East and discuss the fine points of Northern Chinese or Indian cuisine. In fact, he says he considers the restaurant sort of a social activity rather than a business. He and his wife earn their money making frozen curry puffs for quality food stores. These little pastries, permeated by the curry flavor in the meat filling, can be ordered à la carte at ten cents each. Mr. Lee's thick, dark curries are served in style in handsome casserole dishes. The tray of eight condiments is replenished regularly, and you get a huge bowl with saffron-flavored rice. Mr. Lee believes in ample portions and you will feel well satisfied if you order just the entree (lamb, beef, chicken, crab, or shrimp curry) at less than $2.50. But if you are really hungry it will be well worth your while to order the complete dinner, including a tart soup and tangy salad. Try and get here during the crab season so you can enjoy Mr. Lee's saffron crab. This is a place where you can enjoy good food and quiet, relaxed conversation at exceedingly moderate cost.

Most famous of San Francisco's curry restaurants is the **India House** (629 Washington Street; EX 2-0744; closed Sunday). The pungent curries are served with éclat by turbaned waiters, and you are charged for the atmosphere, about five dollars for dinner. Also atmospheric and less expensive, about three dollars for dinner, are **Taj of India** (825 Pacific Street; EX 2-0089) and **Little India** (40 Jones Street; MA 1-7789).

Filipino

Bataan Lunch   836 Kearny Street. À la carte dinners about $1.25. DO 2-0486. Duncan Hines would never have recommended this place. It is not for sticklers for cleanliness or for the conservative. The juke box blares maddeningly; sailors wander in and out. But if you like to try unusual dishes, you can get authentic Filipino food here. It is very spicy and tasty, similar in some ways to Creole cooking. You have to know what to order—the waitresses are exceptionally casual. A small glossary: *manok,* chicken; *ampalay,* bitter melon; *sotanghon,* long-grain rice; *sarciado,* tomato sauce; *baboy,* pork; *carne,* meat; *hipon,* shrimp; *isda,* fish. We particularly recommend the *hipon* and the *tapang carne* (a pungent meat-stuffed omelet). There is a highly flavored chicken soup, *tinolang manok,* well blended with garlic and bitter melon. You'll never be able to eat canned chicken broth again. The hot peppers ought to wear a "keep off" sign. Also stay away from dishes with *dinuguan* (blood).

Italian

The Italian motif is the strongest in San Francisco eating out. While higher-priced Italian restaurants sometimes call themselves "continental" and offer French dishes, the Italian influence on other restaurants is even more pronounced. Where else do German *hofbraus* offer Yankee pot roast with *tagliarini?* There are more Italian restaurants than those of any other nationality, and there are good ones at every price level. They offer a variety of dishes and of seasonings and sauces and herbs which will startle those who equate Italian cooking with mushy spaghetti or doughy pizza.

Henry's Fashion   22 Davis Street (at Market). Closed Sunday. Dinner about $5. SU 1-8485. This restaurant has just about everything for a gala dinner out, especially if you're not on an expense account and yet want to be free of worrying about how much it is costing you. This is a traditional (since 1919) San Francisco restaurant. The service is superb. You can eat at leisure without being rushed. And the food is outstanding. This is essentially an Italian restaurant; it even serves *antipasti assortiti* rather than the hors d'oeuvres of other "continental" restaurants. But there are some French dishes on the menu. *Saltimbocca à la Bolognese,* a specialty of the house, is a standout. *Saltimbocca* means "jump in the mouth," and it is appropriately named. This dish, featured in several San Francisco restaurants, is veal wrapped in *prosciutto,* the thin Italian ham, and served with a delicate wine sauce. Boneless king squab, breast of capon, and sweetbreads are also recommended. The complete dinner is an excellent value, unless you're not up to a gargantuan meal.

Amelio's   1630 Powell Street. Dinners $5–$7. SU 1-9643. This is a first-class Italian restaurant with prices that are relatively high for San Francisco but far from astronomical, considering the quality of food and service. As in all San Francisco Italian restaurants, the dinners are simply enormous—beginning with a substantial tray of hors d'oeuvres, a salad or soup, *pasta,* followed by a meat or fish entree, coffee, and dessert. The more lavish desserts, such as cherries jubilee, are extra. Amelio's chicken dishes are the least expensive on the menu, but are among the best of the gourmet dishes. The rich cream sauce of Chicken Raphael Weill, named after the department-store tycoon who loved it, may be a little too much for some palates. We prefer the Chicken Jerusalem, baked in a more delicate white wine sauce. A very staid and respectable restaurant indeed, Amelio's recalls discreetly on its menu the more wicked times of the past: "Persons entering these premises unescorted must remain unescorted while in this place of business."

If Henry's Fashion and Amelio's seem to us the archtypes of good San Francisco Italian restaurants, there are several others offering similar food, although with individual specialties and variations on the theme, in the same price range. You won't go wrong in any of them.

Vanessi's   498 Broadway. GA 1-0890.
Oreste's   118 Jones Street. GR 4-5811.
Panelli's   453 Pine Street. DO 2-7198.
Torino's   130 Leidesdorff Street. YU 1-2211.

Excellent Italian food can also be found in many lower-priced restaurants, among which are the following:

New Joe's 540 Broadway. À la carte lunches and dinners. EX 2-9979. San Francisco is full of Italian restaurants with some variation of *Joe* in the name. There is an Original Joe's No. 1, and also an Original Joe's No. 2. Suburban entries include Joe of Westlake, Sonoma Joe's, and Marin Joe's. The common denominator of most of them is that there is nobody called Joe in the place. According to legend and Herb Caen, New Joe's is the real original Joe's; Caen says that the "new" was put in the name to make it clear that the Joe who started the restaurant as a front for a gambling joint was no longer around. After this preface, let it be added that New Joe's on Broadway is still an original. The place has been gussied up with a fancy cocktail bar and modern decor. But the quality of first-rate Italian cooking at moderate prices remains. New Joe's Special, the justly famous mishmash of hamburger, spinach, eggs, and onions, has inched up to the two-dollar mark. But it is still special. The hamburgers (sacrilege to use the same word that describes the nineteen-cent variety) are the best in town, good-quality ground meat on a quarter of a loaf of delectable French bread. Or try the cheeseburger, made not with a thin slice of packaged, pasteurized American cheese but with a thick slab of fresh, tangy Monterey Jack. The most fun eating here is to sit at the counter and watch the chefs at work. They pour olive oil lavishly, deftly toss hamburgers high in the air, or adroitly trim the fat off the veal to be used in *scallopini*. When they make chicken sauté, the flames shoot high in the pan as the olive oil heats; onion and green pepper are added; wine is carefully ladled on and the dish is lovingly coaxed along. The chefs assume a nonchalant air, chattering in Italian among themselves. But they are aware all the time of the admiring eyes upon them. The same food is available here from early in the day until late at night; there are no formal lunches or dinners. But you can have a good special dish and coffee for about two dollars, or a more rounded meal for four to five. One word of warning: New Joe's is usually crowded.

Lupo's Pizzeria   1042 Kearny Street. À la carte. SU 1-9938. You get the best pizza in town here, not the soggy, pasty stuff which passes by the name in some restaurants. You can watch the chef toss the paper-thin dough high in the air, cover it with the delicately flavored fillings in more than twenty varieties, and pop it in the big stainless-steel ovens. There are also many other fine specialties here, all à la carte at about $2.50 for main dishes. Our favorite is *calamari sauté à la Lucien*—squid made into a most tantalizing dish. Other highlights are a savory and unusual spaghetti with lobster sauce and a lush veal *parmigiana*. The vinaigrette cold vegetables make good side dishes. Lupo's seems to have everything, a good location in a dimly lighted cellar at the edge of North Beach, candles on the tables for those who like that kind of thing, excellent food, and good service. But it lacks some of the little touches you would expect in a restaurant where a complete à la carte dinner would run about five dollars. The portions are small, there is an additional charge for each coffee refill, and paper napkins are used instead of linen. A lack of showmanship may account for the fact that this is the least crowded of the good North Beach Italian restaurants. In the meantime, you can enjoy an unusual meal here in quiet surroundings without the annoyance of waiting to be seated.

The Iron Pot   639 Montgomery Street. Lunch about $1.50, dinner about $3. EX 2-2100. In the days when the fabulous Montgomery Block was nearby, the local Bohemians used to gather here at night over a bottle of red vino and a platter of Italian cheeses. Legend has it that an iron stew pot was constantly simmering on the stove, and that many an artist received a lavish helping of its contents in return for one of his paintings. What is left now is a good Italian restaurant with red-checkered table-cloths, with candlelight and paintings on the wall adding a dash of culture and atmosphere. Near the bar is a little sign which explains carefully that the house takes no sides in the different fields of art expression and gets no cut from the paintings; the proceeds go to the artists. The paintings cover quite an artistic range. Some large canvases have the slapdash effect of the action school; others are conventional watercolors of cable cars. Over the bar there is a romantic painting of Rima in *Green Mansions*. Getting back to food, *Lasagne a pesto* (a garlicky parsley herb sauce) is inexpensive gourmet eating, as is the roast chicken served with tasty vegetables.

You may have heard of the good old days when you could get a fine Italian dinner, complete with wine, for thirty-five cents. That was true before World War II. But you can still get good Italian food, a complete seven-course dinner, for about $2 to $2.50 at several restaurants.

La Pantera Cafe   1234 Grant Avenue. EX 2-0170. Here you eat family style at long tables. Great bowls of soup, huge platters of salad, fish, *pasta,* and meat are passed around. Sometimes a sauce on the fish or meat course has a touch of greatness. You get wine with the dinner, but they do charge extra for coffee, and you have to be willing to sit at a table with strangers in a plain, unadorned eating place. This is one of the best food values in town.

North Beach Cafe   1512 Stockton. SU 1-9316.

Caesar's Restaurant   2299 Powell Street. Closed Monday. DO 2-1153.

Montclair Restaurant   550 Green Street. DO 2-5188.

Green Valley Restaurant   510 Green Street. EX 2-9290.

Buon Gusto   555 Broadway. Closed Sunday. GA 1-9938.

One of the old-time North Beach family-style restaurants, Buon Gusto recently reopened after a short and unhappy life as a Dixieland jazz bistro. Food is simple, inexpensive; always available is *pasta peso* and fresh basil—parsley, garlic, butter and olive oil worked over into a fine, smooth green sauce over spaghetti or, better still, over *tagliarini*.

There are even a few Italian restaurants left in North Beach where you can get an adequate if uninspired dinner for slightly under two dollars.

New Lucca   631 Broadway. SU 1-5731.

New Pisa   1268 Grant Avenue. DO 2-4726.

San Remo   2237 Mason Street. OR 3-9090.

French

In the latter decades of the nineteen century San Francisco became famous for such great French restaurants as the Poodle Dog, the Maison Riche, and the Maison Dorée. The story goes that these and other celebrated eating places were started as a result of the numerous transcontinental trips of New York financiers and railroad kings who came west to inspect their properties. The tycoons, of course, took their chefs with them in their private railroad cars. When their business was done they returned to the East—but without their chefs, who stayed in San Francisco to open glittering temples of the French cuisine. San Francisco's French restaurants first gave the city its long-enduring reputation as a gourmet's paradise. They did not give the city its reputation for wickedness; it had that already. But they added to it a romantic and sophisticated aura. All the French restaurants had private dining rooms upstairs with couches and doors that could be securely locked, making them favorite rendezvous for lovers as well as gourmets. The old haunts are gone, but the French influence on San Francisco's food tastes remains strong.

San Francisco can boast good French restaurants in all price ranges. Among those in the four- to six-dollar category are the following:

Le Trianon   242 O'Farrell Street. Closed Sunday. YU 2-9353. We'd rate this as the best medium-priced French eating in town. Table appointments, candlelight, smooth service all suggest the "class" restaurants. So does the food. Soup and salad are above-average quality. The chicken livers sauté and the *entrecôte* beef filets are especially fine. For dessert you can splurge on a Grand Marnier soufflé. Portions are ample but not overwhelming. There is an excellent wine list of both French and domestic wines. Trianon is apt to be crowded week ends, and reservations are a good idea. Large parties are handled with ease and assurance. The over-all impression is one of Gallic elegance at moderate cost.

Chez Leon   124 Ellis Street. Closed Sunday. YU 2-1093. Run by the former chef of Romanoff's swank, now-defunct San Francisco restaurant, Leon likes to consider his cuisine continental, but the *coq au vin* and other specialties are distinctly French. You are given meticulous service and attention along with the food and wine.

Ritz Old Poodle Dog   65 Post Street. SU 1-1918. The last survivor of the French restaurants of San Francisco's golden era. It is, of course, now chaste and respectable. The food is no longer so divine as it is once said to have been. But it is still good. And the Poodle Dog still exudes plenty of old San Francisco atmosphere.

There are at least three surprisingly good low-priced French restaurants at which you can eat well for about three dollars:

Koe's Auberge   1205 Stockton Street. Closed Sunday. EX 2-1608. On the fringe of Chinatown is an exquisite and inexpensive little French restaurant run and operated by Chinese. Koe's has a plebeian-looking storefront and is sandwiched in most unpretentiously between a family shoe store and a grocery. The elegance within, soft taupe walls, glittering chandeliers, and an intimate atmosphere comes as a surprise. The seating capacity is quite small and adds to the feeling that you have made a find. Everyone who has eaten here refers to Koe's as a gem, but this one is rapidly becoming as well known as the Hope Diamond. Harold Koe, assisted by a brother and two sisters, makes good on the adage that the Chinese are the French chefs of the Orient. The *boeuf à la bourguignonne,* flavored with pearl onions and served in a charming copper bucket, is a real treat. The frogs' legs are meltingly tender; there is also a delectable chicken curry. The service is excellent, as is the wine selection. A few years ago you could get a good meal here at $1.50. Mr. Koe admits frankly that his prices have gone up with the spruced-up decor. Dinners are à la carte, and by the time you add all the trimmings you will probably spend about $3–$3.50. But still a spectacular value and a find for those who don't know about it.

Hotel de France   780 Broadway. GA 1-9528. This is country-style French cooking with decor to match: red-checkered table-cloths, brightly colored woodwork and posters. The emphasis here is on good, substantial French food, not on elaborate delicacies and sauces. You get a complete dinner, and a very good one indeed, for $2.50. But you get no choice. You take what is on the menu, which changes every night. Friday night, for example, you get clam chowder, hors d'oeuvre, rex sole in a *meunière* sauce, roast beef, salad, dessert, and coffee. The service is good. It is hard to beat this place at the price.

Des Alpes   732 Broadway. Closed Monday. GA 1-9909. Mme. Catherine Bardalampe greets all customers warmly and the old regulars with a kiss on the cheeks; her mustached husband John officiates genially over the bar. They leaven with a personal touch the otherwise rather routine manner in which an excellent French family-style meal is slapped down before the customers. If plain, unadorned surroundings and indifferent service don't bother you, you will get here one of the best and biggest under-$3 dinners in town. We found Hotel de France more pleasant and relaxing. But the almost identical type of food at Des Alpes is perhaps a shade more distinguished. *Vol-au-vent,* tasty veal with wine sauce served in a patty shell, is especially good. This is just an appetizer, served once or twice a week, before the main chicken or roast-beef course.

Russian

The best thing that has happened to the flatlands of the Richmond residential district (in the northwest part of town) is the influx of Russians who have brought in their wake a number of good small restaurants. These are run by recent émigrés, displaced persons who have come via Shanghai or Germany. They usually start as small bakeries or delicatessens and branch out to serve lunches and dinners.

Mary's Fountain   301 Balboa Street, at Fourth Avenue. Dinners about $2. Closed Monday. EV 6-9459. Boris and Mary serve authentic Russian food in what looks like a neighborhood soda fountain. Don't be fooled by the unpretentious appearance. The food is good and inexpensive. Try the tasty chicken cutlets, the stuffed cabbage, or the *pelmeni*—savory meat dumplings served in a pot of chicken broth. These are excellent. The beef Stroganoff is good here but lacks the extra elegance this dish requires.

Luchina Restaurant   1829 Clement Street. Dinners $2–$4. SK 2-5629. Lots of atmosphere, including a highly decorated Russian peasant-style-art front. Specialties of the house, all served with flair, are *shashlik* on swordlike skewers, chicken with sour cream, and *pelmeni.*

Miniature Restaurant   433 Clement Street. Inexpensive snacks, lunches, and dinners. Closed Sunday. SK 2-4444. Behind a tiny delicatessen with exquisite goodies is a plain dining room offering hearty, low-priced, excellent Russian food. The *piroshki,* deep-fried dumplings filled with ground meat, are out of this world. You can have an excellent lunch with a big bowl of luscious sweet-and-sour cabbage borsch, good rye bread, two *piroshki,* and a cup of coffee for about ninety cents. A fine dinner will come to about two dollars. Or you can just drop in for a snack. There is no attempt to create atmosphere. The predominantly Russian clientele knows this place is genuine. The broad-faced waitresses

may have a little trouble with your English, but they will do
their best to make you feel at home. On your way out, you can
stock up on Russian smoked fish, chocolate-covered waffle pastries,
and excellent hard candies.

Helen's Bakery and Coffee Shop 1801 Clement Street, at
19th Avenue. Low-priced snacks. SK 2-7484. You can drop by
on a Saturday or Sunday afternoon for a couple of *piroshki* and
a cup of coffee and see middle-aged expatriate Russian ladies
smoking, chattering, and sipping tea. Helen Kashikow waits on
you while her husband John works in back preparing the *piroshki,*
dainty French pastries, *baklava,* strudel, honey bread. The quality
is exceptional at the price. You can't beat *piroshki* to take home at
fifteen cents each.

Armenian

Bali's 615 Sansome Street (in the financial district). Dinner
Friday, Saturday, Sunday, 6–11 P.M. About $3. YU 2-5059.
Despite a name suggesting the South Sea islands, this modest little
restaurant serves first-class Armenian food—and at exceedingly
low prices, considering the quality. The story of Bali's started
before World War I, even before the Armenian refugees who
now run it were born. Their parents fled north into Russia from the
ravages of the Turks, then across Siberia to China at the time
of the Revolution. That was how Aram and Armen Baliantz
came to be born and married in North China. The family's
long hegira was not yet over. Mr. Baliantz had an Iranian
passport, and since Iran was allied against the Axis, the couple
and their infant daughter were arrested by the Japanese and
held in a concentration camp for two and a half years during
World War II. A son, Arthur, was born in the camp. Finally,
they came to San Francisco and after a few years of searching
set up a cafeteria across the street from the Immigrant Service
headquarters on Sansome Street. The location helped business
(it also recently helped daughter Janet, now a beautiful young
woman, get a job with the Immigration Service in New York).

Bali's now leads two lives. It is still a cafeteria during lunch
hours, serving (among more prosaic dishes) an excellent stuffed
cabbage. On week-end nights the steam table is decorated with
Middle-Eastern brass vases, the lights are dimmed, and Bali's
blossoms into a delightful dinner restaurant. Mrs. Baliantz is a
vivacious and charming hostess. Excellent meats are used for
the specialties of the house, the *sedlo* (rack of lamb) and *shish
kebab*. Mrs. Baliantz personally marinates the meat, which is well

and strongly seasoned. The dinner also includes marinated fruits and vegetables, salad, and coffee. The salad dressing, always a test of a good restaurant, is piquant and unusual. One of San Francisco's best and most inexpensive intimate restaurants.

Cairo 77 Fourth Street, between Mission and Market. Dinners $2.50–$3. Closed Sundays. SU 1-6819. If you don't mind crossing over Market Street to the wrong side of the tracks on the fringe of Skid Row and climbing up a long, steep flight of stairs, you can get authentic Armenian food at bargain prices. Main courses include *sarma* (stuffed grape leaves); lamb *kebabs* broiled with onion, pepper, and herbs; and an assortment of entrancing eggplant medleys. On the full-course dinner you also get a piquant egg-lemon soup and the many-layered splendor of *baklava* —compounded of nuts, honey, and silver-thin dough.

Jewish

David's 474 Geary Street. Lunch, dinner, and à la carte specialties. PR 6-4770. David, an enterprising Jewish refugee from Poland who still looks athletic and young despite the rigors of a spell in a concentration camp, broke a long San Francisco jinx on kosher-style food. Numerous Jewish restaurants had been opened and closed over the years, never quite making it. David started with a small place in the downtown theater district and introduced a couple of innovations. He offered immense pastrami and corned beef sandwiches at surprisingly low prices, ditto for huge slabs of cream cheese and *lox,* all on good dark bread or rolls. Patrons were surprised not to receive a check. They were put on an honor system, just telling the cashier what they ate. David's was soon doing a land-office business, drawing big lunch and dinner crowds as well as after-theater customers from the Geary and Curran theaters across the street. David expanded his seating capacity and spruced up his decor. The sandwiches gradually slimmed down, and the honor system was abolished. But portions remain generous enough and the food good if not spectacular. The blintzes are probably the best in town. You can order sandwiches and specialties à la carte which, with coffee, will come to between $1–$1.50. Dinner comes to about $3.

Solomon's 424 Geary Street. Lunch, dinner, and à la carte specialties. PR 6-3525. Solomon kept going during the lean years before David's hit the big time. Now his little Jewish delicatessen and a restaurant a few doors away catch some of the spillover business and he has been forced to expand. High-quality food, less expensive than David's. Try the excellent meat blintzes with sour cream and applesauce.

Lisa's   186 Eddy Street. Lunch, dinner, and à la carte specialties. PR 5-6155. The success story on a somewhat smaller scale than David's of a Polish refugee couple. Slightly lower-priced, and less elegant, than David's. Substantial lunches and dinners. Also good sandwiches, gefüllte fish, chicken-noodle soup, and potato pancakes.

German

Schroeder's   240 Front Street. Lunch about $1.50, dinner about $3. Closed Saturday and Sunday. GA 1-4778. A madhouse during lunch hours, when it draws a big crowd from the financial district. Schroeder's has gone quite a way from its old *hofbrau* atmosphere with a strong smell of beer and with the menu scrawled on a blackboard. Success has led to expansion and prettifying the decor. But it is still a hearty men's restaurant serving hearty food. In fact, ladies aren't admitted during lunch hours, but they can come for dinner. The potato pancakes and *Sauerbraten* are old favorites. Or you might want to try *Schweitzer Bratwurst* with red cabbage or garlic sausage and lentils. There is a good selection of German beer.

The Rathskeller   602 Turk Street. Lunch about $1.50, dinner about $3. PR 5-3188. Located in the basement of the California Hall, which has for generations served as a meeting place for the German community, this is probably San Francisco's most unpretentious and authentic German restaurant. *Sauerbraten* is served for both lunch and dinner. *Hasenpfeffer* (rabbit) is a speciality of the house. Or you can come here in the evening just to drink beer and perhaps join some of the German community activities in the building.

The Shadows   1349 Montgomery Street. Dinners about $3.50–$5.50. EX 2-9823. A quiet romantic spot way up on Telegraph Hill with a fine view of the Bay. *Sauerbraten* and other German specialties featured, but the atmosphere takes precedence over the food and even the wine.

Austrian

Maximillian's   637 Sutter Street. Dinner about $4. Closed Tuesday. PR 6-7875. Very good food and service for dinners in this price range. Also lots of atmosphere—including Viennese music, paneled rosewood walls, and soft lights. French and Russian specialties are on the menu. But try the chicken paprika or one of the veal specialties.

Mexican

El Sombrero 5800 Geary Boulevard. Dinner $2.50–$3. Closed Monday. EV 6-9661. A pleasantly atmospheric restaurant in the Richmond district, with pleasant murals on the walls and attractive waitresses in gay skirts. If you feel up to it, the combination plate, including *tamales, tacos,* beans, and salad, is both good and filling. Almost equally filling is the chicken *tostada;* it comes in the shape of a huge pyramid with many layers to excavate, including thick slices of chicken, ripe avocado, and spicy vegetables.

La Piñata 1701 Polk Street. Dinner about $2. PR 6-3129. A quiet and charming little place with the usual Mexican specialties and excellent Mexican Carta Blanca beer.

The Guitar 449 Mason Street. Dinner about $3. Closed Sunday. GA 4-4312. Good Mexican food and beer in the downtown area, suitable for either lunch or dinner. *Huevos* and *rancheros,* Mexican-style eggs with beans and rice, are a specialty. Or try the subtly flavored beef *tostada.*

Sinaloa 1416 Powell Street. Dinner $4–$5. Closed Wednesday. SU 1-9624. More in the night-club or theater-restaurant line. But you can get a good Mexican dinner here while watching a colorful floor show.

Spanish

Martin's Español 674 Broadway. Under $3. Closed Tuesday. GA 1-9412. Amid Spanish posters and guitars hanging on the walls, you can have a gargantuan Basque dinner here very inexpensively—and served in style by waitresses in peasant costumes. You get salad, soup, platters of beans and veal stew, or other preliminary dishes, a substantial main course, and dessert and coffee. Order the *Paella à la Valencia* and you will be brought a huge bowl of chicken, seafood, and rice. If you choose what is described as "Veal Scallopini (Basque Style)" you will get a pungent, tasty veal cutlet. The food is good as well as filling, but just misses distinction.

La Bodega 256 Columbus Avenue. About $2. SU 1-9408. This is an intimate spot for a romantic date—and a light dinner. The atmosphere is pleasant, and it is less noisy and crowded than most of the North Beach restaurants. The *Paella Valencia* is excellent, but portions are a bit on the skimpy side. There are no menus and no choice of entree, but you are certain to come up with some variety of *paella.*

El Patio Andaluz 1601 Powell Street. About $3. Closed Monday and Tuesday. SU 1-9784. Spanish and Mexican specialties are served in a brightly decorated and unpretentious little theater-restaurant. On Friday, Saturday, and Sunday evenings you can enjoy flamenco dancing and music for the price of the dinner—if you make reservations for before 9 P.M. The owner keeps busy as a bartender and as a guitarist between drinks; he is a virtuoso in both capacities.

Seafood

Tadich Grill   545 Clay Street. À la carte. Lunch and dinner. Closed Sunday. SU 1-9754. As the oldest (established in 1849) San Francisco restaurant still operating, Tadich's could get by on tradition alone. But many practicing gourmets are convinced it serves the best seafood in town, even though it has neither view nor waterfront breezes. Hangtown fry with Olympia Oysters, said to have been a favorite of Forty-Niners, is one of the specialties of the house. Against stiff competition from other good seafood places, Tadich's serves what is probably the best rex sole in town. Or try the baked sea bass with crab meat *en casserole*. Prices are à la carte and extremely reasonable; most of the heaping platters are between two and three dollars. It is probably wise to have dinner here rather than lunch; the portions are huge and liable to make you drowsy in midafternoon. Between its tradition and the excellence of its food, Tadich's has found no necessity to put on any swank. The atmosphere is unpretentious and there is no modern decor. Truck drivers and financiers both come and are equally welcome. You don't even have to wear a tie if you don't feel like it. Service is good, but the waiters are brisk and don't mollycoddle you. If you like seafood, you shouldn't miss this one.

Big Ben   645 Montgomery Street. Lunch about $1.50, dinner about $3. GA 1-3972. A favorite of old-timers, Big Ben in the financial district serves exceedingly high-quality seafood of all kinds along with very good, crunchy French bread. Don't pass up the big special Dalmatian salad, bountiful quantities of shrimp and crab served with a tangy dressing containing some mysterious and delightful ingredients.

The Fisherman's Wharf restaurants, all pretty similar in quality and price, serve good solid seafood at a relatively modest $3 to $4 for dinner and about $1.50–$2.50 for lunch. Two restaurants favored by old-time wharf devotees are:

Exposition Fish Grotto   Fisherman's Wharf. OR 3-9565.

A. Sabella's Fish Grotto   2766 Taylor Street. GR 4-8770. Standbys at most of the wharf restaurants are crab and shrimp Louis, combination seafood platters, broiled salmon, and crab *cioppino,* the traditional Italian fish stew cooked in wine. If you try the latter, you'll have to use your hands to dig clams, prawns, and crab out of their shells. But you get a big bib, and a hot wet cloth when you finish. There are also somewhat fancier but also tasty specialties. Sabella's features turbot stuffed with deviled crab in wine sauce and Antone—swordfish baked in wine-butter sauce, stuffed with deviled shrimp, topped with white sauce and parmesan cheese.

Attention Steak-eaters

San Francisco is not a haven for steak-lovers. Its steak houses do not on the whole compare with those of New York, Chicago, or even—let's face it—Los Angeles. But there are some restaurants that specialize in serving a pretty good steak for $4.50 and up. These include:

Grison's Steak and Chop House   Van Ness and Pacific avenues. OR 3-1888.

Le Boeuf   545 Washington Street. GA 1-2914.

Alfred's   886 Broadway. SU 1-7058.

The Big Splurge

Here is a sampling of San Francisco's more expensive restaurants.

Jack's   615 Sacramento Street. Lunch and dinner. GA 1-9854. One of the most cherished memories of middle-aged San Franciscans is being taken to Jack's by their parents when they were little boys and girls. Many have kept up the custom over the years. Others who return after a long lapse are startled to discover that nostalgia has played no tricks on them. The decor is still the same; a plain dining room, no fancy lighting, a few unpretentious gold curlicues on the woodwork suggesting that Jack's has been around for a while. The food has changed little over the decades; it's still great. Even the waiters look and act as if they come with the place. "What's filet of sole Marguery?" a newcomer asked recently. "If you haven't tried it, it's time you did," the waiter replied. And indeed it was. Jack's steaks, chops, and roast beef are superior. One of the fish or chicken dishes with a French sauce is, however, the *pièce de résistance.* Try chicken *sauté a sec,* or *en casserole* with vegetables. As at many of the older San Francisco restaurants, the cuisine is French–Italian–American. At Jack's the French flavor predominates. The prices have, of course, advanced with the years. If you have a couple of drinks and wine and a big meal from the à la carte menu, it will come to about ten dollars per person. (There are complete dinners at five dollars, but selection is limited and many of the better dishes aren't on it.) By skimping on the drinks and the trimmings and skipping dessert, you can eat well at Jack's for five to six dollars. Whether you skimp or splurge, dinner at Jack's will be an occasion.

Trader Vic's 20 Cosmo Place, off Taylor between Post and Sutter. Lunch and dinner. PR 6-2232. Starting from behind a small bar called Hinky Dink's in Oakland, Trader Vic Bergeron has built up a formidable empire with imagination, showmanship, and good food. Make reservations in advance if you want to get in. Come well dressed if you want the red-carpet treatment. And be prepared to spend at least twenty-five dollars for dinner for two, including drinks. If you can afford to enjoy it, you will get your money's worth.

Vic has adapted essences and aspects of the Polynesian style to American taste, although he also features "continental" and Chinese dishes. And he does it with a flair, as befits a showplace. The decor is a blend of authentic island artifacts, bamboo, straw matting, and seashell lamps. He flies in special limestone lettuce from the East and *mahi mahi* (dolphin) from Hawaii. He has been known to fire half his kitchen staff if he spots a dirty glass or finds the crab not quite up to snuff.

The Chinese barbecue ovens in their special glass-enclosed room are important both to the decor and the food. The white-coated chefs can be seen making the spare ribs and the barbecued filet steaks and the Indonesian marinated lamb, all specialties of the house. Other specialties are filet of sole and San Francisco crab in numerous versions—especially pake crab, sort of a Polynesian crab Newburg served in a rich sauce in coconut shells. Vic's salads are tremendous creations put together for dramatic effect, fruit salad served in scooped-out pineapples, crab and shrimp with Green Goddess and other dressings.

The rum drinks are almost as important as the food and the decor, and their variety is enormous. They often come in ceremonial bowls for four or six and some are served in special mugs which can be taken along as souvenirs. If you want the full treatment, start with a Mai Tai rum drink, followed by a salad of limestone lettuce, Bongo Bongo oyster soup, and either an Indonesian lamb or a barbecued filet. Ice cream with praline sauce is a choice dessert.

Fleur de Lys 777 Sutter Street. Dinner. Closed Sunday and Monday. OR 3-7779. This is the French *haute cuisine,* featuring delicate sauces, careful preparation, dishes that look beautiful and also taste that way. The green salad is superb. So are many of the specialties. Try boned breast of chicken folded over imported cheeses. It looks like a perfectly shaped baked potato, but is considerably better than even the best Idaho. À la carte only, and you will find it hard to pass up the tartes and Napoleons for dessert. At least ten dollars per person, especially if you order wine with the dinner. The mink-coat crowd comes here, and it is usually noisy and jammed as well as expensive. But the French cooking is the best in town.

Ernie's 847 Montgomery Street. Dinner. EX 7-5969. A San Francisco institution like the Top of the Mark and the cable cars. Ernie's was the best-known eating place in town even before Kim Novak swished and swirled through it in *Vertigo*. The red-brick front, the plush but not hushed Victorian atmosphere, and the elegant service recall what San Franciscans like to think of as the old days. The food is predominantly Italian, with a dash of French. The hors d'oeuvres on the dinner are among the best in the city. The *tortellini,* little rings of stuffed pasta with a delicious cheese sauce, are outstanding. Be sure to phone a reservation, then be prepared to wait. Twenty to twenty-five dollars for a couple, including wine.

Lunch

Many of the restaurants above serve lunch, and many of those below serve dinner. In grouping eating places under the lunch category, we have considered prices, the type of food offered, convenience of location, and other variables. But with some exceptions, the two categories are not mutually exclusive. (Don't forget the Chinese tea-lunch houses mentioned earlier.)

Bardelli's 243 O'Farrell Street. Lunch about $1.50–$2.50. Lunch and dinner Monday through Friday. Saturday, dinner only. Closed Sunday. YU 2-0243. You can have an excellent lunch here and rub elbows with newspapermen, advertising executives and *cognoscenti*. But you don't need an expense account to afford it. For this price you can eat well in one of San Francisco's older and more atmospheric restaurants. You get good service— including the attention of "Stu" Adams, one of the city's most skillful and better-known *maître d*'s, sparkling linen, and coffee in a silver pot. The inexpensive *lasagne* lunch is a favorite. But try the spinach *fritata* (eggs, onions, and spinach in a savory omelet) or the delicate seasoned baked rex sole *à la Bardelli*. Good for dinner too, when Italian meat specialties are the thing.

Original Joe's 144 Taylor Street. À la carte lunches and

dinners. PR 5-4877. Original Joe's may be newer than New
Joe's in North Beach, but the food is good and very similar.
Huge sandwiches—hamburgers, roast beef, roast pork, and meat
balls—served on great slabs of crunchy French bread with
generous helpings of French fries or olives and *pepperoncini*. Also
excellent meat dishes as daily specials. The restaurant and bar
are always crowded, but the turnover is fast and the service good.
You can get an excellent lunch for between $1.25 and $2.50.

Golden Rule   765 Market Street. À la carte. DO 2-3274. Plain
but fresh and tasty seafood served in unpretentious surroundings.
Try the clam chowder, or the thick and meaty pea soup (served
every Monday), the kind which includes a vast medley of ingredients and is cooked for days. About $1–$1.50.

Opus One   738 Montgomery Street. À la carte. SU 1-5526.
You can get good crisp Caesar salad here or a lean roast-beef
sandwich while good classical music comes over the hi-fi in this
very atmospheric, moderate-priced, and offbeat hangout in an old
warehouse.

Jake's   673 Union Street. Lunch only. $1.50. Monday–Friday,
12 to 2 P.M. EX 2-9854. This is one of the best lunch values in
town, if you're up to a first-class Italian dinner for your lunch and
are willing to go to North Beach to get it. Jake's doesn't advertise,
and there isn't even a sign on the door. In fact, the door is
usually locked and you have to go through the bar on the corner
to get in. You walk through a bar adorned mainly by a big
moosehead, then through the kitchen where a lovely middle-aged
lady called Tilly is busy fussing over pots and pans, finally into a
small dining room with a few oilcloth-covered tables. Don't be
misled by the absence of swank. Tilly is a real artist, specializing
in genuine, home-cooked Italian meals. A tureen of delicious
steaming soup and a basket of French bread are put before you.
Then a crisp salad and an excellent main course. If stuffed *zucchini*
is available, be sure to order it. A good sour Italian wine comes
with the lunch. The vegetables are not overdone and are well
seasoned. Even the potatoes taste different here. The strong
Italian coffee arrives just in time to wake you up. But don't
count on doing any serious work after the lunch. On your way
out be sure and tell Tilly what you think of her food. She'll
never get rich at her present prices; she ought at least to get
compliments. She gives the whole place a warm, homey atmosphere.
Even the waitresses are maternal, anxious to make sure you
enjoy everything. Most of the patrons are steadies, and newcomers may get a quizzical look. Jake's is usually crowded. You

might be wise to phone a reservation, and even then count on a drink or two in the bar while you're waiting. To tell or not to tell about this one was a painful moral dilemma.

Mike's Famous Sandwich in Dante's Billiard Parlor   521 Broadway. À la carte. EX 7-0454. This place is revered by old-time North Beachers almost as much as New Yorkers do McSorley's Saloon. It really *is* a billiard parlor, frequented mainly by middle-aged Italians, with a long counter where food is served and a few booths if you want to eat in privacy. Mike's claims to be the original home of the "hero" sandwich. There is still nothing quite like the variety it serves—fresh crunchy Italian rolls filled with loads of salami, *prosciutto, gorgonzola,* or Monterey cheese, and a slice of onion if you wish, served with hot little *pepperoncini.* Or you can order a cavernous bowl of minestrone for sixty cents. Or try a *fritata* and watch the omelet skillfully thrown together with many herbs and vegetables. If you wonder about *osso buco,* featured on the menu stuck up on the fall, this is veal shanks braised in Italian sauce. There was consternation not long ago when a socialite bought this place and began sprucing it up. He offered the help a wage boost—and prepared to raise prices accordingly. The waiters and cooks rejected the increase and begged that the prices and everything else remain the same. So far Mike's hasn't changed too much, and the billiard tables are still there.

Veneto's   389 Bay, near Mason. Lunch and dinner Monday through Friday. Dinners only Saturday and Sunday. YU 6-4553. If you're on the two-hour-lunch level, this is the place to eat in a leisurely Italian atmosphere, even a bit romantic, away from the downtown treadmill. You can get a really cold dry martini and a fine plate of spaghetti or succulent veal. The meal winds up with a lovely fruit basket and cheese. Waiters are pleasant, and it's all very relaxing. Not even any problem about parking. Count on about $2–$2.50 per person.

Buon Gusto Pastry Shop   414 Columbus Avenue. GA 1-1937. While still offering rum cakes, *panettone,* and *cannoli,* this bakery has taken to serving lunches. For about fifty cents you can get a three-layer sandwich accompanied by a delicious little whipped-cream-filled puff. Disappointingly, none of the sandwiches are served on French bread—just the standard white, whole wheat, or rye. The businessmen's luncheon, about a dollar, is substantial and well cooked. With only a small seating capacity, the place is crowded and the young waitress somewhat harassed. It looks as if success has caught them a little unawares. At one table you can

see a young girl reading *Hamlet,* at another three ladies discussing
Saks Fifth Avenue fashions, or earnest young men going round on
politics. An unobtrusive sign says "no loafing" for fear beatniks
should wander in. As you pay your bill, the luscious pastries
behind the counter will trap you.

A few San Francisco restaurants that serve hearty sandwiches
and meat platters are favored by men for lunch. The only one
that specifically excludes ladies during lunch hours is Schroeder's
(see p. 102). Ladies are welcome in the others but may find
both the food and the atmosphere on the masculine side.

Hoffman Café and Grill   619 Market Street. About $1.50 for
lunch. GA 1-1467. Big platters of Yankee pot roast with *tagliarini,*
or sauerkraut with frankfurters, served by waiters who know their
own mind and yours too, in a restaurant that spurns decorations
apart from aged paneled walls and a solid, impressive bar.

Tommy's Joynt   1101 Geary, at Van Ness. $1–$2. PR 5-4216;
and Mason and Market Streets. Open from 11 A.M. to 2 A.M.
daily. If you don't mind waiting in line during the 12-to-1:30 rush,
you can get an excellent hefty sandwich (roast beef, ham,
corned beef, turkey, etc.) served cafeteria style and cut to your
order as well as a stein of imported beer at Tommy's Joynt. At
your table you'll find an assortment of relishes, including the
superb pickles which are among the many reasons for going
there. The cold salads and cheesecake are above average. Decorated
in deliberately bad taste, Tommy's has an ersatz German flavor.
The Joynt at Geary and Van Ness is older and more authentically
hideous, but the one at Mason and Market is closer to the
business and shopping districts.

Day's   24 Ellis Street. $1–$1.25. GA 1-2894. A big barn of a
cafeteria offering some of the best sandwich values in town. Big
helpings of corned beef, roast beef, pastrami, or turkey. Be
sure and get your sandwich on a French roll dipped. The meat
and fish special plates aren't quite up to the sandwiches. You can
get a good martini for twenty-five cents at the huge bar.

Several restaurants cater primarily to women shoppers; men
can come along but may feel out of place.

Iron Horse   19 Maiden Lane. $1.50–$3. Closed Sunday.
DO 2-1349. New Orleans atmosphere and rather expensive prices.

Chuckburger Heaven   8th floor of H. Liebes department store,
Grant and Geary. $1–$1.25. Closed Sundays. GA 1-6240.
Delicious broiled hamburgers, milkshakes, diet plates, and sand-

wiches served cafeteria style in a large, cheery room. Usually not too crowded after 1 P.M.

Normandy Lane City of Paris department store. $1–$2. Stockton and Geary. Closed Sunday. DO 2-4500, Local 404. Good, although not distinguished, lunches are served in the gourmet food center of this downtown store. The tiny hot cinnamon rolls are outstanding and the atmosphere is relaxed and pleasant. On your way out you can buy some East India tea or fragile French pastry.

Breakfast

Buena Vista 2765 Hyde Street. GR 4-5044. (See page 120.) Best known for its Irish coffee, this hangout and bar also serves a good breakfast. Try the sausage and eggs. But unless you have lots of time, stay away on Sundays, when it is mobbed with customers who come in for brunch. A fine view of the Bay along with the food.

Cliff House 1090 Point Lobos Avenue. SK 1-7220. Sunday brunch at the Cliff House is an old San Francisco tradition. But the view of the ocean takes precedence over the food.

Sear's Fine Foods 529 Powell Street. Inexpensive. DO 2-9938. Justly famous for its pancakes. The plate with eighteen small pancakes served with whipped butter and maple syrup is something to behold and to taste.

Pancake Palace International Airport. JU 3-4364. All kinds of pancakes, including chocolate. Light, fluffy, very tasty. Some San Franciscans drive out here for Sunday breakfast. But certainly if you're at the airport in the morning, you shouldn't miss it.

Juanita's Galley Gate 5 Road, Marinship, Sausalito. Open daily 2 A.M. until 6 P.M. ED 2-9977. If you like lots of local color, a good view of the Bay, and good food but aren't too fussy about cleanliness and don't mind waiting before you eat, Juanita's, on the Sausalito waterfront at the old Marinship yards, is the place for you. You punch a time clock, write your order on the card, and then wait. Juanita, a huge woman with a temper well publicized in local newspapers, is in no hurry to serve you. But the huge platter of ham or bacon and eggs you get in the end is well worth your time and money.

(*Note:* Count on spending about two dollars per person at Cliff House and Juanita's Galley, between one and two, depending on how hungry you are, at Buena Vista, Sear's and Pancake Palace.)

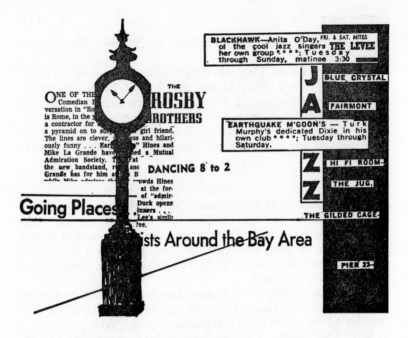

6: NIGHT LIFE

ONE OF Oscar Wilde's quips rather fits San Francisco. "In Paris," he said, "one can lose one's time most delightfully, but one can never lose one's way." San Francisco is a wonderful town to while away an evening over a cappucino or a Scotch and soda, just talking, or listening to jazz or classical music or even opera, or taking in the fast patter of sad comics. But anyone trying to get lost in the city's notoriously sinful night life is liable to turn up at his hotel disillusioned and probably in time for a good, long sleep. This is a town where the most respectable bars and night clubs affect the decor of old bordellos and where the sidewalks are rolled up at 2 A.M.

San Francisco is in the position of the distinguished dowager who enjoys looking back on her wicked past. But there is a difference. The dowager keeps her old sins secret. San Francisco flaunts them and keeps its present virtue under wraps. A paperback book, *How to Sin in San Francisco*, was a local best-seller until fairly recently, long after it was hopelessly outdated. Until a few years ago there was a pathetic pretense that the Barbary

Coast still existed; a few decrepit honkytonk bars operated on a once-notorious block on Pacific Street behind a concrete arch with the label *International Settlement*. Nobody seems to mind that this is now the locale of swank decorators' shops. For all their bravado, San Franciscans overwhelmingly vote down an occasional mayoralty candidate who campaigns on an open-town platform.

This isn't to say that the city is pure or stuffy or completely closed. You can see old-fashioned burlesque of the kind they used to have at Minsky's at the **President** (80 McAllister Street). There are several bars that are homosexual hangouts and that seem to keep going despite repeated and well-publicized crack-downs. There are bars where sailors get rolled and pay heavily for watered drinks, and there are still ways to get select addresses and phone numbers. But other cities have more to offer in this line.

San Francisco's night life isn't an antediluvian throwback to the Barbary Coast. Nor is the city particularly strong in the girlie-show type of night club or in the expensive, exclusive café-society type. The city's most distinctive night spots tend to a faintly European or Bohemian or longhair flavor. San Francisco excels in intimate cellar night clubs with offbeat and sometimes excellent entertainment, in places which feature Italian arias or Spanish flamenco dancers, in clubs for jazz aficionados, in a wide assortment of atmospheric bars, hangouts, and coffee houses.

Out of these haunts have come first-class entertainers, fresh in approach and breaking with old clichés. Here were nurtured Mort Sahl and other so-called sick comics with their acid comments on contemporary life. Small San Francisco night clubs provided a refuge for traditional Dixieland jazz and then fostered its revival. Barbara Dane, now making a national reputation as a serious interpreter of the blues, first won acclaim in modest local bistros. San Francisco audiences had had the opportunity to discover groups like the Gateway Singers, the Kingston Trio, and the Limelighters—who have adapted the folk song to a night-club milieu without corrupting it in the process.

The most unique aspects of the city's night life are to be found in relatively inexpensive and informal spots clustered mainly on the fringes of North Beach. San Franciscans keep returning to them, outnumbering tourists except on occasional summer week-end nights.

The Dark Cellars

The hungry i   599 Jackson Street. EX 7-0929. Three shows nightly, starting at 9 P.M. Closed Sundays. The lower-case *i* in this most spectacularly successful of San Francisco's intimate night clubs stands for intellectual. But long gone is the snobbish joy of discovering what used to be a quiet, inexpensive, highbrow joint. Owner Enrico Banducci's black beret is one of the few remnants of the hungry i's hungry days. Prices and attendance have climbed upward at the same dizzy rate. Customers range from Berkeley students (a few can still afford it) to visiting conventioners and Pacific Heights society. They line up outside to sit knee to knee inside in smoky intimacy, all sharing the illusion that they are not the usual type of night-club goers. An informal art gallery and a continental-style restaurant are among the expanding attractions. But spending a whole evening here would give you the feeling of being cooped up in an air-raid shelter. The entertainers are still the i's principal drawing card, and these have ranged from really terrible girl torch singers to good folk-song groups to the incomparable Mort Sahl.

Success has not completely spoiled the hungry i, although the days of its dollar cover charge are long over. It still has something, namely Banducci's flair for occasionally stumbling across a first-class comic or musical group. He took a chance (at seventy-five dollars a week) on an unshaven young intellectual from Berkeley whose only props were a rolled-up newspaper and a sweater. Sahl's incredibly rapid-fire jibes at practically everything from hi-fi to McCarthyism—including along the way police corruption, sports cars, psychiatry, the FBI, jazz buffs, politics, and the H-bomb—took San Francisco by storm. Everyone liked the sophisticated feeling that came from catching even a tenth of his fast patter and being able to repeat it afterward. Staunch Republicans, who would have thrown Sahl out of their living rooms, applauded him wildly at the i, and Democrats swallowed his acid comments about their party. Sahl went on to the big money, and Banducci became the proud owner of a king-sized yacht. They still appreciate each other, and Sahl will occasionally appear at the hungry i for a cut-rate $5000 a week.

The Purple Onion   140 Columbus. SU 1-0835. Performances start at 9. Closed Sundays. Similar to the hungry i and almost as successful, this place discovered the Kingston Trio when its members looked and sounded like gawky amateurs. It goes in heavily for folk singers and jazz musicians, avoids the kind of social satire of which Mort Sahl was the most spectacular exponent at the i.

Now closed, **The Jazz Cellar** (576 Green Street) was one of the best-publicized of San Francisco's informal, inexpensive night clubs. This is where the national poetry and jazz vogue started in 1957 when Kenneth Rexroth and Laurence Ferlinghetti read their poems against a jazz background. The experiment was a great success, but the patient died. Business was poor, and the Cellar closed down.

The Continental Touch

Just as old newspapermen dream of editing little country weeklies, retired Italian opera singers in North Beach used to dream of starting little cafés where the strains of the familiar arias would be heard. Some of them did just that, and the local aficionados would turn out and shout prolonged bravos when a promising young tenor or mezzo-soprano turned up. There are still a few of these places, and they have a slight whiff of the old flavor left.

Bocce Ball. 622 Broadway. SU 1-9507. No substitute for the San Francisco Opera, much less the Metropolitan. But you can hear arias from *La Bohême, Rigoletto,* or *The Marriage of Figaro* while you sip "Venetian" coffee—brandy laced with coffee and topped with whipped cream. The singers are accompanied by piano and accordion, and the quality varies. Scouts for major opera companies have been known to haunt this place and to sign up talented youngsters, and you still occasionally hear an exciting if not fully disciplined voice. Although schmaltzy popular ballads are now interspersed with the arias, some North Beach opera-lovers come around on weekday nights when it isn't too crowded. On week ends the tables are pushed close together and the clinking and talking almost drown out the opera. There is no cover charge. Although drinks are energetically pushed, you can spend an hour or so for the price of only a couple of drinks. And if you want to get away from the noise and smoke, just walk out in back to the bocce ball courts where old men, impervious to the night-club clatter inside, play their traditional bowling game.

La Casadoro 720 Broadway. EX 2-9570. Similar to the Bocce Ball, but smaller and more informal. The bartender is liable to break out in song at any moment. There is also the same mishmash of popular ballads and arias.

Flamencophilia is San Francisco's latest fad, and several spots feature "authentic Flamenco" with artists just imported from Spain. Some of the performers are actually local kids who have seriously studied the flamenco art. One guitarist, who sings and plays as if he just got off the boat from Barcelona, was born across the Bay with the very un-Spanish name of Brown.

The pyrotechnics of **Los Flamencos de la Bodega** are displayed Thursday through Saturday nights (admission $1.50) in a small, weirdly decorated room of the **Old Spaghetti Factory** (478 Green Street; GA 1-0221). The performers stomp and sing and strum the guitar intensely enough to make you forget the clutter of wine bottles and old wax dummies and African masks all over the walls and ceiling. Coffee and wine are served. Or you can drop in at a flamenco dinner club like **El Patio Andaluz** (1601 Powell Street; SU 1-9784; see p. 103) or **Casa Madrid** (406 Broadway; EX 7-2881) and eat inexpensively while watching the show.

For spirited Mexican entertainment, try the **Sinaloa** (1416 Powell Street; SU 1-9624). This is a reasonably priced supper club. The food is ample and peppery, and so are the three floor shows a night. Wandering troubadors and zaftige señoritas, all billed as recent sensations in Mexico City, come and go, while this North Beach standby, run by Luz Garcia for more years than she cares to remember, just goes on and on.

While folk-dancing falls into the do-it-yourself category, the **William Tell House** (630 Clay Street; GA 1-9405), an unpretentious, homey place, has a German band playing Thursdays through Sundays, 9 P.M. to 1 A.M. You can see young men in *lederhosen* and girls in swirling peasant skirts doing polkas and waltzes. Observant wallflowers are permitted, but dancers are preferred.

Le Jazz

During the last decade San Francisco has risen rapidly to increasing prominence in the jazz world, a development that is the result of responsive audiences, high-quality performers, and the crusading efforts of a first-class critic and columnist, Ralph J. Gleason.

Jazz buffs consider San Francisco second only to New York in the number and quality of its progressive jazz spots. Most are small and inexpensive, and usually have only a modest cover charge. The two best-established are the **Black Hawk** and the **Jazz Workshop.** Both are showplaces for first-rate groups and combos which like to perform there because the audiences are made up largely of the hip and of local musicians who come to listen, not to discuss world affairs or their own troubles.

Black Hawk   200 Hyde Street. GR 4-9567. Cal Tjader, who graduated from San Francisco State College with teaching credentials but switched to jazz, put this place on the map. Dave Brubeck was also featured here. There are frequent guest stars and visiting combos. One feature of this spot is a special gallery for teen-agers. Enthusiastic young jazz buffs are kept out of most night spots by a California law barring persons under twenty-one from bars. The Hawk devised a wire cage to separate the impressionable young from the guzzling adults, and battled Mayor Christopher and local police for the right of teen-agers to listen to live jazz.

Sugar Hill   430 Broadway. SU 1-3872. Barbara Dane has established (at the locale of Barnaby Conrad's unsuccessful El Bordell) the country's first room devoted exclusively to the blues, which she considers "the greatest song form ever invented." Barbara is not only a remarkably authentic blues singer but a student of the field as well. She is backed at the piano by Kenny (Good News) Whitson and by seventy-year-old Wellman Braud, Duke Ellington's first bass player. Her motto, "True blues, fine booze, and easy dues."

Jazz Workshop   473 Broadway. DO 2-9246. Owned and run by a young attorney who digs cool jazz and correctly proportioned cocktail waitresses. Programs change at least once a month unless a featured group or star, like the Mastersounds or Cannonball Adderley, go over big.

The Jazz Workshop is a real hangout for local jazz fans who brave noise and crowds and even stand in line to hear their favorite music expertly played.

Stereo Club   350 Divisadero Street. Friday and Saturday nights. MA 1-9826. No big names here yet. But they really swing here week ends in the midst of a quiet neighborhood.

Jimbo's Bop City   1690 Post Street. Opens 2 A.M. Soft drinks and breakfast only. Cover charge. FI 6-2412. A favorite after-hours hangout for jazz musicians, both the famous and the unknown. When they're through blowing for a meal, they come here to blow for each other. Here you will find musicians of both sexes and all races improvising music and sociability. Jimbo officiates quietly over his popular joint. A tall, immaculately dressed Negro, he affects one eccentricity; he won't be seen without a cap whether indoors or out.

Traditional jazz continues to draw good crowds in San Francisco, and there are several places that feature Dixieland music.

Black Sheep   645 Geary Street. Closed Sundays. PR 5-7611. Earl "Fatha" Hines still plays his wonderful brand of traditional jazz. This is no place to go for conversation; the music is loud and jumping.

On-the-Levee   987 Embarcadero. Friday and Saturday evening. EX 7-2452. Long a stronghold of Kid Ory and his Creole band. Now features visiting combos.

Pier 23   Embarcadero off Greenwich. Open every evening. YU 6-6440. Jazz piano and trio alternate.

Beer and Sawdust

A number of dens, nicely scrubbed and the sawdust neatly distributed, offer old-time atmosphere, beer, peanuts, and lots of noise to the college or career crowd as well as a chance for Miss Lonely Heart to meet a nice young man on the way up and vice versa. All go in for banjo-thumping community singing and cute names. **Red Garter** (670 Broadway; YU 2-7483) is mobbed almost every night, with lines waiting outside. Roaring Twenties music is banged out by the Strugglers (banjo, piano, gutbucket, and saw). Sheet music is handed out for the community songfest, featuring numbers like "California, Here I Come!" The **Monkey Inn** (2025⅞ Van Ness Avenue, behind the Hippo restaurant; PR 5-1758) draws the young white-collar set for beer and popcorn. Other places where boy meets girl amid sawdust are **Crazy Horse** (1659 Market Street; UN 3-0296), **Honey Bucket** (3158 Fillmore Street; WE 1-7027), and the **Copy Cat** (2244 Fillmore Street; FI 6-9764).

Miscellany

The closest thing to a big, swank New York night club in San Francisco is the **Venetian Room** of the Fairmont Hotel, California and Mason Streets; DO 2-8800. It's fairly expensive; count on spending about twenty-five dollars for a couple. But if you feel like an occasional splurge, this is the place to catch the big-name entertainers like Lena Horne and Ella Fitzgerald. Even Mort Sahl appeared here once, somewhat out of place in his sweater. Or if you feel like dancing to a smooth band, try the **Mark Hopkins** (EX 2-

3434) across the street, or the **Sheraton-Palace** (EX 2-8600) downtown.

In the traditional night-club category, about the only places where convention-goers out on the town will find a chorus line are **Bimbo's 365** (1025 Columbus Avenue; GR 4-0365); **Moulin Rouge** (412 Broadway; EX 7-6488), and **Forbidden City** (363 Sutter Street; DO 2-6550), which features "Oriental dolls." **Goman's Gay Nineties** (345 Broadway; SU 1-1899) goes in for the closest thing to old-fashioned vaudeville with corny jokes and schmaltzy songs on the "Grandpa's Follies" theme. **Roaring 20's** (807 Montgomery Street; YU 2-3150) features melodeons, silent movies, Charlestons, and Lindy Hops in a flapper-era decor. **Bustles and Beaus** (247 Powell; YU 2-7330) is a recent competitor; sexy waitresses in bustles slide down a brass pole to entertain the customers. One shocker that never fails to pull the crowds is **Finocchio's** (506 Broadway; DO 2-9913), which features female impersonators. Tourists on the Gray Line night-life tour really pop their eyes here.

Hangouts

This is an ephemeral category which includes mainly spots serving beer and wine or coffee but also a couple of restaurants and bars. The only sense in grouping these places together is that the refreshments, whether liquid or solid, are only an incidental reason for going there. Atmosphere is a principal item on their bill of fare.

Old Spaghetti Factory Café & Excelsior Coffee House   478 Green Street; GA 1-0221. This is a whopping name for one of the more whimsical and genteel North Beach hangouts, established in what really used to be an old spaghetti factory. The furnishings look like they were salvaged from every attic in town that survived the 1906 fire and then put together with a sense of humor. Strauss waltzes and corny old tunes are provided by a record-player. Spaghetti is served, of course. But the food is undistinguished and overpriced. The idea is just to sit around over a beer or a glass of wine, in one of the smaller side rooms if you prefer intimacy. There are live chamber-music concerts Sunday nights at eight-thirty.

Opus One   738 Montgomery Street; SU 1-5526 (see p. 108). Classical music is offered over a good hi-fi system in a partially converted old warehouse. There are also occasional live concerts; while food is served, most people just come in for a drink or two.

There is lots of room to sit, no pressure to keep ordering or get out.

Vesuvio's 255 Columbus Avenue. DO 2-9808. The sign "Booths for Psychiatrists" in the painted glass window is sure to catch your eye. Don't expect a community-sing atmosphere inside. There is a medley here of weird paintings and weird characters, pseudointellectuals and Bohemians, organization men, tourists. There is a good selection of wines and imported beers. Or you can have a wine, coffee, and whipped cream concoction called Danish Coffee, not quite as bad as it sounds.

Enrico's Coffee House 504 Broadway. EX 2-6220. A swank offshoot of Enrico Banducci's hungry i, this is supposed to be an open-air, European-style café. It must have something because it is crowded until three every morning, but just what is hard to say. It often gets chilly, and braziers have been installed to provide some heat. The food is poor, the pastry often stale, the prices ridiculous. It's probably the carefully cultivated place-to-be-seen reputation which attracts.

Trieste Caffe Espresso 601 Vallejo Street at Grant Avenue. EX 2-6739 (see p. 64). If you just want some espresso and pastry at reasonable prices, this is the place to go.

Brighton Express 580 Pacific Avenue. Thursday through Monday, 5:30 P.M. to midnight. SU 1-9947. In the heart of what was once the International Settlement, this coffee house draws a mixed bag of entertainers and customers from nearby night clubs, Bohemians, and the teen-age crowd attracted by dim lights, inexpensive dinners and a gooey ice-cream dessert called a Mudpie. The food is continental-style, is surprisingly good for the price— under two dollars for a dinner. All the traditional coffee-house beverages plus *maté,* the South American tea, and imported beer from Japan and elsewhere.

Bars

There is no difficulty defining this category, but it is hard picking a few from among the hundreds (or is it thousands?) in San Francisco. The sampling below is sketchy indeed.

Buena Vista Beach and Hyde, end of Hyde Street cable car line. GR 4-5044. Jack Koeppler, a former waiter on the Richmond –San Rafael ferry as well as the Buena Vista, hit the jackpot when he took over this place in 1940. Endowed with an atmospheric location overlooking the Bay, the Buena Vista has had one break after another. During the war this was one of the few bars near the Presidio not declared out of bounds. Trade flourished, and many San Francisco romances burgeoned over a couple of drinks. A few

years ago, columnist and client Stanton Delaplane discovered Irish
Coffee on a trip abroad and the Buena Vista was the first bar
to introduce the Irish whisky, coffee, and whipped cream concoction. The Buena Vista has been fighting off customers ever since.
Koeppler and his French wife, a former City of Paris saleslady,
are on a first-name basis with hundreds of regulars. Customers
include furred dowagers driven to lunch in a Rolls, newspaper and
TV people, even occasional refugees from the North Beach coffee
houses. One of the waitresses claims they come in sections and
labels days "Art and Culture," "Brooks Brothers," "TV production," and "Off-Beat." Although it draws a terrific tourist trade,
the BV has a steady clientele of San Francisco residents willing to
battle the crowds for a heavily poured and reasonable drink and
a man-sized portion of whatever the daily special happens to be.
Irish Coffee and Ramos Fizz are the best-known drinks. Regulars
also order drinks like Danish Aquavit, Tequila Sangrita, Pimms
Cups, the house martini made of Tanqueray gin, and Pisco Punch,
an old San Francisco favorite with mysterious ingredients.

La Tosca   242 Columbus Avenue. GA 1-9651. Recordings of
arias from the great operas come free with the drinks. And the
fancy mixed drinks are among the best in town. This old Italian
bar introduced San Francisco to the local version of *cappucino*—a
hot brandy-and-chocolate drink suffused with steam on impressive
and gleaming espresso-type machines. Now you can get it all over
town, but experts still prefer the way it is made here. If you like a
somewhat sweeter drink, you can have a White Nun—hot milk,
brandy, and coffee liqueur. Or you can have a smooth cold Piçon
Punch—Piçon, grenadine, and seltzer. Baskets of crisp anise-fla-
vored cookies are served with the drinks. Unhappy modernization
has routinized the decor of the lounge in back and removed the
mural of Dante and Beatrice, although there are still some faded
murals opposite the bar. There was a time when Tosca prided itself
on playing only a choice selection of original 78 rpm recordings that
included the best of Caruso, Galli-Curci, and Chaliapin. But a few
of the great favorites are still on the juke-box. Tosca has retained
enough of its original flavor to make it one of the city's most distinctive bars.

El Matador   492 Broadway. GA 1-3348. Barnaby Conrad,
writer and ex-bullfighter, officiates here over one of the city's
swankiest watering spots. The Pacific Heights crowd mingles with
movie and television celebrities amid posters and other momentos
of old bullfights. In the men's room there is a blackboard with
chalk so customers can get rid of their inhibitions. On Sunday

nights the regulars gather to watch reruns of bullfighting movies with guitar accompaniment. Despite the mannered atmosphere, this bar isn't as offensive as it might sound. The drinks are not exorbitantly priced. And Johnny Cooper's jazz piano is superb.

XII Adler Place   The address on an alley off Columbus Avenue near Broadway. EX 2-9612. On the fringes of Chinatown and North Beach, this is a quiet, tastefully decorated, well-stocked bar frequented by young businessmen and women, some of the prosperous art group, and occasional theatrical celebrities. It is also a story of two generations. Frank Guidera, Jr., operates this successful and sophisticated watering place. But walk up a flight of stairs and through a corridor and you come to a modest working-man's bar (you can also walk in through the front door at 529 Broadway) operated by Frank's father. Here come fishermen, longshoremen, and Italian working people. At Frank, Sr.'s, try a traditional Compari over ice with a twist of lemon. At Frank, Jr.'s, the more sophisticated Negroni cocktail is the drink to order.

Gold Street   56 Gold Street, in an alley off Montgomery Street between Pacific and Jackson streets. EX 7-5626. This bar goes in heavily for Victorian decor. In a gesture to the old times, it offers nickel sandwiches; but the ample drinks are $1.25. Noisemakers and hats are produced at midnight in an every-night-is-New-Year's push. So stay away if you want a drink or two in quiet.

The Gaslight   1144 Pine Street. TU 5-1532. Sally Stanford's old "house is not a home" changed hands, but people still come around to see the gas chandeliers and the lush bordello decoration. Dinner is served, but you can merely drop in for a drink.

Shanty Malone's   570 Clay Street. EX 7-6919. This financial-district bar is a gathering place for sports enthusiasts and politicians and newspapermen who drop in to reminisce with Shanty. The walls are covered with hundreds of action shots of historic California sports and with old newspaper layouts, all donated by customers.

The Happy Valley Bar   Sheraton-Palace Hotel. EX 2-8600 (see p. 15). Drinks served in authentic old-San Francisco atmosphere.

Day's   24 Ellis Street, near Market and Stockton streets. GA 1-2894 (see p. 110). You can still get a pretty fair martini at the huge bar for twenty-five cents.

French Bread for Night Owls

The night clubs and the bars close at 2 A.M. What then for those who are still not sleepy or tired? One possibility is to go to Jimbo's after-hour jazz hangout (see page 117). Another, more unusual and favored by some old San Franciscans as the way to finish off a night on the town, is to drop in on one of the French-bread bakeries in North Beach, near many of the good night spots and restaurants. The bakeries start working about 1 A.M. so that the bread will be fresh for early morning delivery to restaurants and stores. And they will be in full swing if you get there any time after that. Of course, you have to appreciate San Francisco sour-dough French bread (see p. 67) to enjoy watching it made. But if you do, you will get a chance to observe one of the city's miracles in the process of creation.

The **Italian-French Bakery Company** (1501 Grant Avenue) is just beyond the Bohemian shops and night spots. The storefront will be closed when you get there. But you will see a light coming through a door past the main entrance. For a moment you may have the feeling of entering a speakeasy or some mysterious off-limits dive. But walk in and ask if you can watch for a while. The foreman and the bakers won't mind. Of course, they'll pay no attention to you, and you will have to stay out of their way.

A wonderful, slightly sour smell permeates the large, brightly lighted room. Men in white, white pants, white T-shirts, white aprons are working at a furious pace; some of the most skilled bakers are neither French nor Italian but Mexican. One will be stirring a great cauldron of dough. An overhead belt stretches the dough and breaks it up into manageable blobs. The chunks of dough are put on a table where several men work it and shape it and pound it, make it into round loaves or rolls or long loaves. These are placed on long narrow boards, about twelve loaves to a board. Quickly the loaves are scored and popped into great tile-front wall ovens that remind you somehow of a French or Italian village bakery. About forty minutes later one of the bakers pulls out the loaves with a big paddle, piles them on a belt which runs along the ovens. The hot bread and rolls are loaded into cars, ready for delivery in a couple of hours. All the while you have to step lively to avoid being hit by a board or a paddle.

The process is slightly more mechanized at the bigger and more modern **Venetian Baking Company** (2200 Powell Street, a few blocks past the night-club area). But the wall ovens look substantially the same. The pounding and shaping and scoring are still done by hand. Men still put the loaves into the oven and take them out. Craftsmanship is still the key ingredient. But an old baker mutters, "The French bread isn't as good as it used to be. We don't work it over as long, don't take as much time." We wonder what makes San Francisco sourdough French bread different. He shrugs his shoulders: "Maybe it's the climate and the weather."

Buy a loaf on the way out. You can get one right out of the oven. But you will have to wait a couple of minutes until it cools enough to break into chunks. The warm soft dough beneath the hard crust will melt in your mouth. If you have the foresight to bring some Monterey Jack cheese and Italian salami, you will be able to make a sandwich better than the most elaborate concoctions of the greatest chefs. You can munch it as you walk along the deserted streets into the gray San Francisco dawn.

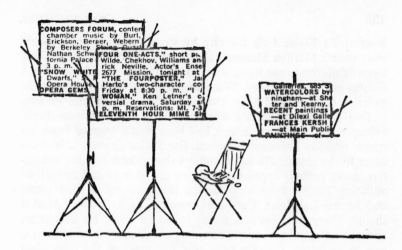

7: THE LIVELY ARTS

Liaison Passionelle

FOR MORE THAN a century San Francisco has maintained a *liaison passionelle* with the arts. The relationship has often been stormy. There have been quarrels, recriminations, separations. But there has rarely been indifference. San Francisco was ever and still remains a city where a poem or a painting or a mural can create a sensation and make the headlines.

Back in 1875, San Francisco was stood on its ear by the mystery of Toby Rosenthal's missing "Elaine." The story is an old-time favorite, no doubt exaggerated in the telling, but it is not altogether irrelevant to the city's helpless infatuation with the arts. Toby was a painter, the son of an immigrant tailor. When he was very young he revealed a flair for making precise little sketches which the elder Rosenthal displayed in his Stockton Street shop. Passersby admired the drawings, and the father decided to save pennies painfully accumulated by stitching away until late at night to send his prodigy to Europe. Toby was a competent craftsman, his work something like that found nowadays on the covers of the *Saturday Evening Post*. After making good in Europe, he was commissioned by a wealthy San Francisco merchant to do a painting based on Tennyson's "Idylls of the King." The result was a five-by-three-foot oil painting of Elaine, victim of unrequited love for Lancelot, on a funeral barge attended by her faithful servant.

Rosenthal's Elaine took the city by storm, became more sought after than a Marilyn Monroe calendar. Fan clubs were organized, more flamboyant than those which have since swooned over Frank Sinatra and Elvis Presley. When the painting was unveiled at the galleries of Snow and May, thousands filed past to gaze in awe.

Two days later the city was rocked by the most sensational kidnaping in its history. Elaine had been neatly snipped from her frame, and San Francisco mourned. But Police Captain I. W. Lees came to the rescue. He heard rumors that sinister-looking characters, most unlikely types to haunt an art gallery, had been seen admiring Elaine. Something clicked in the captain's alert mind, and he tracked down Cut-Face Donahue to a South-of-Market shanty. There, sure enough, neatly rolled up under the bedclothes and camouflaged by a custom-house report, Elaine turned up, virtue and looks intact. Captain Lees was the toast of the town, and everyone rejoiced when Elaine was safe in the gallery again. Elaine has since been consigned to the University of Illinois art gallery, but Rosenthal's "Cardinal's Portrait" can be seen at the Palace of the Legion of Honor in San Francisco.

The excitement, though less flamboyantly displayed, was almost as great in 1953 when a death sentence hung over the Anton Refregier murals at the Rincon Annex Post Office. The villain this time was not a Damon Runyonesque criminal but a dastardly politician.

Refregier, a modernist at the opposite pole from Toby Rosenthal's romanticism, had won a hard-fought commission against eighty-three other artists for a series of panels on California history. The result was brilliant art and searing social comment (see page 23). Refregier touched on several of the sore points in San Francisco's past. He was unkind to the vigilantes of the fifties; he was explicit about the persecution of the Chinese, and he told the story of what may euphemistically be called the city's labor troubles. The Daughters of the American Revolution and veterans' organizations were outraged from the outset. By 1953 it became possible to condemn the murals as Communist propaganda and a congressman from a rural Northern California district did just that. He put a resolution into the hopper demanding removal of the murals. Support for the resolution mounted in the House. The Refregier panels appeared doomed.

Then the city rallied to the defense. Political and artistic hatchets were buried as bankers, trade unionists, society matrons, artists, businessmen, museum directors joined in pleas to save the murals. Straw votes were conducted to sample public opinion, and the results were reassuring. The California Historical Society gave the murals the equivalent of the *Good Housekeeping* Seal of Approval when it pronounced them "historically accurate." George Stewart, the prominent writer and University of California expert on the West, found them "remarkably sensitive" rather than derogatory of either San Francisco or the state. A San Francisco Citizens Committee to Protect the Rincon Annex Murals was formed. Representatives treked to Washington to enlighten Philistine congressmen. And in the end art emerged triumphant. The murals still delight and disturb and excite in the otherwise drab Post Office.

The story, alas, does not always end so happily. Beniamino Bufano's massively gentle statue of St. Francis has endured a painful and rejected existence. Bufano sculpted his St. Francis in Paris in 1928, hoping that it would be proudly displayed in the city named after the warm-hearted saint of Assisi. He waited twenty-seven years, and even then his dream was realized only briefly.

Local art patrons attempted in 1932 to have the statue moved to San Francisco, but they couldn't raise the necessary funds. Bufano proposed a few years later to place a giant 180-foot replica of his St. Francis on top of Twin Peaks, where it would extend a perpetual welcome to the city. Again the funds failed to materialize. Finally, in 1955, the Reverend Alvin P. Wagner helped rally parishioners and art patrons behind a plan to put the statue in front of the Church of St. Francis in North Beach. There it stood appropriately and splendidly for six years, rescued at last from its long sojourn in a Paris warehouse.

Unfortunately, Father Wagner's successor was less enthusiastic about the statue, complaining that it cracked the pavement and interfered with funerals and weddings. The battle of St. Francis was fought out for weeks on the front pages of the newspapers, and art lost. On a nippy March day in 1961, hundreds of North Beach residents, poets, businessmen, Chinese, Italians, stood mournfully in front of the church while St. Francis was uprooted by jackhammers and acetylene torches. "They could use those hacksaws and jackhammers for something constructive—like tearing down the Embarcadero Freeway," one artist muttered. The statue was carted away to Oakland, of all places, where it was used to promote a fancy new shopping center.

There are no cracks in the pavement any more at the Church of St. Francis, but to San Franciscans passing by something seems irreparably missing. Bufano says he still hopes his St. Francis will wind up in San Francisco. Perhaps he is right. Perhaps the city will yet reclaim its statue and its reputation.

Captain Vioget's Impulse

San Francisco began its tempestuous liaison with the arts even before it was properly born. In 1837 Captain Jean Jacques Vioget, later the city's first surveyor, dropped anchor at Yerba Buena Cove, then promptly started painting a scene of the Bay from his trading bark. The captain yielded to what later became a mass impulse, and he provided a clue to the city's appeal to artists of all kinds. The beauty of the city's setting has always proved irresistible to writers and painters. It may also condition its residents to be receptive to the arts.

The city's early frontier conditions seemed to be hostile to the esthetic. But the reverse was the case. Perhaps because many of them were crude and unwashed, San Francisco's pioneers worshiped all the more ardently at the theater, the opera, and other temples of culture. One of the stated objectives of the Bear Flag revolt of 1846, an enterprise of tough soldiers and adventurers, was "to encourage virtue and literature." The saloons of the brawling town decked their walls with paintings and entertained their patrons with "musicales." The city's first literary review, the *Golden Era,* was started in 1852, and Horace Greeley was amazed at "its power and influence when the population is so sparse and the mail facilities so poor." The *Era* was full of sentimental verse at first, but later it turned to the lusty humor and exaggeration of Bret Harte and Mark Twain, who drew their materials from the tales and legends of the prospectors. Some years later the city's free and easy atmosphere permitted the mordant criticism and bitter whimsy of Ambrose Bierce.

San Francisco's romance with the arts never ran smoothly. Bret Harte and Mark Twain left early, and many others have deserted since for New York or Paris. Nor has the city always been kind to its artists; enough of them have gone hungry in it. The love affair has waned and waxed. The splendors of the 1870s and 1880s, touted as San Francisco's golden age, often smothered the artists or brought out the worst in them. Creative artists were hardly needed when the mining and railroad barons could import the most expensive and atrocious bric-a-brac from Europe. But only a few years later Jack London, Frank Norris, and George Sterling heralded a new literary renaissance. New artists began painting, and new Bohemias flourished. The socially conscious 1930s were a productive time for San Francisco's painters and writers, and there are many who think San Francisco is in the throes of a new cultural upswing now.

Not all San Franciscans are art-lovers. But enough of them are to create an atmosphere in which artists feel at home. Art isn't the exclusive province of a few longhairs, society women, and wealthy collectors. A man can be a poet or a painter in San Francisco without being considered an eccentric. Perhaps the frontier's respect for culture has never been totally eliminated. Perhaps the city's cosmopolitan population is a factor. Some observers suggest that the city's cultural climate, due to its substantial Italian and other Latin groups, has been more Mediterranean than Nordic and therefore more hospitable to the arts.

Whatever the reasons, San Francisco provides a mass audience for most of the arts. The city's annual Art Festival draws a cross-section crowd running into the tens of thousands. The city maintains, although perhaps not too generously, an opera company, a symphony orchestra, even a ballet company. Potters, ceramicists, jewelers have flocked to the area, making San Francisco a national center for skilled practitioners of the arts and crafts who attempt to give an esthetic lift to everyday objects. There is a flourishing and well-attended little-theater movement, making up in verve and dedication what it lacks in professionalism. There are literally thousands of practicing writers in the area, full-timers and part-timers, successful and unknown, some beats and Bohemians, others eminently respectable teachers at colleges and universities. Poetry readings are an established institution, and a visiting poet will usually pull a substantial and enthusiastic crowd. It is hard to keep track of all the little magazines publishing local writers. The city is literally sprinkled with bookstores, and sales are among the highest in the country. San Francisco's cultural life, never dull and often lively indeed, is one of the city's most appealing and distinctive features.

The Seacoast of Bohemia

Cincinnatus Heine Miller was probably San Francisco's first practicing Bohemian, back in the 1870s. Weary of the cumbersome name he never chose, he decided to call himself Joaquin after Joaquin Murieta, the romantic Mexican Robin Hood whose exploits he immortalized. On a trip to England he titillated aristocrats and literary lights by appearing everywhere in a red flannel shirt, high boots, and long hair falling Indian-style to his shoulders. His personal life was not above reproach, and he was known to improve on the truth. He demonstrated beyond doubt that the artistic temperament sometimes includes a dash of the poseur as well as a willingness to defy convention.

While Miller was creating a sensation in England, a number of artists, writers, and journalists, partly inspired by his example, decided to form the San Francisco Bohemian Club. The members had only a bare room with a few tables and chairs in which to meet. There they held their monthly "High Jinks" discussions followed by a supper, and all accompanied by considerable liquid refreshment. The story goes that one speaker pulled out a revolver along with his manuscript and announced, "This is to shoot the first Bohemian galoot who stirs from his seat before I end this paper."

For years the favorite haunt of San Francisco Bohemian painters was the Montgomery Block, a super-colossal four-story building conceived by General Henry Wager Halleck. Occupying an entire square block at the corner of Montgomery and Washington streets, it was called "Halleck's Folly" at first. It was considered far too big for the needs of the city when it was completed in 1853, and its construction was bizarre, millions of bricks on the foundation of a huge redwood raft set deep in what was then the mud of the waterfront. Most people expected it to stand empty for years, but its offices were quickly filled by the city's leading business firms and attorneys. Historic events, from the vigilante violence of 1856 to the overthrow of the Manchu dynasty in China by Sun Yat-sen, were plotted there. Practically all the great names of San Francisco art and letters lived or had studios there or at least used to drink potent Pisco Punch at the famous Bank Exchange in the building's early days or eat at Papa Coppa's restaurant at the turn of the century.

When the building reached middle age, the more prosperous tenants moved out and fortune-tellers, Chinese herbalists, and secondhand-clothes dealers moved in. Finally, in the 1890s, when the rents and the building had really run down, painters began to notice that the big high-ceilinged rooms would make fine studios. The painters were followed by a miscellaneous crew of musicians, sculptors, poets, and newspapermen.

The Monkey Block, as it was called, was just the right place for Giuseppe Coppa, an excellent cook who sported a flowing mustache and concealed a long-held desire to be a painter himself. The Bohemian tenants took to Papa Coppa at once. The food was good, the prices were low, and the wine flowed freely. Without consulting his customers, Papa Coppa once ventured to redecorate his walls with bright red wallpaper. The artists revolted at this conventional elegance. Mounting wobbly tables and armed with big jugs of Italian red wine and an assortment of chalk, they covered the wallpaper with gay murals. Portraits of many of the artists were part of the mural, and a popular pastime for hangers-on of the arts was to visit Papa Coppa's and figure out who was who on the walls.

There is a story about a young man who so much enjoyed the gay company of the Monkey Block's artists that he decided this was the life for him. He persuaded his well-to-do father that he was a potential Rembrandt who needed only a studio and time and money to realize himself. Every once in a while when the father would drop in to see him, the young man would hastily hire a model, borrow a couple of paintings, and get busily to work impersonating an artist. But real artists lived and painted at the Monkey Block up until the late 1950s, when the hallowed wreck was torn down to make way for a parking lot.

San Francisco has ever been one of Bohemia's favored seacoasts. Over the years successive Bohemian colonies have flourished on Russian Hill, on Telegraph Hill, now on Potrero Hill, nurturing new generations of artists and writers. Frequently the city was scandalized, but its prevailing attitude was a somewhat dismayed tolerance. One night George Sterling decided to take a swim, without a bathing suit of course, amid the water lilies of Stow Lake in Golden Gate Park. An unsympathetic cop ran him in. But legend has it that the Chief of Police formally gave Sterling permission to take a nude swim any time he wanted to anywhere in the city. San Francisco police have not always been so sympathetic to Bohemian antics, and perhaps the anecdote was later embroidered to prove how San Francisco loved its finest poet.

A historian would probably interject that time mellows the shenanigans of vanished Bohemias. Generations of schoolchildren have recited "Columbus" by Joaquin Miller, now an eminently respectable if unimportant literary antique. The once-lively Bohemian Club is now one of San Francisco's stuffiest and most exclusive clubs, so respectable indeed that Herbert Hoover was a frequent guest for many years at its 2500-acre redwood grove on the Russian River. A logician might add that, while many artists and writers have been Bohemians, not all Bohemians have been writers or artists.

The Beat Generation

These truisms apply to San Francisco's most recent crop of Bohemians, the so-called beatniks who were sensationalized and publicized far beyond their number or their importance. Time has not yet glamorized their antics, and many have still to produce anything more creative than that morning-after feeling. They were for the most part a fringe group, the hangers-on of practicing writers and artists.

In the late 1950s they began to flock to North Beach, finding "pads" in which to live and haunts in which to sit and talk. They considered themselves members of the beat generation, camp-followers of Jack Kerouac, Allen Ginsberg, and other literary spokesmen of revolt against the middle-class status quo. If you have read Kerouac's *On the Road* you will understand something about the lost young men and the sad-eyed girls who used to sit around all day and most of the night at the now-defunct Bagel Shop and a few of whom can still be seen wandering aimlessly on Grant Avenue.

Like Kerouac's Dean Moriarty they sought refuge in a nirvana of jazz, sexual excess, marijuana, and fast automobiles. But unlike Kerouac's wild, holy fool, they were not children of the slums and graduates of reform schools. They were for the most part the sons and daughters of middle-class suburbia engaged in a brief and superficial revolt against a conformity to which they would soon return.

If they could not change the world they knew, they could at least withdraw from it. If they could not challenge the power of Madison Avenue, they could at least have no part of its rewards and its slickness. Their revolt was something less than complete; many of them were described as the modern remittance men, wheedling a monthly stipend from their parents so that they could write or paint. Others took low-paid, casual jobs, and exchanged the split-level comforts for squalid, inexpensive flats. They discarded the gray-flannel uniform for uniforms of their own, beards and black sweaters for the men, black stockings and sandals for the girls. "They are the most conforming group I have seen," says a craftsman with a shop on Grant Avenue. "They all need to look alike, dress alike, swagger alike, think alike." Some of the beats were serious young people genuinely interested in the arts. Others were interested mainly in themselves and in the unexplored frontiers of sensation and experience.

What were they looking for on Grant Avenue? Were they just looking for kicks and excitement? Or were they searching for their own identity in a conformist world? And what did *beat* mean anyway? Did it mean down and out and defeated? Did it mean revolt against the conventions and sexual mores of society? Did it mean the beat of jazz? Did it, as some claimed, mean the beat in beatitude, the search for purity and holiness in the midst of sin?

Oddly enough, many of the beats were attracted to religious ideas if not practices. Some clustered around the Reverend Pierre de Lattre's short-lived Bread and Wine Mission on Grant Avenue. Others followed Kerouac, a part-time San Franciscan and the most frenetic Buddhist in history, into the contemplative mysteries of Zen.

Most of them probably didn't know, and whatever it was they sought they didn't find it. For they left Grant Avenue either in search of other Bohemian haunts or to return to the suburbs. At high tide there were perhaps two hundred full-timers on Grant Avenue, supplemented on week ends by commuters from Bay Area colleges. But high tide did not last very long. The beat Bohemia was undermined from without and from within.

An enterprising headline writer coined the term *beatnik,* and soon the Grant Avenue regulars were engulfed in a tide of publicity, tourism, and commercialism. At best a fringe group whose excesses attracted notoriety, the beats became a center for other fringes. Dope peddlers and other criminal elements were reported active on Grant Avenue. Tough young kids came around to check the action. Entrepreneurs moved in with bars, night clubs, and gift shops. Soon the curious far outnumbered the beats. One result of the exploitation was to drive out many of the beatniks, a transient group anyway.

But the internal crisis among the beats was more serious. Rejecting the values and standards of Madison Avenue, they replaced them only with a hectic social and moral nihilism. Kids from sheltered middle-class homes burned the candle at both ends, and the light it gave was not always lovely. Kenneth Rexroth, a prominent poet and critic who was for a time the gray eminence of the beat writers, warned in the San Francisco *Examiner* that the beat generation was committing "emotional suicide." Indeed, there were actual suicides as well as nervous and physical breakdowns. Among some of the youngsters there grew an awareness that they were achieving neither happiness nor self-expression and they deserted Grant Avenue, before it was too late, to continue their seeking in other ways and other places.

Rexroth called for drawing a line between the "poorly organized schizophrenia" of the beatniks and what he describes as "the great creative upsurge" in San Francisco since World War II. It was not always easy to find the line; many San Francisco writers and artists were in some measure part of the beat-generation trend. But when the beatnik sensationalism subsided the distinction became clearer. The so-called beatniks were only the fellow travelers of a literary movement with plenty of excesses, but with some talent too.

The Poets' General Store

When you say **City Lights** in San Francisco, you're not talking about the old Chaplin movie but about the city's original paper-back bookstore (261 Columbus Avenue), started in the early 1950s by Lawrence Ferlinghetti, a prominent practicing poet. City Lights is also a publishing house, a literary center, and a hangout for many of San Francisco's beat (and non-beat) poets.

It is next door to Vesuvio's pseudo-Bohemian bar and on top of an old Evangelical mission. The latter fact turned out to be important. The mission had a spacious cellar headquarters as well as a tiny cramped street level and a balcony up a narrow stair-case. There was plenty of room for expansion; now all three floors are jammed with books and customers, some of whom have the economical habit of doing their reading in the store. Old "I Am the Lord" and "Sinners Repent" signs are interspersed with abstract and other contemporary paintings.

The store carries a wide selection of paperbacks, even some murder mysteries. But its strong points are psychoanalysis, Zen, and poetry. A fantastic magazine display includes publications from all over the world, literary, philosophical, liberal, radical, and homosexual. A section marked "new releases" keeps patrons abreast of the latest paperbacks. And all the pamphlets, books, broadsides, and mimeographed sheets of the San Francisco poets are lovingly and prominently exhibited.

City Lights is the post office address of many local poets. They use the store's bulletin board as a messenger service to reach friends and colleagues and as a free advertising exchange where they can pick up jobs or flats. There are also occasional notices like the one by a "gassy looker" who needed work as an artists' model.

The store has something of the atmosphere of a beat cracker-barrel general store. Poets who have been out of town come by to check in and find out what's new. Others come by to read each other their latest poems or discuss trends in contemporary litera-ture. Robert Duncan, one of the founders of the San Francisco poetry renaissance in the late 1940s and who looks more the spectacled, absent-minded college professor than the stereotype of the poet, is a frequent visitor. So is Vincent McHugh, a poet and occasional interpreter of the new poetry for the San Francisco

Chronicle. Ferlinghetti puts in a couple of evenings a week at the cash register.

The regulars here are more interested in poetry than in conspicuous Bohemian display. Ferlinghetti had a romantic enough past. Born in New York of French ancestry, he seems to have been connected during World War II with both the French and Danish undergrounds. After the war he studied at the Sorbonne and wrote novels, then was attracted to San Francisco by the new poetry movement. But the curious will find him disappointingly conventional in appearance—lean, clean-shaven, almost ascetic. Shigeyoshi Murao, the clerk and general manager, more obligingly sports a luxuriant beard camouflaging both a shrewd business sense and a keenly humorous appraisal of the store's unending stream of students, beats, poets, book-lovers, and tourists.

City Lights has weathered both success and a most unorthodox financial setup. As Ferlinghetti describes it, the proceeds are divided among the five employees of the store and publishing firm, with any surplus poured into new publishing ventures. City Lights has published many of the better-known San Francisco poets, including Duncan, Ferlinghetti, Allen Ginsberg, Kenneth Patchen, and Rexroth. It has also published a curious assortment of other titles, among them *Basic Chinese & Japanese Recipes, Beat Zen, Square Zen, and Zen,* and *What's Really Happening in China?* All the books are paperbacks, none selling for more than a dollar. They are nationally distributed, and some even make money. Of course, there is also an occasional fiasco. Ferlinghetti was one of the backers of *Beatitude,* a mimeographed poetry magazine whose editor ran off with the funds.

The most sensational City Lights venture was publication of Ginsberg's *Howl,* a chaotic, Whitmanesque poem of protest which began with the compelling and often-quoted line, "I saw the best minds of my generation destroyed by madness, starving hysterical naked. . . ." The poem was also liberally sprinkled with four-letter words. City Lights had the book printed in England, and the customs collector in San Francisco seized one shipment, stating, "You wouldn't want your children to come across it." Murao was arrested for selling the book, and both he and Ferlinghetti were charged with publishing and distributing obscene writing.

In a courtroom filled with civil libertarians, poets, beats in turtleneck sweaters, and the curious, the prosecution demanded the extreme penalty (six months and $500) on the ground that youth had to be protected, while the defense argued that adults had the right to read books unsuitable for children. The defense also

produced nine critics who discussed the poem as literature, some
claiming that it was one of the most significant long poems in many
years. The trial was well covered in the press and was generally
taken as a test of whether San Francisco could be turned into
another Boston. The verdict, in a thirty-nine-page opinion, was a
complete victory for Ferlinghetti, Murao, City Lights, and freedom to publish and read. One minor consequence was that Murao,
now something of a celebrity, began publishing his own little
magazine, *Shig's Review*.

The New Poetry

The *Howl* decision suggests one reason poets have been flocking
to San Francisco during the past decade. They consider the
atmosphere freer than in most American cities. There is an availability of casual work as sailors, warehousemen, agricultural
laborers, giving poets both a measure of economic independence
and time to write; Ginsberg shipped out on a long Arctic voyage and
returned with enough money to travel in Mexico and Europe. The
most important reason is that the poets can get published and find
an audience. There is an abundance of small presses like City
Lights and of tiny magazines. There are also two more ambitious
quarterly reviews, *Contact* and the *San Francisco Review*. Besides,
poets can establish direct contact with a literate, interested public.
They can and do read their poems at homes, art galleries, bookstores, small night clubs, community centers. Some poets go around
North Beach and elsewhere selling their own little books and
brochures.

There are now literally hundreds of practicing and more-or-less
serious poets in the Bay Area. Not all of them can by any means
be characterized as beat, nor do all of them cluster around City
Lights. A rival group, challenging the beat approach, has long existed
around the San Francisco State College Poetry Center, which runs
some of the city's best-attended poetry readings. The beat poets
have appeared at its readings. So have more conventional poets
and visiting celebrities like Stephen Spender and Langston Hughes.

No common denominator of style and content can easily be
used to identify the San Francisco poets; there are rather several
central influences and trends. Robert Duncan said once, "This is
what I wanted for the last poem. A loosening of conventions and
return to open form." If the word *painting* had been substituted
for *poem,* the same statement could have been made by one of San
Francisco's abstractionists, and the poets do have in common with
many of the artists a revolt against conventional form. The same

search for "unbound space" is found in some of the huge, bold abstractionist paintings and some of the sprawling, undisciplined poems. The impact of jazz is strong, in a search for the same throbbing rhythm, the same "gone" mood, for a kind of poetry that can be read aloud against a jazz background and communicate directly and aurally with an audience. There is a strong religious impulse in some of the poets; William Everson, a one-time Guggenheim Fellow, is now Brother Antoninus, a lay member of the Dominican Order, but continues to write experimental lyrical poetry. The strains of the older modernists Ezra Pound and William Carlos Williams can be found among the works of the local poets, but so can the even older influence of Walt Whitman.

A dozen different currents conflict and converge sometimes in the same poet. There is ugliness and obscenity in Ginsberg, and there are also tender, lyrical lines. Some of the poets celebrate the antisocial beat revolt, but the same poets sometimes express social concern. There is both escape from responsibility and commitment to social goals and ideals. Obviously, the poets are still searching and groping. They are confronted with much the same dilemma as their bearded and sandaled camp-followers. Does their revolt against middle-class conformity end in chaos and self-destruction? Does it lead to some form of coherent social protest? Does it wind up with a religious conversion, whether Buddhist or Catholic?

Rexroth and Ferlinghetti, perhaps the most influential of the local poets, have both in different ways condemned the nihilist alternative of rejecting all human and social values. According to Ferlinghetti, "The Wiggly nihilism of the Beat hipster, if carried to its natural conclusion, actually means the death of the creative artist himself. While the 'non-commitment' of the artist is itself a suicidal and deluded variation of this same nihilism."

The new poetry is still in flux, and it is difficult to get perspective on the beat-generation writers. It is perhaps enlightening to turn the pages of *The Improper Bohemians* by Allen Churchill. This book is a history of Greenwich Village in its heyday, of that other Bohemia when it was a mishmash of poseurs and phonies, talented artists and writers and young female schoolteachers in revolt against convention. Churchill does not soft-pedal the zaniness of the Village in those days, and there was plenty of it. But he concludes with an interesting anecdote about the ceremonies of the National Institute of Arts and Letters in 1958. Malcolm Cowley, the poet and critic, "at one point let his eyes range over the faces of the distinguished men and women sharing the platform with him. All these diverse talents, Cowley realized with a start of pleasure and surprise, shared one thing in common. Each had, at one time or another, been an improper Bohemian in Greenwich Village."

Only the most optimistic will hope that San Francisco's Bohemian colonies of the 1950s and 1960s will prove as fertile, or that the work of San Francisco's new poets and writers will prove as enduring as that of Eugene O'Neill, Sherwood Anderson, Sinclair Lewis, Edna St. Vincent Millay, Theodore Dreiser, and others who wandered through the Village. But many critics believe that the San Francisco poets, for all the groping, uneven, chaotic quality of much that they have written, are nevertheless producing a body of worthwhile and promising poetry. *The New American Poetry 1945–1960*, edited by Donald M. Allen, includes more poets associated with San Francisco than with any other place or school. The reader could do worse than pick up this or some other collection with work by the new poets and try to decide for himself what it is all about.

Art in the Streets

Art in San Francisco isn't confined to the city's three art museums and countless galleries. A lot of it is out in the streets, and people seem to prefer it that way.

Every September a few acres of City Hall Plaza, or sometimes the Marina or Fisherman's Wharf, are turned over to a glorified country fair with a brass band playing and with hot-dog, beer, and soft-drink stands. Instead of the usual sideshows and rides for the kids, there is a vast conglomeration of painting, sculpture, photography, and crafts. More remarkable than the art—which ranges from distinguished to terrible—is the attendance. Tens of thousands of San Franciscans visit the annual four-day Art Festival—men, women, children; businessmen, socialites, truck drivers; people of all races and nationalities, including, of course, the Bohemian. An attempt was made one year to hold the show in the city's big barn of a Civic Auditorium rather than right out in the streets, and somehow that put a damper on things. It was never tried again.

The city's Art Commission, which runs the festival, has the bigger and thornier assignment of planning the use and improving the esthetic standards of artwork in public places. The results of its efforts are usually controversial. When it picked a modern tapestry for a new library a few years ago the Library Commission turned thumbs down. There was an even greater furor when the Art Commission rejected on esthetic grounds a mural for the new Hall of Justice already selected and contracted for by the architect. The Art Commission probably makes more headlines than any other city commission. There has never been actual violence at its meetings, but artists, sculptors, and patrons of the arts have been known to threaten to punch each other in the nose during a heated session.

The city is literally sprinkled with sculptures and murals, often where you least expect them. Even the battered old lamp posts on Market Street display the work (not among his best) of Arthur Putnam, the city's most celebrated early twentieth-century sculptor. Much of the statuary and other art work is awful; the scores of statues cluttering up Golden Gate Park are particularly undistinguished. But some of the miscellaneous scattered art is excellent, and all of it suggests at least the good intentions of decorating the city and making art available to the public.

Patrons of the bar at the **Hoffman Café and Grill** (619 Market Street) unknowingly gulp their beer or Scotch-and-soda under an elaborate interpretation of Shakespeare's Ophelia. The artist, Italian-born Domenico Tojetti, was the unchallenged favorite of the city's gaslight era. Now almost forgotten, his work was once purchased eagerly by the gold and silver and railroad barons. At another bar, **Via Vai** (1203 Polk Street), hangs Tojetti's huge "Progress of California," which suggests in classical style such modernities as the airplane.

You run into the work of Beniamino Bufano, one of the world's great contemporary sculptors, in the most unlikely places. On the veranda of the **Maritime Museum** (Aquatic Park at foot of Polk Street) are perched his sleek black seals. The lawns are unkempt and the buildings worn by time at the **Valencia Gardens Housing Project** (15th and Valencia streets in the Mission district). But Bufano's lustrous, humorous animal figures help create a make-believe backdrop for the children playing jump rope and tossing balls. Here are a mother bear with two little bruins in warm marble. Here are seals, rabbits, and all kinds of cats—a whimsical one with a mouse on its back, some with Cheshire grins and others with devilish grimaces. If you stop in for a snack at **Moars Cafeteria** (33 Powell Street, near Market), you will see another facet of Bufano's work; his bold, colorful mosaic tile panels of St. Francis of Assisi, including children with one eye—symbolic of the oneness of purpose and destiny—and other figures brooding over the imperfections of humanity. A San Francisco legend has it that Bufano was given a lifetime meal ticket to the Moars cafeterias as part of the payment for his work. More striking examples of Bufano's virtuosity are to be seen in the Sun Yet-sen statue at St. Mary's Square (see p. 54) and in the huge peace shaft at the International Airport.

Walking through the downtown financial district, you may be startled by the massive proletarian sculptures of Ralph Stackpole on carved pylons on either side of the **San Francisco Stock Exchange** (301 Pine Street). A group of female figures represents "Earth's Fruitfulness." Male figures on the other pylon represent "Man's Inventive Genius." The emphasis is on the strength of the common people hewn out of the earth. Financiers and investors passing the sculptures daily have apparently grown accustomed to being overshadowed by Stackpole's sturdy workers. Stock Exchange clients enjoy a more private display of art in the Lunch Club quarters on the tenth and eleventh floors of the building, which are decorated by Diego Rivera frescos of California history.

When the great Mexican artist died in 1957, the city suddenly recalled that he had done a huge mural on seventy-three–by–twenty-three-foot movable panels for the 1940 Golden Gate International Exposition; it had been stored away for years at a special warehouse at San Francisco City College. The original plan was to put the Rivera work in the college library, but then the claim was made that the building was not suitable and that no other public place of the right proportions was available. There may have been other reasons. Some groups protested when the mural was first displayed against the lampooning of Hitler and Mussolini. Or perhaps some timid souls were frightened by Rivera's political radicalism, which certainly never seems to bother the stockbrokers who eat in full view of his frescos every day. In any case, the Rivera mural was literally an artistic skeleton in the city's closet for two decades. Finally the work, grandiosely titled "Marriage of the Artistic Expression of the North and South on this Continent," was unveiled early in 1961 at the City College campus little theater. Dominating the mural is a giant figure, half machine and half Aztec symbol, carrying out the theme of the title. Both critical and public reaction were favorable.

For a long time the only place in the city where Rivera's artistry was easily accessible was the **California School of Fine Arts** (800 Chestnut Street). A forty-by-thirty-foot fresco panel depicts the artist's conception of San Francisco. Painted in 1931 in his flat, broad style, the panel shows various figures typifying various slices of city life—the construction worker, the laborer, the

financier. When he laid down his brush, Rivera is reported to
have said, "And that's what I think of San Francisco." The
pudgy artist's own backside is prominent in the central panel. But
perhaps he meant that as a compliment.

The school is worth visiting for any number of good reasons
besides the Rivera fresco. Steeped in history and tradition, it was
one of the first schools in the United States devoted to the visual
arts when it opened in 1871 in a loft over a fishmonger's shop.
It then moved up to Mark Hopkins' Nob Hill palace, and is now
located in an elegant pseudo-Spanish mansion on the slope of
Russian Hill. The sweeping view of the city and the Bay should
inspire, if it doesn't overawe, the fledgling artists. In the school's
Art Bank you will see a representative collection of the work of
more than two hundred members of the San Francisco Art Association, with trend and tendency in contemporary art on display.
The show changes every three weeks. Faculty and student shows
are also frequent. The gallery is open Monday through Friday,
10 A.M. to 4 P.M., and the staff also enjoy taking visitors through
the school when it is in session.

If you want to give the youngsters a grim history lesson or feel
nostalgic yourself about the tumultuous 1930s, scamper up to
Coit Tower (top of Telegraph Hill, see p. 216) and study the
murals inside. A Works Project Administration cooperative effort
in which many San Francisco artists participated, the murals
remain memorable chiefly as a pictorial record of the *Sturm und
Drang* of the Depression era. The style, heavily influenced by
Rivera, seems derivative, and the quality of the work is quite
uneven. The murals seem to have a flat quality without the
consciousness of texture which makes contemporary painting particularly exciting. This is in part due to the fresco technique, which
consists of painting when the wall is still wet so that the color
becomes part of the plaster. It is the most permanent way of
painting on walls, but, as seen here, probably not the most
stimulating. However, the newspaper headlines of the era come
alive. "I'm a Tough Guy," FDR warns Congress in one panel.
There are the taut faces of striking miners, of families in their
Hoovervilles, of the demonstrating unemployed. Reproductions
of magazine covers recall the days when Mae West was the
nation's sex queen. A volume by Karl Marx is prominent in a
library panel. The murals reflected the radicalism of the period,
and in recent, more conservative years they were marred and
scribbled over by vandals. But a restoration project has been
in progress for some time. Some of San Francisco's better-known

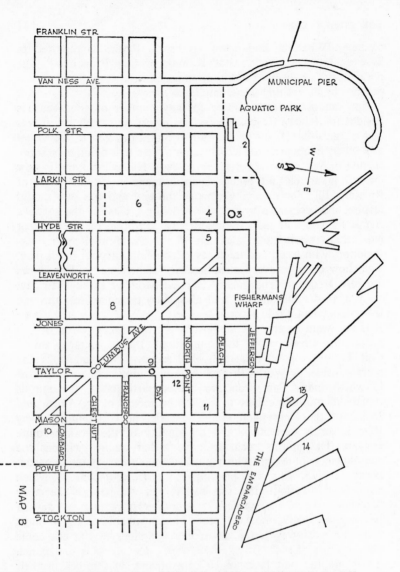

MAP C: FISHERMAN'S WHARF AND AQUATIC PARK

1. Maritime Museum
2. Aquatic Park Beach
3. Hyde St. Cable-car turntable
4. Buena Vista Café
5. Playhouse Repertory Theater
6. Russian Hill Park
7. Lombard Street serpentine road
8. California School of Fine Arts
9. Cable-car turntable
10. North Beach Library
11. Longshoremen's Hall
12. Cost Plus
13. Harbor Tours
14. *Balclutha* (Pier 43)

artists are represented—Ralph Stackpole, Lucien Labaudt, Ralph Chesse, José Moya Pino, Clifford Wight, Bernard Zackheim, and Victor Arnautoff.

The WPA Art Project in San Francisco, one of the biggest and most active in the country, was a major factor in the decoration of public buildings. The themes of its artists varied from the social protest in the Coit Tower murals to the placid panels of "Noah and His Ark" and "Children and Their Animal Friends" in the Mothers' House (a glorified rest room) at the Fleishhacker Zoo. Many of the WPA artists acquired both fame and money in more prosperous times, and a number of them turned from the prevailing realism of the thirties to modern abstractionism.

San Francisco artists have no trouble getting their work displayed, whether in public buildings, museums, or galleries. They have only one complaint against the city. It is not a good town in which to sell paintings. New York and even Dallas and Los Angeles provide a better market. This is partly because there isn't as much easy money around in San Francisco. Cynics add that it is also because the art-buying public here has a more developed critical sense.

The Museums

M. H. de Young Memorial Museum   Golden Gate Park. Open daily 10 A.M.–5 P.M. BA 1-2067. This institution was started in 1895 with much enthusiasm. Founder Michael de Young, publisher of the *Chronicle*, scoured Europe for art treasures, while eager citizens cleaned out their attics, contributing Grandma's fan and ball gown and Grandpa's hat and boots. It is still a miscellany of almost everything except contemporary art, which is shown only at special exhibitions. Its permanent collection stops at about 1850. It has some good old masters—Rembrandt, Velásquez, Goya, Rubens. It also has pioneer memorabilia, old fire engines, pre-Columbian Indian baskets and pottery; Greek, Egyptian, and Oriental art; and European paintings that reflect the art tastes of wealthy San Franciscans *circa* 1895.

The really exciting development at the museum is the addition of the Avery Brundage collection of Oriental art, described as the world's finest private collection of Asian art treasures. In 1959 San Franciscans approved a bond issue to build a separate wing to house this treasure. The Brundage collection spans thirty centuries of art forms, predominantly Chinese. It is a dazzling display of sculpture, pottery, and pictorial art—and at the same time a vivid re-creation of Oriental life, revealing how men prayed and thought and worked. Here are crude utensils designed to meet daily needs, and then the paleolithic working in bone and stone gives way to the bronze culture. Here are to be seen the early dynamic clay forms of the Han dynasty (220 B.C. to 228 A.D.), the carvings of rhinoceri and serpents, the movement from art prescribing religious rituals to pictorial art. The influence of Buddhism which swept over China in the fourth century A.D. is strikingly evident; note the Bodhisattvas wearing Chinese-style clothing and how the images of the gods are slowly transformed from Indian to Chinese. Note too the great Tang dynasty innovations in ceramics with new glazes and hues and dappled streaking, and the intricate Ming dynasty carvings in jade so light it is transparent.

This museum is a crowd-catcher. Attendance averages 100,000 a month, a record for a city the size of San Francisco. Museum officials concede its location in the Park doesn't hurt, and they ruefully admit that the convenient rest rooms are an attraction. But attendance does vary sharply with the exhibitions. When something exciting occurs, like a comprehensive Van Gogh collection or a first showing of the Brundage treasures, the crowds are phenomenal.

California Palace of the Legion of Honor   Lincoln Park. Open 10 A.M.–5 P.M. daily. BA 1-5610. Clement bus from any downtown point on Sutter Street will get you to Clement and 33rd Avenue; from there a walk to the museum through Lincoln Park.

Very French, from the statue of Joan of Arc at the entrance to the inscription *Honneur et Patrie* and an exact replica of the Palais de la Legion d'Honneur in Paris. Donated by Adolph B. and Alma de Bretteville Spreckles (sugar fortune) as a memorial to California's dead in World War I. Take this one in even if you don't appreciate eighteenth-century French architecture as represented by this classic pile, approached through a Roman arch and double rows of Corinthian columns. The view alone, overlooking the western end of the Golden Gate where the narrow gorge becomes ocean, it worth it. There is a permanent collection of eighteenth-century French art, also a scattering of El Greco, Corot, Pissarro, Rembrandt, Degas, and Jacob Epstein's "Weeping Woman." Don't overlook Room 11, devoted to the sculptures of Arthur Putnam, one of California's top artists. His animals are remarkable for litheness and whimsy. The closest thing to a native son, Putnam was brought here when he was seven. The self-taught artist created a sensation at the Panama–Pacific Exposition in 1915 and was commissioned to do iron bas-reliefs on the bases of 238 lamp posts along Market Street. Most of his early work was lost in the earthquake. But many of his best pieces are on display here. Overshadowing all else here is the Auguste Rodin room, displaying "The Kiss," "St. John the Baptist," "Youth and Old Age," and a bust of Victor Hugo. One of the five original bronze casts of "The Thinker" is in the courtyard. There are also special exhibitions, changed monthly. Organ concerts are usually offered Sunday afternoons.

San Francisco Museum of Art   Veterans Building, McAllister Street and Van Ness Avenue. Saturday, Sunday, Monday and holidays 1 to 5 P.M., Tuesday through Friday 12 noon to 10 P.M. HE 1-2040. A front-runner for modernism on the West Coast. The museum was a real innovator in showing abstract contemporary painting when it was opened by the San Francisco Art Association in 1935. Now that modern art has become respectable, the museum is having trouble adhering to its chosen role of pioneer, opening the way for the "growing edge of art." A more mundane difficulty is its location. It is out of the way on the fourth floor of the Veterans Building in Civic Center. The building's classic style—it is a twin of the Opera House—hardly prepares one for artistic experimentation; the museum shares the building with veterans' organizations and the genealogical library of the Sons of the American Revolution. The museum's permanent collection includes a strong representation of Mexican artists, a striking Jackson Pollock, and a sampling of work by Matisse, Picasso, Cézanne, Bracque, Klee, Bernard Buffet, and surrealist Yves Tanguey. Bay Area artists receive special attention in the regular monthly exhibitions. Frequent photography and architectural design shows are featured. Art movies and concerts are another attraction. There is a library where you can linger over luxurious art books, also a bookstore which displays inexpensive prints and paperbacks on art. Although the museum is privately financed, there is no admission charge except for occasional special shows. A pleasant way to while away an afternoon or an evening inexpensively.

The Galleries

Eric Locke Galleries   2557 California Street. Call WA 1-2494 to check hours. In the middle of a dull Victorian gingerbread block, one comes across this delightful continental gallery. It might he dubbed free forms among the ivy; the garden patio offers a splendid setting for modern abstract sculptures and strik-

ing brass mobiles. This gallery specializes in sculpture and prints.
If you have sometimes thought modern sculpture on the grotesque
side, see it in this landscaped garden. The brass wire mobiles
of Ruth Asawa blend into the swaying branches of the trees. The
gallery is one of the oldest in the city.

The owner is Eric Locke, an old movie star who was discovered by Erich von Stroheim and worked with Ernest Lubitsch.
He always loved art, and he had the good sense to start his
gallery before he was too old and too poor. Locke came up
with an original solution to a familiar problem: how to tell good
abstract art from bad abstract art. His answer was to retreat to
original prints. He claims that the defects of poor and sloppy
work are glaring in reproduction and that the very process of
printing demands skill and craftsmanship from the artist. Now
his gallery has a fantastically large graphic arts collection representing both American and foreign artists; woodcuts, etchings,
engravings, lithographs. The colorful, bold Italian prints are among
the most attractive. Locke is assisted by Ernest Jordi, a Swiss-
born connoisseur who will be most helpful in discussing the
"sooner eye" of artists (who paint today what we will accept in
fifty years), the tremendous technical advances in print-making,
and the value of good original prints. Each print here is from a
limited edition and is signed by the artist. The battle-cry at Locke's
is "Why spend two dollars for a poor print and thirty for an
elaborate frame? Why not spend thirty dollars for a first-class print
and two for a simple frame?"

Lucien Labaudt Gallery   1407 Gough Street. Wednesday–Saturday 1–6 P.M. Tuesday 1–9 P.M. Closed Sunday. JO 7-1850. This
gallery, tucked away in a quiet, residential area, is a tender love
story as well as a place to see the work of some of the city's
most interesting artists. Mme Marcelle Labaudt, a tall, quiet
woman with a streak of iron determination, maintains the gallery
as a memorial to her husband, one of San Francisco's most
venerated art figures.

Labaudt was instrumental in bringing the modern-art movement, especially the French impressionists, to the city. He
painted, lectured, propagandized. He pioneered in many areas—
from the low-slung modern upholstered sofa to contemporary
art. Born in France in 1880, from a long line of craftsmen, he
arrived in San Francisco in 1910. He first turned his talent to
costume design, then to stage scenery, finally to painting. His
work can be seen at the gallery, in the Coit Tower murals, and
at the Beach Chalet (Great Highway at Golden Gate Park).

Labaudt was always searching for new theories, new techniques, new materials in which to work. Most of all, he was searching for new artists whom he encouraged and helped.

The Labaudts had worked together for twenty-five years in costume design. In 1940, when Lucien was close to sixty, they were married. Three years later he undertook a wartime assignment for *Life* magazine in China. The plane crashed en route in Burma. Mme Labaudt determined to perpetuate his spirit in an art gallery. She makes no money on it; in fact, she works on the side to keep the gallery going. "Some people go to night clubs and such," she says. "This is my extravagance."

Once a year she arranges a show of Labaudt's work, but at other times the gallery isn't dominated by her husband's painting. It is his spirit that prevails, his interest in new talent. Mme Labaudt is always looking for promising newcomers. She is interested in artists and their work, not in art cults or schools of painting, and she has given a number of now-successful modern artists their first showing.

Bill Pearson 1814 Union Street. Tuesday through Saturday 10 A.M.–5:30 P.M. WE 1-2712. Compact, lithe, and turtle-necked, Bill Pearson started out as an art student, then became a jockey, finally returned to his old love as an art collector and gallery owner specializing in pre-Columbian art. The publicity and money he won on the *$64,000 Question* TV show as the jockey who was an art expert helped make his galleries (he has one in Texas and another in Southern California) a reality. Pearson wears the mantle of fame lightly, but he maintains his Hollywood associations and gets his name in the columns frequently. Although he has some early California paintings in his tastefully decorated gallery, the emphasis is on pre-Columbian art of the Zapotecan and Tarascan cultures in Mexico. The pre-Columbian influence is marked in modern ceramics, and there is an amazingly contemporary flavor in the urns and statuettes with their simple, squat human forms and in the vessels in the shape of animals. Pearson says he specializes in pre-Columbian art objects because they are the only originals left within the reach of those with moderate means; his prices range from $100 to $30,000. The pre-Columbian art vogue is now strong, and Pearson's gallery is catching on among the socialites.

Artists Cooperative 2224 Union Street. Open Tuesday through Thursday, 12 to 6 P.M., Friday through Sunday, 12 to 9 P.M. JO 7-0464. More than one hundred Bay Area artists, known and unknown, good and mediocre, have banded together to form the cooperative which runs one of the largest and best-selling galleries in the West. This is a temple for True Believers in the faith that original paintings should not be owned exclusively by millionaires or movie directors. Here you will find art works within the reach of everyone's budget.

Founder and guiding light of the cooperative gallery—its members speak of him in reverent tones—was Thadee Skaar (Count Thadee Skarzynski), a Polish nobleman who died in 1960. The gallery reflects his conviction that the important thing is not to play up the big names but to uncover new talents. This is where young artists are given a boost upward. As the artists win recognition, they usually begin to display in the prestige galleries. But there are no hard feelings.

Each member, whether a Sunday painter or an acknowledged professional, is allotted space for two or three paintings. The pictures are hung alphabetically and rotate so that each number circles the gallery twice a year and nobody hates anybody on this account. The members have to spend six hours a month selling, and signs on the bulletin board announce "Hanging Party—Hang Your Friend, Hang Yourself."

The nonprofit, low-overhead, low-rent policy (the gallery is situated in a former grocery store) makes it possible to keep prices down. Business is brisk. Doctors may be unreconstructed when it comes to socialized medicine, but they have certainly taken to modern art. They are the gallery's best patrons. Of course, a large volume business creates problems. Many a buyer has second thoughts at home or feels the painting does not match the draperies.

All schools, trends, styles are represented. There are water-colors, oils, and sculptures. The quality varies sharply, and it is easy to lose your bearings in the mass of paintings. But to separate the wheat from the chaff there is a special-award gallery where only paintings of merit, chosen by a jury of artists, are shown. There is a new award show every month. There is also a more carefully combed selection of work at the downtown branch of the Coop in the Women's City Club, 465 Post Street, open daily 12–6 P.M.

If you take your time and exercise some discrimination, you can find some excellent buys at the Coop gallery. A large number of the paintings reflect San Francisco and its environs. You can get an original, competent watercolor of the city for about twenty-five dollars or an oil for about seventy-five.

Maxwell Gallery   551 Sutter Street. Monday through Saturday

9:30 A.M.–5.30 P.M. GA 1-5193. This is the town's posh gallery, located in the proximity of Elizabeth Arden and her ilk. If you look the part, you will be shown original Van Goghs, Rouaults, or Delacroix in a private alcove to which the Old Masters or the Moderns are lovingly brought from their vaults. There are also frequent exhibitions of top-flight Bay Area artists. Stop in the room which features Emil Janel's amazingly expressive detailed wood carvings; he has a flair for wizened old men. The artist, who does all his work in alder wood without models, lives in the Russian River area. But his creations are straight out of *Heidi* and the Swiss Alps.

Bolles Gallery 729 Sansome Street. Monday through Friday 10 A.M.–6 P.M., Saturday 12–4 P.M. EX 7-4140. In the Jackson Square decorator preserve, John S. Bolles, an eminent San Francisco architect, opened a gallery in 1958 with the aim of giving a boost to local artists struggling for recognition. Bolles is a serious collector of modern painting and a leading exponent of using contemporary art in architectural settings. The gallery shows only oils and sculptures, including the work of the European moderns. Its self-image is an "experimental" art gallery which will stick its neck out. This means that you will see mainly the action school of uninhibited paintings (à la Jackson Pollock). The gallery has been quite successful in renting paintings to the new, handsome office buildings; perhaps it is in these spacious bare halls that this type of painting is most at home.

Feingarten Galleries 535 Sutter Street. Monday–Friday, 10:30 A.M. to 5:30 P.M.; Saturday 12 noon–5 P.M. EX 2-8542. This gallery has the distinction of enabling contemporary local artists to find a broader market for their work. With branches in New York, Chicago, and Carmel and another gallery in Paris, it can and often does help talented San Franciscans obtain more general recognition.

Dilexi Gallery 1858 Union Street. Monday through Saturday, 11 A.M.–6 P.M. WA 2-1394. Farthest-out of the galleries, the only thing modest about Dilexi is its size. The paintings and sculptures are big, bold, and extreme, to put it mildly. This place goes in for shocking the public and is particularly partial to innovators. If you enjoy guessing games, drop in here and try to figure out what the artists had in mind.

Gallerie Gildea 811 Bush Street. Monday through Saturday, 12–6 P.M. TU 5-5200. You will find a mixed bag here. This gallery realized the dream of a career woman in public relations who always wanted to go into the art field but has no particular axe to grind. Old West and contemporary abstract paintings hang comfortably side by side. There is usually a good one-man show by a local artist.

The Brunn Gallery 17 Adler Place (off Columbus Avenue near City Lights Bookstore). Tuesday through Thursday 12 to 5 P.M., Friday through Sunday 12 to 9 P.M. EX 7-6094. A surprisingly varied and interesting selection of work by local artists is shown by this small gallery. It plays no favorites, and most of the clashing schools find representation here.

The Scene 1420 Grant Avenue 8–11 P.M. Probably the most interesting of the avant-garde galleries along Grant Avenue, this converted storefront art show is run by two San Francisco artists with distinctly different interests and styles. Avrum Rubinstein goes in for whimsical horses, animals, and human figures that are often reminiscent of Chagall but sometimes achieve a haunting originality. Earl Thollander exhibits paintings with a more realistic flavor.

Music

San Francisco may have no seasons, but when it comes to musical events, there is orderly rotation and sequence. In the summer, it takes music on the light side, with the San Francisco Symphony offering Pops concerts in the **Civic Auditorium** in something of a carnival air. Or you can relax on the grass at the **Sigmund Stern Memorial Grove** (19th Avenue at Sloat Boulevard) and watch a varied fare ranging from Gilbert and Sullivan to ballet. Or you can attend the Sunday afternoon band concerts at the **Music Concourse** of Golden Gate Park, the traditional brass-band type. In September San Francisco begins to get serious about music and the ponderous **War Memorial Opera House** becomes the locale of the big events. The opera season bows in to the accompaniment of social and sartorial fireworks. This lasts six weeks, and then the San Francisco Symphony gives regular concerts for eighteen weeks at the Opera House, usually into May. (Call UN 1-4008 or EX 7-0717 for opera and symphony information and reservations.) In between, the ballet takes over for the Christmas season.

The San Francisco Opera Company continues an old and honored tradition. Opera has been a San Francisco favorite since 1879 when the Tivoli Opera House ran light opera eight months a year and grand opera the other four. William H. Leahy, manager of the Tivoli, was a prominent San Francisco character for years and a keen musical scout. He discovered Luisa Tetrazzini while visiting Mexico City; after her San Francisco debut in 1905 she became the city's most beloved singer, returning repeatedly for concerts over the years and for her memorable performance at Lotta's Fountain in 1910 (see p. 20). The present opera company was founded in 1923 by Gaetano Merola, and opera's status in San Francisco is suggested by the fact that this was the first United States city to have a municipal opera house, completed in 1932.

The opera company is smoothly guided by Kurt Herbert Adler, who has made many innovations in modernizing both repertoire and staging. Because the season is a short one and starts in September, it has been possible to get stars who later perform at the Metropolitan and in Europe. Rising young stars find it easier to break in here. San Franciscans acclaimed Leontyne Price and Eileen Farrell several seasons ago; both made their Metropolitan debuts only in 1960. There have been some impressive San Francisco firsts in American productions, including Cherubini's *Medea* and *The Carmelites* by Poulenc. In the latter Dorothy Kirsten and Miss Price had top roles.

Despite artistic success, high prices and the short season limit the company's ability to reach audiences. Reserved seats are a jealously guarded family treasure. (Former buyers always have first opportunity for the same seats next year.) One apocryphal tale concerns the hundreds of phone calls to the ticket office when the death of a prominent box-holder was announced. He, of course, had passed on the box in his will. And when tickets go on public sale, the lines are so long many music-lovers don't even try to get them. Visitors to town may find that a few top-priced seats may be left and, for the young and hardy, there is standing room usually available among the true aficionados, at $3.50 per ticket.

The opera-lovers' answer was a Spring Opera Company, independent in management and operation but cooperating with the San Francisco Opera Company. Launched in 1961, the spring opera features popular prices and gives opportunity to young artists. Adler believes the new program brings "a fresh approach to opera that will create an extensive opera-loving community here."

The San Francisco Symphony Orchestra, celebrating its fiftieth anniversary in 1961, is justly proud of having fostered such prodigies as Yehudi Menuhin, Ruth Slenczynski, Ruggiero Ricci, and Grisha Goluboff. It was the first major orchestra to admit women players. Pierre Monteux, the ebullient and colorful little

Frenchman who long directed the symphony, was a popular favorite—something of a local character in fact. It has taken Enrique Jorda, his more subdued Spanish successor, a while to catch on. Jorda is, however, highly regarded by the critics. The symphony's hundred musicians also form the nucleus for the opera and ballet orchestras, an arrangement that makes for a more-or-less regular paycheck. Although it is still the only symphony to be assisted regularly with public funds, it is in almost chronic financial crisis and is forced to engage in frequent fund-raising appeals.

Even apart from the opera and symphony, San Francisco is usually alive with musical events of every variety and quality. Outstanding foreign performers very frequently make the San Francisco area one of their American musts. There are fine concerts at San Francisco State College, the University of California, Mills College, and Stanford University. The San Francisco Municipal Chorus and the Bach Choir present ambitious although not always successful programs. The San Francisco Conservatory of Music, one of the nation's outstanding music schools, has initiated an annual summer Festival of Contemporary Music. There are even regular chamber-music concerts at some of the city's bistros, among them Opus One and the Old Spaghetti Factory. The music-lover has to watch the calendar of events in the local newspapers to keep up with the busy schedule.

Ballet

The San Francisco Ballet is in the position of the prophet who makes good everywhere except in his own home town. The Ballet has performed throughout the world and won high praise for its modern neoclassic style. The State Department has sponsored performances in Latin America, the Far and Near East, and audiences everywhere have greeted the dancers with great acclaim. Here in San Francisco, the Ballet company has no place to call home. It has use of the Opera House for only a few days during the Christmas season. In 1960 the company found a temporary home—the Alcazar Theater—and for nine weeks the local fans came and stayed to applaud the Ballet Jubilant. Proud that it is the oldest permanent performing ballet company in the U.S. (established 1933) it matches or outranks other American ballet companies in drawing audiences on tour, but plays second fiddle to the Sadler's Wells or Royal Danish companies. Under the direction of imaginative choreographer Lew Christensen the San Francisco Ballet has done many new, bold productions and the dancers are achieving increasing maturity and polish. It looks as if they are on the verge of really scoring a local hit.

Little Theater

San Francisco has been building up an indigenous theater of its own. It is of the type that would be called "Off-Broadway" in New York, only more so here since it is made up mainly of amateurs. San Franciscans do get a chance eventually to see most of the big Broadway productions (check the newspapers to see what's on at the Geary, Curran, and Alcazar theaters). But this stage-crazy city got tired of waiting around for road companies to put on the Broadway shows. And it had lots of knowledgeable theater-lovers around. The result has been the development of one of the most active and creative little-theater movements in the country.

While the polish of expensive first-run productions may often be missing, the little-theater offerings usually have excitement and enthusiasm and sometimes display real talent and originality. Besides, San Franciscans get a chance to see frequent showings of Shaw, Shakespeare, Brecht, O'Casey, and other greats not considered money-makers in New York. The scope and success of the little-theater movement may also lead eventually to a full-time San Francisco repertory theater. The Actor's Workshop, finest of the local groups with a few full-time actors at minimum scale working among the amateurs, has been heading gradually in this direction.

There are literally hundreds of actors, directors, stage designers, and light men who are warehousemen, carpenters, stenographers, and schoolteachers during the day but become devotees of "The Method" at night. At times there are as many as twenty-five groups operating within a radius of twenty-five miles. All suffer from a shortage of trained personnel, funds, and adequate facilities, and the level of the performances is often uneven. They put on their plays in old warehouses, converted stores, broken-down old theaters. One uses an abandoned champagne factory. Only about six or seven of the groups have stuck together long enough to be considered permanent, stable operations.

Everybody in town takes the little theaters seriously. Some of the biggest names in San Francisco business and social life headed a fund drive recently to help the Actor's Workshop match a Ford Foundation grant. The daily newspapers help with generous publicity, and their critics do serious and lengthy reviews.

Most of the groups perform only on Friday and Saturday nights. You will find listings in the newspapers. It is wise to phone for reservations since most of the theaters are small. Tickets run about two dollars up.

Actor's Workshop Marine's Memorial Theater. 609 Sutter Street, MI 8-9918; also at the Encore Theater, 430 Mason Street, EX 7-3195. This group won an international reputation by presenting *Waiting for Godot* at the Brussels Fair in 1957. Many questioned the selection as a typical offering of the American theater, but there is no questioning of the high professional quality of Actor's Workshop productions or of its serious and dedicated approach to the theater. As a matter of fact, with the boost of Ford Foundation funds the Workshop has gone off somewhat into experimental left field. Beckett, Ionesco, and the angry British young men are staples. Every once in a while they do Shaw or Anouilh or revive their superb production of Arthur Miller's *The Crucible*.

Interplayers Bella Union Theater. 825 Kearny Street. SU 1-9909. In a historic and rundown theater off Portsmouth Plaza, this group puts on a wide variety of plays, ranging from the work of local playwrights to Tennessee Williams to William Wycherly's *Country Wife*. Productions and performances tend to be uneven.

Playhouse Repertory Theater 2796 Hyde Street at Beach. PR 5-4426. A high level of acting and directing and an unusually wide and balanced selection of plays. You may be treated to a sparkling Bernard Shaw comedy, an adaptation of Mark Twain's bitter *The Man Who Corrupted Hadleyburg,* a somber drama by Lorca, or a bold experimental play by Brecht. Coffee is served free during intermissions, and after the play you can join the throngs at the Buena Vista Café (see p. 120) across the street for Irish Coffee.

Company of the Golden Hind Bella Pacific Theater. 529 Pacific Avenue, EX 7-6673. An imaginatively redecorated theater on the site of an old Barbary Coast joint, the Golden Hind, now finds itself in the midst of the fashionable Jackson Square decorators' area. This company goes in for intriguing stage sets, exotic costumes, and stylized acting. Frequently it spoofs a spoof, as in its production of *The Boy Friend*. It has also done Shaw, Molière, and T. S. Eliot.

Opera Ring 123 South Van Ness Avenue. UN 1-1208. This hard-working group of amateurs, presenting opera (and operetta) in the round, has done everything from *Cavelleria Rusticana* to *Guys and Dolls*. It has also put on productions of *The Three-*

penny Opera, Can-Can, and *West Side Story.* The performances are uneven, but usually provide a pleasant and entertaining evening.

Lamplighters Harding Theater, Divisadero at Hayes, SK 2-2726. Lighthearted, rollicking performances of Gilbert and Sullivan operettas by serious amateurs in an old movie house.

Films

In keeping with its cosmopolitan air, San Francisco boasts a number of small movie theaters that feature foreign films. In fact, many a resident has maintained a weekly diet of movies without patronizing a single Hollywood production. The town gets an early crack at new British, Italian, Swedish, French, Japanese, and Russian films. The recently instituted annual Film Festival in November gives the city an opportunity with new and sometimes experimental foreign films even before they are shown in the local art houses. The **Cinema Guild** and the **Studio** (2436 Telegraph Avenue; TH 8-2038), twin theaters in Berkeley much frequented by University of California intelligentsia, put on reruns of top foreign and American films, providing movie-lovers with a chance to catch up with those they've missed. A monthly bulletin available at the above address contains some of the most concise, caustic, and informative movie criticism extant.

Folk-dancing

Folk-dancing is one of the liveliest of the popular arts in San Francisco. There are literally hundreds of different folk-dance groups in the Bay Area, and several major folk- and square-dance festivals are put on throughout the year. Information can be obtained from the Folk Dance Federation of California (150 Powell Street, SU 1-8334) or the San Francisco Recreation and Park Department (SK 1-4866).

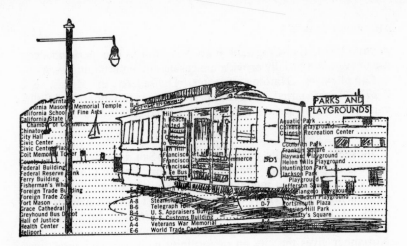

8: FAMILY STYLE

GROUPED rather arbitrarily together in this chapter are some of the sights and activities families with children may enjoy together. But it isn't necessary to be accompanied by a child to visit Fleishhacker Zoo. Middle-aged men and women consume more Cof-fiestas and other mountainous ice-cream concoctions at Blum's than do the young fry. And Golden Gate Park is a constant delight no matter what your age. There is no suggestion, implied or otherwise, that grown-ups minus children who enjoy these particular pleasures suffer from retarded development.

Ocean Beach

Take a walk along Ocean Beach, either on the pavement above or on the sand. (No. 2, No. 5, and No. 38 buses will get you there.) You can see the fishing boats and the freighters and the tankers sailing west toward the horizon or approaching the Golden Gate. San Franciscans flock here on an occasional if rare warm summer evening. Every once in a while it even gets sunny enough for picnicking on the beach. But don't count on it. Besides, the wicked undertow makes the city's long, sandy public beach extremely dangerous for swimming. The beach, however, has attractions impervious to tide and weather.

Playland-at-the-Beach   Great Highway and Cabrillo Street. Most adults will consider this amusement park a miniature, somewhat dilapidated Coney Island. They will be quite right.

But the kids go right on enjoying the death-defying rocket rides and the Fun House full of tunnels and pratfalls and distorting mirrors.

Cliff House Great Highway at Point Lobos Avenue. Once a pleasure dome for San Francisco writers and mining millionaires, this was also a showplace where every visiting President since the days of Grant was taken. Repeatedly burned down and rebuilt, it's now a combination restaurant, gift shop, and tourist area. But it does offer a close view of Seal Rocks (you can explain that the inhabitants aren't seals but sea lions). And you can get a ride(fifty cents for adults, twenty-five cents for children) in an aerial tram suspended from two great cables, to Point Lobos. This will delight the youngsters and make you slightly nervous. But it's perfectly safe.

Sutro Heights Point Lobos and 48th avenues, near Great Highway. Climb up a few steps and you will be in a rundown but curiously attractive park. From this two-hundred-foot-high dune you will get an unbroken vista of ocean, superior to that from the Cliff House. Both the park and the Cliff House below were once the property of Adolph Sutro, the German-born engineer who dug a tunnel under the Comstock Lode in Nevada and never had to work after that. He bought up a good part of the Ocean Beach area. He also became a philanthropist and mayor of San Francisco. On the site of this little park he built one of San Francisco's great mansions and supervised the decoration of the grounds. You can still see remnants of his taste, palm trees incongruous among windswept cypresses and an odd assortment of Victorian statuary, including two reclining lions which look like exact replicas of Bert Lahr as the cowardly lion in *The Wizard of Oz,* also a new rather disconcertingly headless satyr. Sutro was so proud of the place he opened it to the public during the day. In 1938 his daughter turned it over to the city, but the next year Sutro's big house burned down. The combination of decayed splendor and ocean view makes for one of the city's more unique spots.

Sutro Baths Point Lobos Avenue, near Great Highway. This massive rococco edifice was Sutro's idea of the greatest pleasure resort of its day, complete with what used to be the world's biggest indoor swimming pools, palm-bordered promenades and curiosities and exhibits drawn from all over the world. Thousands of San Franciscans used to come every Sunday to see what was new at Sutro's, and a great many still do. It remains an intriguing bit of Old San Francisco, its incongruous collection including Egyptian

mummies, a talking-bird show, what are described as Tom
Thumb's personal belongings, a cable car and maritime exhibits.
Sutro's also has one of San Francisco's ice-skating rinks; there are
only two in the city.

Maritime Attractions

Youngsters will get a bang out of visiting the Embarcadero and
Fisherman's Wharf (see Chap. 3). They are guaranteed to enjoy
playing captain for a day on the historic *Balclutha,* looking at
models and photographs of old ships in the Maritime Museum, and
wandering around Fishermen's Wharf. While visiting the Ferry
Building, be sure they don't miss the **Mineral Exhibit** of the
California Division of Mines on the second floor. On display are
replicas of famous gold nuggets including the "Welcome Stranger,"
the largest authenticated nugget ever discovered. There is also
a 201-ounce piece of crystallized gold found at Spanish Dry
Diggings in El Dorado County. There are photographs of historic
mines and lushly mustached miners. Also on display for the
serious-minded are meteors, rocks, and fluorescent minerals.

Bay Model   One mile north of Sausalito. Wednesday through
Friday, 9 A.M. to 4 P.M. Call the Army Engineers office at
YU 6-3500, extension 3665, to arrange group tours. Here
sprawled all over a vast warehouse is a model of the San Francisco
Bay where the Army Engineers study all the movements and
problems of this inland sea. With this model they can determine
the accumulation of silt, the effect of tides, the battle between
land and sea and between salt water from the ocean and fresh water
pouring in through Carquinez Strait. They are also studying
here a plan to control the Bay devised by a strange, dedicated
man named John Reber, a former actor, playwright, and stage
director who fell in love with the Bay some fifty years ago. Reber
devoted his life to crusading for his Bunyanesque plan to put
two great earth dams across the Bay. These would provide two
immense fresh-water lakes, solving California's water problems
forever. They would provide the bridge and auto and rail
facilities across the Bay needed for generations to come. They
would also moderate the Northern California climate and create
year-round beach and vacation resorts around the Bay. Reber
died in 1960 while the study was in progress. If the model of the
Army Engineers show the plan works, Reber's name may become
as well known at those of John Muir and other great conserva-
tionists who helped preserve California's resources. Scientifically

inclined youngsters are always fascinated by this working model
of the Bay.

Golden Gate Park   As no San Franciscan ever wearies of re-
peating, there isn't a single "Keep off the Grass" sign in the Park.
There are picnic areas with benches and tables, but you can
picnic anywhere you want. The Park houses the De Young
Museum of Art, an aquarium, a planetarium, a science museum,
a music concourse where there are band concerts, an arboretum for
thousands of imported plants and flowers, a Hall of Flowers, a
conservatory for tropical flowers. It has baseball diamonds,
a football stadium, tennis courts, polo fields, a chess-and-checkers
pavilion, a bowling green, bocce ball courts frequented by
elderly Italians, and miles of trails and walks. It is an outdoor
recreation area. It is a center of cultural activity. It is an
oasis for escaping the city and its cares. Tens of thousands of
people come here every week end. But it never really seems
crowded except in the area around the music concourse where
the museums are clustered. Perhaps the most remarkable thing
about the Park, even more remarkable than the feat of creating
it out of barren, windy sand dunes, is the fact that the most
crowded Sunday or holiday week end you can find lonely spots
to sit and read or deserted trails to walk.

Of course, most people laughed when the Park was started in
1867. For a long time it seemed that they were right. No green
thing would grow in this narrow strip of land between Stanyan
Street and the ocean. Finally, the sand met its match. A Scottish
gardener named John McLaren was appointed superintendent
in 1887—and he stayed on the job until he died in 1943 at the
age of ninety-six. McLaren's long fight with nature in the formative
years of the park is a San Francisco legend. He planted trees
again and again, only to have them covered with sand each
time. He persisted until the dunes were covered with soil-holding
shrubs, bluegrass and manzanita, oak, eucalyptus, and madrone
trees. "Uncle John" McLaren always referred to himself as "the
boss gardener" who conquered the sand.

But when he was through with that job, McLaren had to
wage the even more difficult battle with politicians who thought
the thousand precious acres of park should be covered with
buildings, statues, and parking lots and that the payroll should be
padded with their friends and relatives. Once he had three oaks
planted at the Park Police Station, only to discover that they
were being replaced by concrete for a parking lot. He put the

trees back, and the Bureau of Public Works took them out
again. In the end, McLaren won and the oaks are still there
obscuring the police station. The old Scotsman didn't win all
his fights. There are more statues, including one of himself, than
he would have wanted. But he did hold back the tide that
would have engulfed the Park, and he established a tradition that
is still in effect. The lawns and wooded areas still predominate
over concrete.

If you're on an extremely short visit, there is probably no
alternative to a fast drive through the Park. Otherwise, you
will want to take leisurely walks through it and make separate
visits to the key attractions. There is no attempt here even to
list them all.

One you shouldn't miss is the **Shakespeare Garden**, right next to
the Academy of Sciences buildings but hidden by a hedge of
myrtle. This is a quiet nook tucked away in the midst of the Park's
busiest area. It is planted with all the flowers and shrubs mentioned
in Shakespeare's plays and sonnets—here are the marigolds and
columbines, the daffodils and primroses, crocuses and forget-me-
nots. There are plaques with appropriate quotations and a glass-
enclosed bust of Shakespeare in an ivy-covered brick wall.

Try to see the **Japanese Tea Garden** in April, when the cherry
trees glimmer with pink blossoms which fall on the multishaded
greens of mosses and shrubs. But it is a place of magic any time
of year. Stand on the Wishing Bridge, feed the squirrels and birds
almond cookies furnished, along with tea, for twenty-five cents by
strikingly costumed Japanese waitresses. Admire the delicate landscaping and the plump goldfish. And come, if you can, on a weekday.

The **Children's Playground** has been the training ground for
generations of San Franciscans whirling away years riding the
carousel or sliding down the circular slide. Right above the
playground, twelve feet high, is a century-old totem pole on which
Tlingit Indians from Alaska carved the experiences of their
ancestors.

Museums

Grouped together in Golden Gate Park across the Music
Concourse from the De Young Museum is the cluster of popular
scientific museums maintained by the California Academy of
Sciences. Founded in 1853, the Academy is the West's oldest
scientific institution. Years of work were destroyed when the
Academy's old building burned in the fire of 1906. But Alice

Eastwood, a plucky little botanist, climbed the fire-scarred staircase repeatedly to lower books and one thousand of the precious specimens in her department by rope. These, along with other exhibits, were moved to the Academy's new headquarters in Golden Gate Park in 1916. Concerned chiefly with the study of the flora and fauna of the Pacific, the Academy has dispatched numerous expeditions to the Galapagos, the Gulf of California, the South Sea islands, and Alaska. But its interests have also long been broad enough to encompass astronomy; it sponsors one of the best planetariums in the country. (Call BA 1-5100 for any of the three institutions in Golden Gate Park listed below.)

Alexander F. Morrison Planetarium   Shows Wednesday through Sunday 3:30 P.M. and 8:30 P.M.; Saturdays, Sundays, and holidays an extra show at 2 P.M. Also extra matinees during July and August. Admission seventy-five cents for adults, forty cents for children under sixteen. Twinkling galaxies of stars are displayed under a sixty-five-foot aluminum dome to space-conscious youngsters and oldsters in the first planetarium that can be operated entirely automatically with the flick of a switch. The big project, which took four years and $140,000 to construct, was the first of its kind to be built in the United States. The planetarium owes its existence to private philanthropists, the contributions of school children and the side interest of the Academy's paleontologist in optical instruments. Dr. G. Dallas Hanna became an expert on microscope lenses in the course of his study of fossils and headed up an emergency project undertaken for the Navy in World War II to repair optical instruments. Thousands of fossils were moved out of the Academy's department of paleontology to make room for the optical workshop. Out of this work grew the staff and the know-how to build a planetarium. At the entrance to the planetarium the Foucault Pendulum, demonstrating the rotation of the earth, always draws a big crowd. Competent and easy-to-understand pamphlets on astronomy are available for fifteen cents.

Steinhart Aquarium   10 A.M. to 5 P.M. daily. Youngsters are endlessly fascinated by the diamond sting ray, the carnivorous piranha, and the talking fishes. The Aquarium's collection of tropical fish is one of the best in the world. Don't overlook the fish from Hawaii with the mouth-filling but accurate name of *Humumumunukunukuapuaa,* meaning a trigger fish with the snout or grunt of a pig. Alligators in the imitation tropical swamp in the sunken tank dominating the lobby examine with gleaming and hungry eyes the juicy little visitors. A recording of jungle noises adds to the atmosphere. Fish are fed Monday, Wednesday, and

Friday at 1:45 P.M., alligators Tuesday, Friday, and Sunday at 3 P.M.

Science Museum   10 A.M. to 5 P.M. daily. Youngsters have a wide choice of exhibits. Simpson Africa Hall is an old-fashioned stuffed-animal exhibit. There are also many stuffed animals and birds in the North American Hall. The museum has one of the world's largest collections of gem minerals as well as impressive collections of lamps and clocks.

Josephine Randall Junior Museum   Corona Heights. Take No. 43 Roosevelt Way bus to Levant Street. Open daily for youngsters using facilities 10 A.M. to 5 P.M., also evenings for special activities. Visitors welcome 12 noon to 5 P.M. Sunday. UN 3-1399. This is a do-it-yourself paradise for children who like to use their hands or dabble in science. Here is headquarters for innumerable clubs and study groups of junior astronomers, naturalists, photographers, puppeteers, and basket-makers. Under skilled supervision, the youngsters use kilns and other facilities for making pottery and working in leather and copper; an airplane-model room is one of the more popular spots. Visitors can watch boa constrictors being fed, inspect live birds and a variety of animals. They are allowed to play with weasels and rabbits. There are displays of rocks, historic ships, and Indian handicrafts. Science movies are shown every Saturday and school vacation days at 12:30 P.M. Nearby is an excellent playground; the setup amounts to an integrated recreation center suited to the interests and tastes of young people. The large attendance from all over the city rebukes the city fathers who long delayed construction of the museum on this craggy height (known locally as Rocky Hill); they were convinced nobody would ever come here. Putting the museum on a hill near the center of the city was the inspiration of Josephine Randall, former San Francisco recreation director.

Wells Fargo History Room and Museum   Market and Montgomery streets. 10 A.M. to 3 P.M. Monday through Friday. SU 1-1500. For youngsters who imbibe Maverick and Wyatt Earp with their milk, this is the Old West come alive. The kids will thrill to the sight of the handsome red Old Hangtown Stagecoach, complete with iron treasure box containing gold bullion, smack in the center of the room. It is all here—the leather boot for luggage, the trusty mail pouch, and the dust whipped up as the stagecoach traveled the overland route from California to Carson City in 1850. Replete with Wells Fargo & Co. memorabilia, this is authentic stuff; the posters proclaiming rewards for Black Bart (who robbed twenty-eight stages single-handed and left mocking verses to taunt the Wells Fargo gumshoes); the display of revolvers, all sizes and shapes; the iron doors from the Wells Fargo branch in China Camp with bullet holes and the legend of the brave agent who died in a lone stand against the bandits; mementos of intrepid Pony Express riders; souvenirs of the gold miners. There is a large book collection of Western Americana. A few treasured photographs of old San Francisco are displayed— one of Market Street in flames after the 1906 earthquake. A desk used by Mark Twain is on exhibit. So is an original proclamation issued by San Francisco's Emperor Norton slyly warning that "no notice be paid to proclamations issued by Pretenders."

Of Fairy Tales and Animals

Fairyland Lakeside Park, Oakland, Grand Avenue, between Harrison Street and Lakeshore Avenue. Across Bay Bridge, through Oakland on US 50 to Grand Avenue. Daily 10 A.M. to 5:30 P.M. Admission fifteen cents for children, twenty-five cents for adults. Oakland's Lakeside Park at Lake Merritt has several attractions, including boats for hire and regular concerts from the bandstand. But the Children's Fairyland has really stolen the show. All the old favorites really come to life here, quite literally in many cases. On Noah's Ark live animals contentedly munch away. A seal show offers excitement and visitors can descend a subterranean exhibit to catch a glimpse of Willie the Whale. For lovers of Pinocchio, there is a replica of old Gepetto's workshop, and a Mad Hatter in full regalia for Alice in Wonderland fans. Imaginative landscaping is combined with wonderful design of buildings and exhibits. Only the most sensitive purists will resent the commercials, such as the sign that Gerber's Baby Food has been good enough to supply the Rock-a-Bye Baby Exhibit or that the Milk Wagon Drivers and Dairy Employees Local 302 sponsors the three-times-daily puppet show. While the youngsters watch the puppets, you can watch them watching the puppets—which is even more fun.

Storyland at the Fleishhacker Zoo. Daily 10 A.M. to 5:30 P.M. Sloat Boulevard at foot of Great Highway. Take L streetcar to end of line. Admission ten cents for children, fifteen cents for adults. A member of San Francisco's Board of Supervisors got tired of taking his daughter across the Bay Bridge to the Oakland Fairyland. That was what the Supervisor said; maybe he was even more riled at the thought that lowly Oakland had something San Francisco didn't. In any case, his ire led to the

building of a San Francisco Storyland sponsored by the city's
Park and Recreation Department, a Mother Goose in stage sets
with imaginative papier-mâché construction and singsong accompaniment. Now there are about twenty exhibits from Old King Cole
to Rapunzel's castle and including, of course, the wolf dressed in
grandmother's cap leering at Red Riding Hood. Sad to relate, this
effort does not yet measure up to the Oakland Fairyland that
started it all. Among other shortcomings, it lacks live animals.
Attractions include a Mad Hatter Munch Bar and a nicely decorated spot for birthday parties. Minimum charge $1 per captive,
sort of a package deal where the "birthday kit" includes ice
cream, cake, hats, balloons. Call MO 1-1699 for reservations.
And dress warmly.

Fleishhacker Zoo   Sloat and Skyline Boulevard at foot of Great
Highway. Open daily 10 A.M. until dark. OV 1-5877. San
Francisco's zoo is full of islands, waterfalls, caves, all intended
to give the animals an illusion of the great outdoors and spectators
an illusion that they are observing the birds and beasts in their
natural habitat. The aviary is a vast enclosure with nesting places
and a running brook, much unlike the usual birdcage. Monkey
Island, honeycombed with bizarre caves that look like nothing
except abstract architectural design, proved so inviting recently
that five co-eds went swimming in the surrounding moat, to
great excitement among both the monkeys and city police. The
pachyderm house and the bear pits, which fool visitors as well
as inmates in their resemblance to natural rock, are among the
permanent attractions.

The zoo was a beneficiary of the Depression as well as of
tycoon Herbert Fleishhacker's philanthropy. Only a few years old
when the WPA was started, it became a major work-relief project.
Architects and builders had a field day, taking off from the
famed Hagenbeck Zoo in Germany. Recent additions have been
mainly of gimmicks or unusual animals rather than of buildings.
The zoo has now instituted "talking boxes" near forty of the
exhibits to disclose details about the animals. A key to the boxes
costs fifty cents, and the investment is particularly worth while
if the kids stump you with questions. For weary parents anxious
for a respite, there is an elephant train which will take the
small fry away for an inexpensive twenty-five-minute tour. A
large playground, complete with a carousel and an old Southern
Pacific locomotive over which youngsters can clamber, is also
guaranteed to keep them occupied. Less successful was Fleishhacker's major contribution to the zoo, the vast swimming pool.

Statistics proving that it is the world's largest—1000 feet long, 150 feet wide—and contains 6.5 million gallons of heated salt water, tend to be irrelevant. It is usually too foggy and chilly at the zoo for swimming.

Cable Car Rides

The cable car is proof positive that San Francisco values the picturesque and the traditional above the practical. In the 1870s, this mechanical billy goat prancing up and down the city's hills was a great engineering advance. By the 1960s it had become an anachronism, expensive to operate and slow and inconvenient as transportation. Moreover, it had become a safety and traffic hazard on crowded Powell Street. But who can deny the thrill of holding on precariously to a pole and standing outside on the narrow running board while the car clangs up Nob Hill? Or the beauty of the view down toward the Bay from the top of the hill? Or the suspense every time the car circumnavigates the monumental curve at Powell or Jackson? Or the sense that every ride is an act of personal participation in a hundred years of San Francisco history, a sharing of experience with Mark Twain and Emperor Norton, with the mining and railroad kings who sometimes took the cable cars to their Nob Hill mansions?

The city has yielded slowly to progress, retreating grudgingly and step by step from the time when the cable car was the principal means of transportation and when its slot proudly divided Market Street and the city in two. There remain only three lines, each peculiarly suited for a sentimental journey rather than for quick or modern transportation. Whenever the proponents of economy and efficiency have urged the final, fatal step of abolishing the cable car altogether, indignant and desperate committees have been formed to hold a line against the twentieth century. The line has held. The cable car survives. In fact, it will probably live forever—or at least as long as San Francisco. Even in that future time when atom-powered subway trains rush deep in the tunneled darkness of the city's hills, there will no doubt be a cable car on Powell Street.

No. 61 California goes from California and Market to California and Van Ness through the financial district, Chinatown, and Nob Hill (see p. 25).

No. 59 Powell will take you from Market and Powell streets to Fisherman's Wharf, after many views and curves and hills, past the shops and hotels of Union Square up to the summit of

Nob Hill. It gives you glimpses of Chinatown and Russian Hill, North Beach and Telegraph Hill. It takes its time getting you to the wharf. But what better or cheaper way is there to experience so many of San Francisco's most delightful aspects?

No. 60 Powell–Hyde line also starts at Market and Powell but winds up a few blocks north on the Bay in a sand lot facing Aquatic Park and the Maritime Museum, across the street from the Buena Vista Café (see p. 120). The two routes are identical to Powell and Jackson; here the No. 60 keeps going until it gets to Hyde and then continues on Hyde to the Bay. The principal difference is that the No. 60 goes higher up Russian Hill and gives you a better opportunity to explore one of San Francisco's most storied and colorful heights.

Russian Hill side trip Get off the No. 60 cable car at Hyde and Lombard and wander around the quiet streets of a hill encrusted with history and cluttered with a medley of cliff-hanging little houses and modern new apartment buildings. If there are small fry along you can show them what is known as the "crookedest street in the world," Lombard between Leavenworth and Hyde. Here is a roller-coaster of a one-way street which only drivers with strong nerves will challenge. Landscaped curves of lush hydrangeas and fuchsias and tiered houses wind around the forty-degree slope.

There is a tiny oasis on the hill (off Lombard between Hyde and Larkin streets) that shouldn't be missed. This is a miniature reservoir park, maintained by the San Francisco Water Department, with an unobstructed view of the city, the Bay, and the Golden Gate. A plaque in this small refuge commemorates George Sterling, long the city's unofficial poet laureate. You can sit here a while and then wander along the little streets and alleys like Macondray Lane which are almost in the heart of the city and yet far removed from it.

Asked why it's called Russian Hill when the Russians really live on Potrero Hill, nobody is sure. It may be, as some claim, because Russian sailors once buried their dead in the clay of the hill or, as others insist, that a colony of Russian farmers once raised vegetables here. In any case, the hill's fame came both as a result of its spectacular views and from the writers and artists who lived here before Telegraph Hill became the home of the Bohemians. Among them were Ina Coolbrith, one of San Francisco's first poets who lived on into a ripe old age to encourage and mother Jack London and other young writers;

John Dewey before he became a famous philosopher; Mary Austin; and Ambrose Bierce.

Cable Car mechanics   San Francisco adults are at least as attached to the cable cars as the children. The only difference is that the former are interested chiefly in the traditions of the cable car while the latter are preoccupied with the mechanics. But the line is thin indeed. Plenty of adults idle a few minutes at the corner of Market and Powell to watch the cable cars being turned around or to help give that extra (and unnecessary) push.

The cable cars are pulled along by an endless steel cable, $1\frac{3}{4}$ inches in diameter and made up of six strands of nineteen wires each, running in a slot between the tracks and below the surface of the street at a speed of nine miles an hour. The cables are operated from a center power plant by a 750-h.p. electric motor that turns huge (twelve-foot) cable-winders.

The man who runs the cable cars is called not a motorman but a gripman, a character fabled in San Francisco poetry and legend. He operates a big handle or lever that controls a hollowed grip mechanism at the bottom of the car. When he pulls the lever, he tightens two heavy hinges that hold the cable firmly as the car moves along.

Turntables are needed at Powell and Market streets and at the terminals of the No. 59 and No. 60 lines because the cable cars used on these lines have only one set of controls. The No. 61 California line doesn't need turntables because its cars have controls at both front and rear. The California cars are five feet longer.

An alert operator in the small shack you see at California and Powell streets, where the cable-car lines intersect, performs one of the most important operations in the miniature system. His job is to keep the grip on the Powell Street cars from slicing the California Street cable. The red and green signals he flashes give the gripmen their instructions.

Don't worry too much while going down hills. The cable cars have four separate braking devices. It is rather unlikely that they will all go out at once. The cable itself acts as a brake; when it is gripped tightly, the car can't go more than the nine-mile-an-hour speed of the cable. The primary braking device is the wheel brake, operated by a foot lever. When the gripman presses it down, a metal shoe on each wheel presses down on the tracks. On the Powell Street car the conductor has to help out on steep grades by turning a hand lever on the rear platform to operate the rear brakes. The gripman also has a lever for the track brakes; twenty-inch wooden blocks between the wheels can be clamped down directly on the rails. Finally, there is an emergency brake—used only as a last resort. When the gripman pulls the emergency lever, an eighteen-inch metal wedge is slammed into the slot. It usually requires a welding crew to melt the brake from the slot.

Since the manufacturers of cable cars have long gone out of business, all repairs and parts have to be made at the San Francisco Municipal Railway's own shops. Here, for example, are made the wooden track brakes which have to be replaced frequently. The Muni shop also casts the brass bells which give the conductor his moments of glory to vie with the gripman. The bells used to be made of iron, but a delegation of civic-minded citizens demanded a more melodious sound. Once a year on July 4 the conductors engage in a bell-ringing contest at Union Square in a discarded cable car.

Baseball

Giants Candlestick Park. April through September. Watch newspapers for home games. Call Municipal Railway at FI 6-5656 for convenient bus schedules. When the Giants fizzled after a fast start in 1960, a group of Stanford professors suggested that a psychiatrist might get the team back on the road to a pennant. The desperate remedy was not attempted, and the Giants kept losing. But San Francisco remains a city of avid rooters for the National League team it acquired in 1958. During baseball seasons the black caps of Giant fans by far outnumber the white caps of longshoremen on the city's streets. Attendance has continued high despite heartbreak and disappointment and gripes that Candlestick Park is too cold, too windy, too hard to get to. Even when the team isn't winning pennants it has spectacular performers like Orlando Cepeda and Willie Mays. And the stadium is usually warm enough—during the day. It is also, perhaps irrelevantly, the most beautifully designed stadium in the country. You'll enjoy both the game and the stadium more if you take a bus rather than drive.

Football

49ers Kezar Stadium. Watch newspapers September to December for home games. Take a No. 7 Haight or No. 6 Masonic bus to stadium. Even more than the Giants, the 49ers have been a razzle-dazzle team. They've won no championships, but they're always tough competition. The famed alley-oop pass to high-jumping R. C. Owens has won many a game. The 49ers are always trying trick stunts like the shotgun formation, in which the quarterback stands seven yards back of the center as against the now conventional T formation. Nobody claims that Kezar Stadium in Golden Gate Park is too cold or too far away. But general admissions at $2.50 are hard to get and reserved seats at $4.50 make a 49er game expensive for a family excursion or even a father-and-son combination.

Ice Cream De Luxe

Blum's Polk and California. OR 3-8500. The most dazzling ice-cream parlor in the city, Blum's is where San Franciscans take their children to celebrate birthdays, graduations, and other notable occasions.

There are now Blum's branches at the Fairmont Hotel, the Palace Hotel, on Union Square, and in the Stonestown apartment development, but the main store is still the place to go for a real family treat. Furnished in the sentimental image of what an ice-cream parlor of the Gay Nineties should have looked like, Blum's decor features an eye-filling pink wherever you look, marble-top tables, properly ornate wire chairs, and chandeliers. Monumental ice cream concoctions with whimsical names are the specialty of the house. You can take your pick of Emerald Isle, Cof-fiesta, Fiddlefaddle, Scheherazade, Schmaltzy Gourmet, and a galaxy of other sundaes, all gooey and sweet with rich, creamy ice cream and whipped cream and sauces and nuts. Blum's has wonderful cakes—the chocolate fudge, coffee crunch, and lemon crunch are especially wonderful—and elaborate pastries. You can get breakfast, lunch, and dinner at Blum's, good tea-shop fare but not outstanding—except for the handsome and tasty fruit salads. While you're at Blum's, buy a tin of Almondettes, a crunchy, delicious candy. Most of Blum's chocolates don't quite come up to the Almondettes. The big deal is the ice cream. You really haven't lived if you've never tried one of these calorific splurges.

Evening Out, Junior Department

The common denominator of juvenile gastronomic adventure is usually, alas, the hamburger in various sizes and shapes. If your children are different and will go for Italian or Chinese cooking, by all means take them to the restaurants listed in Chapter 5. If they lean to simpler fare, the suggestions below may be helpful:

Zim's 10th and Market; 18th and Geary; 19th and Taraval; Lombard and Steiner. Zim's serves among the best hamburgers in town at its four locations. For seventy cents (and liable to go up again), you get a huge slab of meat, tomato, pickle relish, melted cheese, and lettuce on a bun. If you're mystified about the difference between a Zimburger and a Hamburger (the only two varieties offered), the former comes on a sesame-seed bun, the other on a plain bun; the difference is not earthshaking. You can also get thick milkshakes and spicy hot apple pie topped with ice cream.

The Hippo 2025 Van Ness Avenue, near Pacific. PR 5-3362. Fancier than Zim's and somewhat more expensive, the Hippo makes a cult of the hamburger. Under a copper dome, busy chefs dish up the once-lowly hamburger in twenty-seven international varieties. There is even one ghastly item on the menu concocted of raw hamburger topped with ice cream. But the burgundyburger and the Italianburger deserve raves. Despite the elegance (you eat by candlelight), you can come dressed very informally. Parking is free.

The Indo-China Restaurant 263 O'Farrell Street. Lunch and dinner. DO 2-9975. Don't be scared by the name. In a typical San Francisco quirk, the Indo-China specializes in excellent Southern-style fried chicken at very reasonable prices. For more sophisticated palates, there is chicken sautéed in garlic and condiments, as well as all kinds of Chinese dishes. Conveniently located in the downtown area.

Bernstein's Fish Grotto 123 Powell Street. Lunch about $2. Dinner starting at $3. GA 1-1938. Trout swimming in tanks and the prow of Columbus' *Niña* in replica may entice youngsters to try the seafood here. You can get a good fish lunch or dinner here right in the downtown area if you don't feel like a trip to Fisherman's Wharf. The clam chowder is a specialty.

San Francisco boasts no automat, but has lots of cafeterias—**Foster's, Compton's,** and **Manning's**—distributed through the city and serving plain but palatable food. **Moars,** operated by the Foster chain, has slightly fancier food and decor. It is worth visiting if only for the Bufano mosaic murals (see p. 139).

(*Note:* Other activities suited for a family group will be found in the San Francisco tours listed in Chapter 11 (p. 213) and in the Bay Area tours in the last chapter.)

9: SHOPPING TOUR

Downtown Treasure Hunt

SAN FRANCISCO STORES are for window-shoppers and for gift-shoppers. They are for women who can afford to be smartly dressed and for those who would like to be. They are for lovers of Oriental art objects, of finely crafted lamps and jewelry, of off-beat imports from all over the world. But by and large they are not for bargain-hunters. If you bear this caution in mind and avoid a frustrating search for the unattainable, you can have a great time in San Francisco shopping or just browsing and wandering through the stores.

Your most rewarding search in San Francisco will be for distinctive shops and unusual items. You will find many of both in the downtown area, but the serious shopper will also have to invade the neighborhoods where many of the most interesting stores are grouped in little clusters. Almost all the arts-and-crafts shops and many of the good import houses are out of the downtown high-rent area.

You can buy almost anything in San Francisco. The department stores and the numerous specialty shops offer a staggering variety of essentials and luxuries. There are good buys, of course. And the bigger stores run sales a couple of times a year. These, however,

171

are nothing like the frenetic Macy–Gimbel price wars in New York. The nearest thing to a bargain basement department store is **Weinstein's,** 1041 Market Street. It will, however, prove tame indeed to those who have elbowed their way to the counters at Klein's in New York.

The major department stores are longer on tradition than on spectacular values. **The White House** (Grant Avenue, Sutter and Post streets) and the **City of Paris** date back to gold-rush days and don't let you forget it. The slightly younger **Emporium** (835 Market Street) compensates with such architectural antiquities as a huge glass-domed rotunda, a long arcade, and ornamented columns on its sandstone façade. **Macy's** (Stockton and O'Farrell), a relative newcomer, adapts to the city's dual worship of tradition and flowers by instituting an annual flower show the week before Easter Sunday.

San Francisco abounds in smart women's shops. Although white gloves and a hat are no longer considered mandatory, San Francisco women still pride themselves on being well dressed. The city is becoming a fashion center, with a growing Apparel City, south of Market Street, manufacturing distinctively California clothes. The accent is on casual fashions, suits, sportswear, and good woolens, displayed during the July shows at Union Square and featured in local shops. A number of shops specialize in imported fabrics and clothes, and modified Oriental styles are a growing vogue.

The city's mink-and-diamonds store is **I. Magnin** (Geary and Stockton), housed in an austere white building and offering high fashion at expensive prices. **Saks Fifth Avenue** (Grant Avenue and Maiden Lane) has moved nearby to engage in a ladylike form of East-West competition. **Joseph Magnin** (Stockton and O'Farrell) features more casual apparel, bold sports clothes, and an unusually imaginative selection of shoes.

San Francisco downtown stores are within easy walking distance of each other. And if you get tired, you can always stop off at **Union Square** (Post, Geary, Stockton and Powell streets), a little park with gay rhododendrons and stately palm trees in the heart of the shopping area. You can sit on a bench or on the grass or on the base of the massive monument to Dewey's victory at Manila in the Spanish–American War—which dominates a park named in honor of the demonstrations supporting the Union on the eve of the Civil War.

On all sides Union Square is surrounded by swank hotels, notably the venerable St. Francis on Powell Street, by airline offices, and by shops of every description. There is often something doing at lunch hour, fashion shows in July, a cable-car-bell ringing contest, and sometimes public rallies of one kind or another. A man with a religious sign may be wandering around. People feed crumbs to the pigeons. The cable car clangs by. But it is somehow a restful refuge nevertheless.

The alleys in the shopping area are a constant surprise to visitors and even to longtime San Franciscans. **Tillman Place** is a tiny enclave in the midst of the fashionable women's shops on lower Grant Avenue with a bookstore, a candle shop, and an art gallery. Nearby **Maiden Lane,** a spectacular misnomer, is a little shopping world all its own on two narrow store-lined blocks.

Maiden Lane used to be Morton Street, the city's most depraved red-light district, where harlots sat in the windows and permitted passersby to stroke their breasts for a few cents; other services were almost equally inexpensive. After the earthquake wiped out the bordellos, a new name was considered essential to cleaning up the street. After some experimentation and the lapse of a number of years, the Maiden Lane label was finally accepted without too much eyebrow-raising. The name is appropriate only in the very general sense that the little alley is a shopping and lunch rendezvous for San Francisco's fashionable ladies who buy their clothes at Saks Fifth Avenue or their unusual and expensive sportswear at **Jax** (134 Maiden Lane).

V. C. Morris 140 Maiden Lane. Glass and silverware. EX 2-5502. Maiden Lane's most glittering ornament and a downtown showplace, this shop is housed in a domelike brick mausoleum designed by Frank Lloyd Wright. The architecture and the wares on display blend in what might be called a series of variations on a circle. Round portholes look in on circular ramps, illuminated by round light fixtures, which take you past round or oval glasses and lucite bowls, one-of-a-kind ceramics and figurines and luxurious silverware. Bought recently by Allan Adler, a Los Angeles silversmith, the store has retained its old name but has added some of its new owner's work, including hand-forged silver flatware and a large selection of jewelry. One traditional V. C. Morris oddity remains: a sleek, fluffy cat is usually in the window, tiptoeing gracefully and apparently without accident over paper-thin glass.

There are a number of small bars and restaurants for shoppers, several exclusive hair stylists, and the **Ansel W. Robinson** pet store (135 Maiden Lane) which features sophisticated canine coiffeurs and sells elegant cats and dogs. In the aviary upstairs Robinson's has some sofa-breasted toucans, in case you're weary of parakeets and canaries. An unusual daffodil festival and occasional open-air art shows brighten up an already colorful and charming alley which seems far removed from its lurid past.

Christian of Copenhagen. 225 Post Street. EX 2-3394. Outstanding for a very representative selection of contemporary, clean-line Danish furniture and for glassware, china, and decorative items. For the child born with a silver spoon in his mouth, you can buy the ideal gift here—a Bangkok teak highchair designed by Dux. But not everything here is for the carriage trade. The salad bowls, black on the inside and colored enamel outside, are good buys and handy gift items at $8.95.

Gump's 250 Post Street. Art objects and gifts. YU 2-1616. This is a hallowed institution and a museum as well as the smartest art and gift shop in town. Billing itself as "the world's most unusual store," it can rise above modesty without losing its dignity. As much a part of San Francisco as Golden Gate Park, it was founded in 1861 by Solomon and Gustave Gump to provide ornate bric-a-brac from Europe to the *nouveaux riches* of the gold-rush era. One of the few blessings of the 1906 earthquake was that it destroyed Gump's original stock. The Gumps (this has always been a closely held and managed family enterprise) turned toward the Orient. Shrewd buyers gathered up authentic Chinese and Japanese art objects, and soon enough the city's elite were wandering through the Tansu Room, the Jade Room, and the Lotus Room. A. Livingstone Gump, father of the present owner, was nearly blind most of his life, but it was said throughout San Francisco that he could determine accurately by touch the value of a jade carving. Now son Richard, a very shrewd merchandiser, has broadened the stock to include imports from every continent; there are even good American craft objects on display.

Gump's buyers remind one of counter-intelligence agents—they scour the globe to win for our side. *Our own imports* is a frequently seen sign heralding well-designed items at moderate cost, like alabaster hand-carved Italian chess sets or luminous Venetian glass in iridescent blues and heliotropes. The Gibson Bayh couturier designs on the third floor make use of rare, shimmering fabrics from the Far East, strongly Oriental in mood. The Steuben Glass room is a haven of smoke-tinted hues, with crystal elegance in leaping dolphins on graceful bowls and decanters. Monkeypod and myrtle-wood salad bowls are prominently displayed on the first floor. The third-floor Art Gallery has a monthly exhibit of contemporary paintings and sculptures. High-flown blurbs by stores offering "romantic woods of amaranth from Africa" and "lustrous Kappa shells from the Straits of Celebes" often lead to disappointment. Gump's, however, is as good as its word. It really does have a vast array of treasures from a twenty-century-old Chinese bronze to a modern stainless-steel fork.

Books and booklets about the much-publicized store are strategically scattered about among the art objects. Richard is the author of a book himself, *Good Taste Costs No More*. He debunks the gilt complex and attacks excessive awe for antiquity and favors judicious mixing of periods, the use of old and new in decorative styling. In line with the title of his book, Richard argues that it is "crazy to live beyond your means." But a visit to Gump's makes one somewhat cynical about this good advice. You can find well-designed bowls and other gifts for five dollars, but most of the china, furniture, Oriental jewelry, and glassware is definitely in the luxury class.

Gump's Jade Room probably has the city's best collection of delicately wrought statuettes, figures, and jewelry of precious stones. Gump's doesn't really expect most people to buy anything here, and you can feel quite relaxed about browsing in this quiet, serene little room. If you think of jade as green, this is the place to get educated. Jade, the Oriental symbol of loyalty and good luck, is here in every hue from dazzling white to deep green. The animals and religious figures have a feathery translucence, a fragility which belies the stone from which they came. The cornelian and amethyst figurines are probably unparalleled in this country. There are in, numerable Buddha images, with strikingly different Chinese, Japanese, Siamese, and Indian interpretations. One incongruous note perhaps captures the mixture of East and West that makes Gump's unique. The magnificent and overwhelmingly sized Guatama Buddha (eighteenth-century Tibetan) which graces the vestibule has a little sign in front: *Donations to Guide Dogs for the Blind Welcomed.*

C. T. Marsh & Company 522 Sutter Street. Oriental art objects. GA 1-5661. Claims to be the city's oldest firm specializing in Oriental art, antedating the Gumps in this field. The first Mr. Marsh designed the Japanese Tea Garden in Golden Gate Park, and the grandson carries on in the family tradition. In the hushed back room of the store you can gape at a breathtaking pair of dark jade parrots or the magnificent craftsmanship of the ivory and rose-quartz carvings. The present Mr. Marsh caters mainly to the carriage trade, designing jewelry of black iron with pearls and real diamonds. He handles diamonds as if they were drops of water to get a light, glistening effect. He has no hesitancy about explaining his philosophy of life. He believes the only way a woman can hold her man is to keep him broke, and Mr. Marsh does his best to accommodate.

W. & J. Sloane 216 Sutter Street. EX 7-3900. In a town crammed with decorating shops, this one stands out. The San Francisco branch of Sloane's was started in the 1870s to meet the insatiable demands of the Palace Hotel for carpeting, but it has, of course, branched out considerably since. It retains, however, a Western flavor which makes it less stolid and awe-inspiring than other Sloane branches. There is an unusually good choice of imaginative accessories, including early American antiques as well as European and Oriental imports. You can find any period furniture and a wide variety of upholstery fabrics. Good gift items are on the first floor. The model rooms are strikingly put together and you can shoplift the ideas. A modern chromium kitchen was enlivened by an unusual decorating note—a pair of weatherbeaten wooden posts from an old home mounted on the wall. Price was $125, but the incongruous accessory suggestion was free. Sloane's won't kid you about antiques and will let you know if they are for real or from Brooklyn.

Profils du Monde 578 Sutter Street. Saris and fabrics. EX 2-0696. Stores which proclaim branches in Beverly Hills and Santa Barbara often scare ordinary folk away, but venture into this one if only to take in the opulent atmosphere. The shimmering silk saris, made up into simple styles, evoke Ava Gardner or Soroya, the ex-queen of Iran, especially when topped by a coat lined with lustrous Italian satin. Prices for one of these outfits run as high as $400—but you can come down to earth with a silk-and-cotton sari evening dress for $59.95, including a stole. Other specialties include India cotton print dresses, Siamese raw silks, gossamer Bengalese silks, handwoven Grecian designs. There are also imported British and Scottish suits, a robust contrast to the exotic saris. All costumes are made to order. Indian jewelry and scarves abound. Sales personnel are very friendly and tolerant of the languorous female sighs.

Treasures of India 625 Sutter Street. OR 3-3490. Bleeding Madras fabric is sold here by the yard, and you can get Madras spreads in unusual color combinations priced from $8.95 to $14.95, depending on thickness of material and closeness of weave. Striking deep-toned red India print spreads are available at $2.95. Also lots of Persian brass and filigree silver jewelry—these at prices befitting the expensive address.

India Imports 429 Sutter Street. YU 2-7777. A bazaar atmosphere and "specials of the week" aim at capturing the tourist trade. A large assortment of Madras spreads starts at $5.95. All kinds of odds and ends including jangle bracelets, silk ascots, handwoven Indian skirts, raw silk by the yard, miscellaneous Oriental decorations that include classically simple teardrop vases in polished brass.

Lew Serbin's Dance Art Company   222 Powell Street. Fabrics and decorations. EX 2-4912. Originally established as a shoe and ballet slipper store for theater people, it has grown into the West's largest theatrical supply house. The lure of showpeople, of glittering rhinestones and grease paint gradually drew general customers. Now the store has three floors filled with every conceivable need of the theater as well as dramatic fabrics from all over the world. A real find for the woman with a flair for decoration or a whim to make her own Christmas ornaments and trimmings.

Scottish Imports   574 Geary Street. EX 7-5460. Two charming little old ladies preside over what they claim is the largest collection of Scottish imports in the country. They've transplanted a touch of the Scottish moors, even to recorded bagpipe music. Virtually everything you've associated with the Scotch is here: toffee, tiles, thistle pottery, tam-o'-shanters, tartan vests, handsome kilts, shetland sweaters in misty shades, striking plaid handbags, even "Moor Heather" perfume. The lustrous mohair stoles at $16.95 are just made for San Francisco's climate. Should you want to dream up an ancient lineage, there are profusely illustrated books on clans and Scottish Highland regiments. Or maybe you have a friend for whom *All About Horsebrasses* at $1.50 would be an ideal gift. There is a large collection of Scottish ballads and books, also inexpensive small items including paper cocktail napkins with coats of arms or Robert Burns' Selkirk Grace ("Some hae meat and canna eat").

Scotch House   950 Geary Street. PR 6-6445. A "wee shop" offering a tidy collection of Scottish, English, Australian, and Irish imports. A musical Koala bear ($19.95) makes Winnie the Pooh come to life. Plaid ties at $2, men's shirts at $15 and robes at $28 could be considered hearty buys. The proprietor has a brisk British air, somewhat reminiscent of the guards at Buckingham Palace. (Next door, the Edinburgh Castle pub opens at 5 P.M.)

Barra of Italy   245 Post Street. Women's sportswear. EX 2-6470. A splash of the Via Veneto in Rome. Bold, exciting sportswear dreamed up by Italian designers. Dramatic sweaters, resplendent evening bags, scarfs, costume jewelry, and quietly elegant knitwear. This is a plush store with prices to match. But drop in, especially if the closest you can come to a vacation on the Mediterranean is through clothes.

Madame Butterfly   347 Grant Avenue. Oriental fashions. SU 1-2417. This elegant outpost on Grant Avenue—before you hit the Chinatown shops—has succumbed to the times. The window displays now discreetly indicate prices—leader items at $9.95 and less, and you can get a cotton coolie coat for $5. But imported coolie pajama sets, mandarin coats, and silk dresses still run high.

Lanz of California   152 Geary Street. Youthful fashions. DO 2-2277. If you have a teen-age daughter, you probably know how high a Lanz cotton rates. The Austrian motifs, classic styling, and good fabrics make it easy to spot a Lanz. Along with the peasant influence, more sophisticated young career dresses have been introduced recently. Prices are steep, but the happy squeals of teenage girls are compensatory.

Rimini's St. Francis Perfume Shop   330 Geary Street. DO 2-0469. Mr. Rimini makes his own perfumes, excellent as gifts or mementos of San Francisco. His pride is Nob Hill Perfume, designed to be "reminiscent of the Comstock, the Mother Lode and days of silver and gold." It is delicately compounded of precious woods and exotic spices. The resulting scent is tangy and not too heady. Price: $2.50 for 1½ drams. Should you want more potent stuff, try Union Square Perfume, which has a stronger dash of myrrh.

Abercrombie & Fitch   220 Post Street. EX 7-2300. San Francisco really became a U city when A&F opened its local branch a couple of years ago, extending civilization's mastery over nature into the wild and woolly West. To rough it with A&F equipment is to have the best of all possible worlds. There are rifles here to bag elephants on safari or to bring down quail. We know a man who ventured in to find out if he could pick up a duck whistle for a friend; he spent an hour rummaging through a drawer full of duck whistles before he could decide which one he wanted. Far from limited to its main role of sportsmen's paradise, A&F also has an amazingly choice selection of adult games, women's sweaters, and shoes. One longshoreman we know wears only twenty-three-dollar A&F boots to work.

Chinatown Note

Chinatown is one of the best places in town to get crockery, housewares, and other imported items at reasonable prices. Your only problem is to exercise discrimination. There are scores of shops, and quality zigzags erratically. Some have excellent-quality merchandise, while others specialize in cheap tourist souvenirs. The **City of Hankow Tassel Company** (406 Grant Avenue; EX 2-5077) has a better-than-average selection of baskets and rattan objects. Philip Klein's **House of Jade** (519 Grant Avenue; DO 2-4978) has a hushed, expensive air. But you don't have to buy rare jade. There are many fine jewelry items here with genuine stones at realistic prices. At **Song Kee** (739 Grant; YU 2-3198) there are arrayed on tall shelves in a long, narrow shop an amazing variety of bowls and plates and china, many featuring the blue fish design which is a familiar item in many San Francisco homes. **Ming's Art Goods** (814 Grant; EX 2-0522) displays ceramics and decorative objects in uniformly good taste; you can get handsome and inexpensive brass Chinese teapots here in which you can both boil the water and brew the tea.

Polk Gulch

Try an informal walking-shopping tour around Polk and California streets, once the center of San Francisco's French community. Although you can still browse among the latest French paperbacks at the **French Book Store** (1111 Polk Street; GR 4-8308) or eat frog's legs at the **Alouette** (1121 Polk; GR 4-1764), all kinds of little gift stores, coffee houses, nearly new shops have begun, displacing the lingering traces of the French. Yet the area still somehow retains the atmosphere of an older San Francisco, a flavor of the city's traditional cosmopolitanism.

Even the name **Freed, Teller & Freed** (1326 Polk Street; OR 3-0922) suggests a more tranquil era when prideful tradesmen reigned supreme and when supermarkets were still unknown. The aroma of roasting coffee beans lures you inside, where you can pick up any variety or color of coffee you want to be freshly roasted while you wait. Freed's offers a bewildering choice in open bags of Colombia, Kona, Java, Arabian, and other coffees. There are also extra-special freshly roasted peanuts.

Genuine antiques are manufactured at **The Intrigue** (1230 Polk Street; PR 5-2935). Brace yourself for the news that many of those venerable inscrutable Buddhas displayed all over Chinatown come from the modest workshop up a flight of stairs over this little store. Fred Feingold and Frank Jameson are specialists in supplying an antiquated, decaying look to all sorts of statuary and decorative accessories. They admit modestly to making Buddhas in plaster molds and shipping them to Chinatown by the carton. You can find them in their shop at exceptionally low prices. If you want to display an accessory that looks like it came out of an Egyptian tomb or a museum of ancient Oriental art, this is the place to buy one. Or bring in a lamp or statuette of your own and have these experts fix it up to look antique. Here are homemade Oriental stone figures, gargoyles, Michelangelo reproductions, and African masks, all looking musty indeed. You can pick up a white-gold antiqued lamp, which might go in the Jackson Square decorator shops for eighty dollars or more, at half the price here.

There is a genteel little outpost of the advanced culture at the **Millard Book Shop** (1548 California Street near Polk; OR 3-6181) where you can browse among books on Zen or booklets by the new poets. Lectures are frequently held on the Hindu or Buddhist Way in a small back room decorated with original paintings. Here on Friday evenings earnest young poets, unshaven and tieless, read their latest offerings by candlelight from a gleaming white-linen-covered table to earnest young listeners. This shop is run by a mother-and-son team who admit to a new infatuation with the world of culture and poetry.

If you get tired of shopping or just looking, you can go in for a cup of coffee and a pastry or a lavish ice cream concoction under the crystal chandeliers and the shocking-pink and black-wrought-iron decor at **Blum's** (Polk and California), one of the city's more solid bourgeois institutions (see p. 169). Or if you are in a more Bohemian mood you can try one of the new coffee houses along the street. The **Coffee Cantata** (1842 Polk; GR 4-0846) features exotic coffees and teas along with tantalizing pastries and snacks. In this uptown variant of the Bohemian North Beach coffee house, you sit back in comfortable lounge chairs while pondering the meaning of life at the bottom of a coffee cup.

Left Bank in Cow Hollow

The area around Union and Fillmore streets, which used to be called Cow Hollow, is conveniently situated for the prosperous citizens of the Marina district and for the even wealthier denizens of Pacific Heights. The proximity of a well-heeled clientele may have something to do with the fact that several blocks in this other-wise undistinguished neighborhood have been blossoming with art galleries and arts-and-crafts shops of all kinds. (The art galleries listed in Chapter 7 include a number of Union Street addresses.) While the Bohemian population in this generally high-rent district is limited, the area is beginning to take on the look of a new and rather plush Montparnasse.

American Indian Art and Handicraft   1843 Union Street. WA

1-3676. At first glance, Marian Davidson appears to be running a little museum of Indian handicrafts here, conveniently located across the street from Bill Pearson's posh pre-Columbian art gallery (see p. 147). But these carefully selected artifacts are all for sale. The shop has an excellent collection of Navajo rugs, clay vessels, turquoise and silver jewelry and belts, and painted wooden dolls—*kachinas*—all made by Indians on reservations in the Southwest. There is also a good display of books on Indian art.

Grete Williams Gallery   2059 Union Street. JO 7-8460. Just a hole in the wall, considerably more modest than some of the other Union Street galleries. Mrs. Williams features contemporary jewelry and paintings by local artists. It is possible occasionally to pick up good buys in both specialties. Mrs. Williams has an eye for up-and-coming artists who haven't yet been discovered, and she is very helpful in chatting with customers.

Jack Nutting   2049 Union Street. Jewelry. Tuesday to Friday, 1–6 P.M.; Saturday, noon to 5 P.M. WA 2-0868. Some of San Francisco's best contemporary jewelry. Modern but not extreme. Graceful, uncluttered designs, especially with gold and pearls.

Collin Wilcox   2157 Union Street. Lamps. FI 6-9415. Some of the best-looking lamps in town at very reasonable prices. An antique or Oriental base with a good linen shade is in the thirty-to-forty-dollar class—considerably less than for the same quality in downtown shops. The cinnabar and other antique finishes seem particularly successful. There are also imaginative plaques and other decorator items. If you have a treasured vase or a distinctive bottle, Mr. Wilcox can turn it into an unusual lamp.

The Daibutsu   3028 Fillmore Street. Oriental art objects. JO 7-1530. Ichiro Shibata, a young man who knows about the Oriental art objects he has on sale, can probably enter a claim for one of the oldest shops of this kind in San Francisco. His grandfather was one of the first Japanese to come to San Francisco in the period following the gold rush, and the family has maintained an Asian art shop almost ever since. Mr. Shibata picks up most of his merchandise on trips to the Far East, but occasionally finds an item he wants in San Francisco. He has a good selection of work from Japan, China, India, Korea, and Java, with some objects more than a thousand years old. A representative item was a thirteenth-century Korean wine-drinking bowl of the Koroyo dynasty. There are sculptures, wood carvings, painted screens, chests, and pottery and porcelain bowls. The shop is in a converted apartment, consisting of a few small rooms and a Japanese garden in back.

Even an amateur expert can find some good buys here. A 150-year-old Japanese folk art pottery bowl decorated with a red and yellow flower design was selling for ten dollars.

Mark Harrington's   3053 Fillmore. Glassware. WE 1-6809. Mr. Harrington sells nothing that isn't made of glass. A former glassmaker and manufacturer himself, he still does glass engraving for Gump's and for San Francisco society clients. His wares are attractively displayed against a background of Swedish modern furniture. The stock includes bowls, glasses, platters, and pitchers in assorted shapes, sizes and colors, with a large selection of imports. If you're looking for an attractive martini pitcher for yourself or for a friend, this is the place to find an exceptionally attractive one. Prices, however, are on the high side.

Waterfront Department

The waterfront is rapidly becoming a center for offbeat import shops. Rents are not prohibitive, and parking is more available than in the downtown area. Besides, there's always the romance and glamor of the Embarcadero.

Cost Plus   2552 Taylor Street, near Fisherman's Wharf. Open daily 10 A.M. to 9 P.M., Saturday and Sunday 10 A.M. to 6 P.M. OR 3-5646. This sprawling split-level bargain basement in an old warehouse pioneered the waterfront shopping trend. Items range from wooden tribal figures from Kenya to Swedish silverware. You can also get an occasional good buy on bottled borscht straight from Brooklyn. Just like the flickers, features change each week and sometimes more often. It is a sound policy here to buy what you like when you see it—you may not see it again. And once you get it, you're stuck; no returns. This is one of the few real havens for bargain-hunters in the Bay Area. One young man about town also claims it is a good, inexpensive place to take a date.

While the emphasis is on home furnishings, there is also an assortment of imported foods, Oriental clothing, and garden supplies. Rattan and bamboo furniture vie with inexpensive Japanese copies of Scandinavian chairs. There are wind chimes, stone figures, planters, straw matting, Madras spreads, and paper lanterns. The potpourri has included Chinese printing plates to hang on the wall, Tanganyika bongo drums, Portuguese tawny wine, Italian minaret-topped bottles, and Hawaiian monkeypod bowls. There is a good selection of Japanese pottery. Roman wine litres selling for three dollars uptown can be bought here for one, if you don't mind a scratch or two. Some of the furniture is of weird design, and much of it is of the do-it-yourself variety. Anyone with imagination can furnish an apartment here fairly inexpensively.

Will success spoil Cost Plus? Operations are so hectic now there is a supermarket-type checking system. There is also an outside display case with choice items tastefully arranged. And prices have been edging upward. But the slatternly atmosphere still predominates, and blemishes are frankly acknowledged. In the slat table-top section, a sign says, "Please take box on top. All benches are equally imperfect."

World Trade Imports   North wing of the Ferry Building, ground floor. DO 2-0701. Excellent buys in teakwood tables and furniture, brass trays and table tops, and wonderful vases for lamp bases. Bargain hunters should sample this place as well as Cost Plus. Open Sunday.

Danish Furniture Importers   1111 Front Street, facing Pier 19 on the Embarcadero. YU 6-3692. A gay, tastefully redone warehouse full of excellent-quality furniture and accessories. Lamps and lighting fixtures are especially imaginative. Prices are only slightly below those in standard furniture shops. However, this outfit does sometimes sponsor occasional "be your own importer" sales right on the docks with real bargains and free Tuborg beer. Open Sunday.

Decorous Barbary Coast

As you wander past the austere and expensive decorators' shops on Pacific Avenue, you come to a little alley called Hotaling Place which is part of the wicked tradition of the area, once the locale of the infamous Barbary Coast. There once stood Hotaling's whiskey warehouse, which supplied liquor to the local bars and bordellos and emerged unscathed from the 1906 fire that swept virtuous San Francisco. Charles Field, a local poet, was prompted to ask:

> If, as they say, God spanked the town
> For being over-frisky,
> Why did he burn the churches down
> And spare Hotaling's Whiskey?

But what earthquake and fire could not achieve has been accomplished by the onward march of commerce. The old Barbary Coast has at last been utterly demolished. It is now called Jackson Square, the center of San Francisco's posh interior-decorator shops. The area still attracts nostalgia addicts as well as window-shoppers. The former can ponder the fact that torts have taken the place of tarts at 722 Montgomery Street, the site of the naughty

Melodeon which once provided lusty entertainment for miners and sailors. The old Melodeon building and nearby 728 Montgomery Street have been restored inside and out to their original decor by Melvin Belli, the very prosperous and proper attorney who has established his offices there. Or you can look at the Gay Nineties decor of the Golden Hind Players, who offer little-theater fare at the old Bella Pacific Theater (329 Pacific Avenue) which once exhibited some of San Francisco's raciest performers. But by and large the interior decorators have taken over.

The old Hippodrome, where exotic dancers performed salacious contortions, is now the home of Herman Miller, Inc. (555 Pacific), exhibiting furniture and fabrics in flawless taste. The displays on Pacific Avenue now are of wallpapers, linens, carpeting, window coverings, draperies, and decorative objects. The shops lining Pacific Street are mainly for the trade. But there are a few that do cater to retail trade; and at least two are outstanding.

Jade Snow Wong   408 Pacific Avenue. Ceramics. YU 6-1923. You may have read Miss Wong's autobiography, *Fifth Chinese Daughter,* which describes her earnest search for a fusion of modern American and traditional Chinese culture. Looking at her work, you can judge for yourself how well she has succeeded in her chosen field. Between lecture tours and books, Miss Wong turns out some of the best-designed ceramics available in a city teeming with good craftsmen. The little copper enameled ashtrays make fine inexpensive ($2.50) gifts; they are distinguished for brilliant and yet subtle effects in the blending of reds, blues, and golds. More expensive ($6.50 to $16.50) are the newel bowl ashtrays, their centers fused with quartz crystals which sparkle like champagne bubbles against the soft texture of the clay. Also suitable for gifts are free-form stoneware dishes at $4.50 and punch or salad bowls, enameled cigarette boxes, and boldly designed earrings. Visitors are made to feel at home even if they don't buy anything.

Takahashi   323 Pacific. Oriental imports. EX 7-4668. This is one of the finest shops in San Francisco for gifts and home accessories. It is also a poignant success story, which started as a gleam in the eyes of Henri and Tami Takahashi when they were still in a relocation camp in central Utah during World War II.

Both American-born and college educated (he in journalism and she in Oriental languages and museum research), they together with thousands of other Americans of Japanese ancestry were suddenly uprooted from their homes and creative work and plunked down in the middle of a desolate desert. The Takahashis don't pretend to have enjoyed the experience, and there is still an understandable edge of bitterness when they talk about it. Henri edited the *Topaz Times,* an oddly poetic name considering the circumstances. Tami gave birth to a baby and sponsored hobby shows to keep up morale.

Somehow the Takahashis and many others kept alive a sense of beauty. She tells how the inmates of what was euphemistically called the Central Utah Relocation Center painstakingly collected bits of rusty wire, scraps of wood, and broken Coca-Cola bottles (only the military guards had the privilege of sipping this heady beverage). Out of these odds and ends they fashioned contemporary sculpture, glass mosaics, and plaques proudly displayed at the hobby shows. The Takahashis kept busy and they dreamed about starting a shop featuring traditional Japanese handicrafts.

When they began to grope for a new life again in San Francisco after the war, they started with this idea, a small private collection of Japanese art objects, and practically no capital. The store, originally on Post Street in San Francisco's Japanesetown, was an immediate success. It attracted neighborhood trade and shoppers from all over the city. Soon the graceful, distinctive items, many made to the Takahashis' own design, began to interest visitors from throughout the country. Orders from shops in the East began to pour in. Now most of the Takahashis' business is wholesale. They place orders with their own factories in Japan and make frequent buying trips. Most of the modern lacquerware throughout the country, they claim, comes from Henri Takahashi's drawing board.

The retail store helps the Takahashis keep track of public tastes and reactions. It also serves as a showcase for their guiding belief that Oriental art objects can be spread throughout America and made acceptable even in Podunk without being vulgarized into cheap junk. If you have been appalled by the quality of some recent Japanese imports, drop in on the Takahashis. There is no lessening of craftsmanship or esthetic feeling. The deep respect for the products of nature which pervades Japanese folk art is seen in the lovingly polished wood bowls where the grain shines through. There is, however, definite adaptation in many cases to American needs and tastes. Although cocktail parties are not indigenous to Japan, the miniature Japanese hibachi is ideal for preparing hot hors d'oeuvres. Most of the wares fit into the American milieu. This is certainly true of the graceful lacquer accessories in soft white, persimmon, and antique gold, designed in the contemporary teardrop shape, of the simple elegance of the white china, the boldly striking casseroles, the lustrous zabuton cushions and the handsome woven table mats. If you have been looking for imaginative party favors, the ones on display here can't be beaten. They help give the whole store a fairy-tale quality.

Since there is no middleman, Takahashi prices are competitive with those all over town, in some cases lower. Many interior decorators spend hours absorbing ideas of color and design. If she is around, Mrs. Takahashi will be helpful to amateurs as well as professionals in discussing Buddhist influences on Japanese art, the esthetic restraint which accompanies the splendid embellishments, and the use of this traditional folk art in modern American surroundings.

Craftsmen in (and out of) Bohemia

The Bay Area is a major arts and crafts center. Even critics who cavil about the merit of some of the paintings on display at the annual Art Festival grant the high quality of the pottery, jewelry and other handicrafts. A number of craftsmen offering this kind of work have opened shops clustered together on upper Grant Avenue among Bohemian hangouts and Italian ravioli factories. No doubt the prevalence of tourists is the explanation. Others have clustered around the Aquatic Park area near the Bay along Beach and Hyde streets, and some have just located at random.

Designer Craftsmen of California   1507 Grant Avenue. GA 1-0465. The work of more than fifty local artist-craftsmen is on display here. The shop is run by the craftsmen themselves, who contribute their creations and their time and share in the profits if any. Their local organization is dedicated to the belief that craft work is vital to the national heritage and is affiliated with the nationwide American Craftsmen's Council. This shop has the atmosphere of a contemporary museum, with many objects that are a pleasure to see even if you have neither the cash nor the desire to buy them.

In all the work from furniture to ceramics and handwoven lap robes there is finesse and artistry unmatched by mass-production machines. The satin-smooth wood salad bowls by Bob Stocksdale have been lovingly molded and polished. The original contemporary jewelry designs by Margaret De Patta, Merry Renk, and Claudia Williams are delicate and supple. On display are an excellent variety of stoneware pottery, the bold Bauhaus ceramics of Marguerite Wildenham, and the vibrant plastics of Frieda Koblick. Prices are the same as at other retail outlets featuring handcrafted contemporary design. Handwoven place mats, tiles, and enamel ashtrays make good and relatively inexpensive gift items.

Silver earrings begin at $7.50. Canny buyers may claim that the distinction between the work here and machine-made objects isn't worth the substantial price differential. The answer of the craftsmen is that their creations have a value, originality, and expressiveness that can't be matched by the machine. If you sometimes feel that the industrial age and the Organization Man are obliterating individual craftsmanship, you can find succor here.

Peter Macchiarini 1422 Grant Avenue. Jewelry. YU 2-2229. An old-timer on the street who got here before the beats and the tourists, Peter Macchiarini is one of the city's outstanding modern jewelers, specializing in free-form rings, pendants, and earrings, free among other things of the tormented shapes of some avant-garde horrors.

Lasnier, the Silversmith 1322 Grant Avenue. Jewelry. YU 2-5643. Striking silver and pearl necklaces quite lovely enough to adorn the throat of any Pacific Heights lady, offered at prices which might bring a strangled cry of anguish from whoever picks up the tab.

The Paint Pot 1356 Grant Avenue. Jewelry and enamelware. EX 7-3259. A tiny nook where a tiny dark girl with big doe eyes and long hair who wants to be known only as Noir turns out some of the most imaginative copper enamel work around. For prices between one and four dollars you can get button earrings, dangles, ashtrays, mad medallions—all splashed with wonderful colors. Noir does her enameling in the back of the shop, and she will make up any shade or mixture you want. One of these days soon she will find retail outlets and the prices of her gadgets will shoot up. For some time they have been among the best gift values in town.

Local Color 1414 Grant Avenue. Jewelry and gifts. YU 2-1977. A little oasis in the midst of the Grant Avenue bustle. Gretchen McAllister, the owner and a fine designer of delicate jewelry in her own right, somehow gives her shop a calm, relaxed, gentle atmosphere. She opened her shop when this was still a quiet Italian family neighborhood, but she took the invasion by beatniks and tourists in stride. Gretchen saw the beatnik furor as a temporary and fleeting excrescence, and she has turned out to be right. Her designs have been sympathetically described as the only jewelry on the block which doesn't look like an archeological find—but she has that kind too. Prices start at $7.50 for silver and $20 for gold. Gretchen's wedding rings seem particularly successful, combining lightness of texture with careful execution. The shop also carries ceramics, contemporary greeting cards, a good choice of inexpensive glassware, and the ubiquitous narrow Ernst ties. Although the emphasis is on California craftsmanship, one rare buy here was a pair of excellent modern machine-made earrings at $1.25.

Bill Sandusky   1314 Grant Avenue. Woven skirts. GA 1-9155. Don't turn away because of the tinseled skirts displayed in the window. That's tourist bait. The shop does a brisk business in what they call cocktail skirts woven with metallic threads. But inside you can find wonderful handwoven tweeds and peasant skirts. All skirts cost $30. Tailors are on hand to make quick alterations—included in the price. You can have floating panels, two, three, or four pleats, flared styles. Every piece is woven by old-timer Sandusky. There is still a loom in the shop, but he has since retreated to the Little River country where he turns out his weaves at demon pace. He is booked up a year in advance, never designs two pieces of fabric alike. On one side you will find handwoven ties, in the narrow shape, at $2—among the most distinctive fabrics in town. Welcome, if for no other reason, than to offer some competition to the fashionable Ernst ties.

Irene Hamel   721 Beach Street. Pottery. PR 5-1464. A few years ago Irene Hamel and her husband, the well-known decorator Carl Rhode-Hamel, purchased the property here, which included a little cottage and a corrugated-iron shed, from an old Italian family. They rebuilt the shed, put in a kiln and expanded what had been Mrs. Hamel's part-time hobby into a thriving business of custom-designed pottery. Mrs. Hamel is known for her unusual effects in glazes and designs, which she achieves through constant experiment; she has made several trips to the Orient to study pottery techniques there. Mrs. Hamel specializes in the use of natural materials such as salt, sand, wood ash, lava, and volcanic ash. Her work ranges from small tiles or ashtrays to one-of-a-kind fireplaces and fountains which run up to $1000. Although she works only to order and limits the number of orders to those she can handle personally, she does have some random items. As a neighborly gesture she keeps her shop open most of December to permit friends and acquaintances in the area to come by and browse for relatively inexpensive gift items, a planter, a pitcher, or an ashtray.

Hal Painter   2721 Hyde Street. Weaver. OR 3-4740. One of the few Bay Area weavers who actually makes a living at it. Hal Painter is mainly interested in designing and making tapestries for private homes and civic buildings. The city of San Francisco has purchased some of his work, and tapestries are coming back into vogue as a form of decoration. Although most of his work is at special order, he usually has on hand place mats at $2.50 or $3, linen tablecloth material at about $10 a yard, and beautifully woven skirt lengths. The window of his shop is gay with swatches of material from raffia to the finest natural wools. He abhors synthetics, believing that natural wools and materials have a more lasting quality and beauty. An experimenter, he uses local mosses, cattail, grasses, plants, fox, mink, and muskrat furs. Painter started out studying painting and ceramics in Europe, at the California School of Fine Arts, and in Mexico. Finally, he found his medium in weaving and synthesized into this craft all his previous knowledge. He has become one of the country's leading weavers and tapestry designers.

Kim's Studio Pottery   1375 Ninth Avenue. MO 1-0609. You would never expect to find this artistic enclave in the solid burgher Sunset district, but here are some of the most imaginative, vital ceramics off any potter's wheel in the Bay Area. Intense and slight, Ernie Kim designs bold patterns in high-fired stoneware which have garnered countless medals. He is surely one of the most successful testimonials to occupational therapy. It was while recuperating in Letterman Army Hospital after World War II that he began to dabble with clay. He has been deeply enmeshed ever since in producing stoneware bowls, and is now in charge of the ceramics department of the California School of Fine Arts. He exhorts his students not to be concerned exclusively with techniques or perfection of glazes but to let feeling and boldness come through. His concern for texture contrast produces startling results. Perhaps most striking are his tall branch vases which reflect a blend of ancient origins and modern techniques. Because of his Korean ancestry, Mr. Kim is often asked if Oriental motifs figure prominently in his work. He answers that he designs the way he feels, and the end result may come out resembling pre-Columbian, Mexican, Japanese, or even Scandinavian design. He doesn't go along with American potters who are always searching for inspiration in other countries. He argues for more uninhibited feeling and less self-consciousness in art.

No utilitarian himself, Kim has never quite resigned himself to the mania for functionalism of American women. Some of the most beautiful pieces in the shop are relatively more functional—but they have been designed by his wife Lise. Kim doesn't fully approve. However, he compromises sufficiently to drill holes in the bottom of his branch vases if you must make lamp bases out of them. As a craftsman with his own retail outlet who keeps coming into contact with customers, he is troubled by people used to machine-made products and inexpensive Japanese imports who express amazement at his prices. He does have ashtrays at $2 and bowls at about $8. But the magnificent larger pieces run upwards of $25. It almost comes down to a moral and esthetic dilemma: would you rather serve food in a Pyrex casserole or skimp on something else and use a dish which is a thing of beauty?

Bonsai   2566 California Street. Miniature Trees. WA 1-1421. Kay Omi is a craftsman too—but in a far different tradition and in different materials than others in the arts and crafts fraternity. He works with trees. In back of an old Victorian house, typical of the Western Addition, he maintains what is probably the most unusual and exquisite private garden in San Francisco. Assisted by his wife and son, he cultivates hundreds of bonsai trees, tiny bamboos, maples, wisteria, ginkgo, junipers, and cypress. *Bonsai* is formally defined as "the Japanese art of cultivating trees in the shallowest containers possible with the purpose of esthetically creating a great tree in miniature." Omi has done just this. The result is a garden with the subtle, haunting quality of a Japanese painting miraculously come to life. Taken over from the Chinese, the bonsai art has been cultivated in Japan for six hundred years. The value of a tree is measured in terms of its age and esthetic appearance. On special occasions, the tree is taken into the house. Basically, it is an outdoor plant. Omi will ship any tree costing ten dollars or more anywhere in the country. But most of his fine specimens are priced at several times this figure. Bonsai are expensive, and, as Omi emphasizes, they are not for the indolent. They have to be carefully and lovingly tended. Along with each sale comes a pamphlet with explicit directions. Bonsai make a superb gift for imaginative and devoted gardeners. But even if you have neither the cash nor the patience for one of Omi's miniature masterpieces, you ought to visit here just for the sheer enjoyment of observing how art, sometimes, can improve on nature.

Books

San Francisco probably has more bookstores per capita than any other city in the country, some carrying a general line, others specializing in rare books or second-hand books or paperbacks. The major department stores (City of Paris, Emporium, Macy's, and White House) all have substantial book departments. The bigger shops are in the downtown area around Union Square, but others are scattered throughout the city.

Tro Harper Books   140 Powell Street. SU 1-7254. Tro Harper likes to refer to his bustling bookshop as the "intellectual's supermarket"—everything from the Manchester *Guardian* to a cherry pitter can be found. Originally a paperback book center, the craze for Japanese imports hit Mr. Harper hard and he has since been on safari around the globe. If you're searching for something and know not what, this is a good base from which to look. Replicas of pre-Columbian jewelry, the sort museums display, make exotic gifts. There are Roman wine bottles, Cornish ovenware, Malabar pepper, Austrian silver buttons, Japanese teapots. And all along the sides there is a comprehensive, well-arranged collection of paperbacks. The walls above are bursting with art print reproductions and bullfight posters at $1. During lunchtime, the aisles are as crowded as a New York department-store bargain counter, with buyers picking at the contemporary greeting cards or trying to sneak in a few pages of Henry Miller.

Mr. Harper considers himself an intrepid pioneer. He introduced hardcover remainders—publishers' overstock—to San Francisco at bargain prices. Recently he decided that some of his customers might want a few impressive leatherbound tomes to add class among the paperbacks. He imported an assorted medley which he offered at moderate prices. It turned out that one buyer found a book with rare Rembrandt etchings valued at about $2000. Harper took it in good spirit. But he is not planning to let the same kind of accident recur.

Newbegin's Book Shop 358 Post Street. DO 2-2808. Full of years, dignity and a choice location on Union Square, this is San Francisco's oldest bookshop. Founded in 1891 by John J. Newbegin, who liked writers as well as books. He was a friend of Ambrose Bierce, Jack London, and George Sterling. A good general bookstore, Newbegin's is strong in Western Americana, rare books, and fine leather bindings.

Paul Elder's Book Store Sutter and Stockton streets. SU 1-2208. Another old-timer in the business, Paul Elder's is the department store among San Francisco bookshops. It offers the widest selection available of current books, and also has a strong children's department and a fine selection of art prints. There are no dollar bargains in prints here, but if you want a really fine reproduction of a French impressionist or an Old Master, this is a good place to look.

Books Inc. 156 Geary Street. EX 7-1555. This is about the only store in the city with a good general stock of both paperback and hard-cover books. There are usually somewhere from 35,000 to 40,000 paperback books in the store. The respect for the paperbacks is hardly accidental. Books Inc. is part of the sprawling Western book empire which includes Paper Editions Corp., Lewis Lengfeld's wholesale house generally credited with sparking the paperback revolution in the Bay Area. Another feature of Books Inc. is a rental library, a fast-disappearing institution in San Francisco.

Charlotte Newbegin   8 Tillman Place, off Grant Avenue between Post and Sutter streets. EX 2-4668. For many years a co-owner of the original Newbegin's, Charlotte Newbegin sold out some years ago and began her own charming little bookshop on one of San Francisco's most atmospheric alleys. A pleasant place to inspect the new books and get into discussions on current literary and publishing trends with other book-lovers and browsers.

Albert Henry Books   524 Geary Street. OR 3-5383. Don't be misled by the tiny storefront or the display of lurid magazines outside. The hole-in-the-wall widens out and extends in back to house a fine selection of better (and more expensive) paperbacks. Without dropping a faithful *Sporting News* and popular-magazine clientele, Albert Henry has gradually built up one of the more interesting paperback shops in town.

Holmes Book Company   22 3rd Street. DO 2-3283. One of the biggest and oldest bookstores in town, Holmes specializes mainly in used books. Book-lovers can find occasional hard-to-get buys in the old books sold on tables outside for twenty-five cents each. Inside is a far-ranging treasure trove, piled high but systematically arranged, with lots of good Western Americana items.

Bonanza Inn Book Shop   (650 Market Street, across from the Palace Hotel; EX 2-8654) has a large assortment of hardcover books on a wide range of subjects and an equally large stock of paperbacks. **Constance Spencer** (450 Post Street, across the street from the St. Francis; EX 2-4229) is, like the Bonanza Inn, among the conveniently located, well-stocked downtown bookstores.

McDonald's Book Shop   48 Turk Street. OR 3-2235. Mr. McDonald (Mac to the regulars) long presided over this big barn of a store bursting with thousands of second-hand books and old magazines. If you have patience you can find almost anything here—out-of-print books on birds, history, economics, and philosophy as well as contemporary whodunits and Victorian novels. While his own tastes run to the more serious sociological tomes, he always dispensed a twinkling smile and bits of good-humored philosophy with every book. A ramrod-straight old-timer with ruddy cheeks and white hair above a stiffly starched high white collar, Mac has retired from active participation in the business. But he still puts in an occasional Saturday at the counter, and his personality continues to dominate the store. Customers still can read Mac's own handwritten reviews of the books on display in the windows. A book about dogs draws this comment, "It is much easier to teach a dog what is right than to teach a man, or even a woman. The dog has less nonsense to get out of his head." And Mac has this to say about a humor anthology, "Learn to laugh. It doesn't cost anything and pays big dividends. Laughing out loud aids digestion and no one who indulges in belly laughs need ever complain about peptic ulcers. The best medicine on the market." The humor book does have a one-dollar price tag, but it seems cheap at the price.

Iaconi Book Imports for Children   300 Pennsylvania Avenue. AT 2-1884. Open Saturdays only, 1 to 4 P.M. Other hours by appointment. In a charming Victorian mansion on Potrero Hill, you will find an unusually wide selection of handsomely designed and illustrated book imports for children—Italian, Spanish, German, French, and other languages. Also a number of bilingual books which make intriguing gifts. The Iaconis started out with a little home mail-order business when they were peeved at not finding foreign-language books for children in their own family. Apparently other parents felt the same need. The idea has really caught on. Children might have fun seeing their favorite elephant Babar all dressed up in German as *dem Kleinem Elfanten* or how the Little Golden Books have swept the world, becoming *Ein Goldene Kinderbuch, Un Petit Livre d'Or, Un Pequeño Libro d'Oro* or the Swedish *Gyllene Bok.* (Realistic adults can meanwhile visualize the gold pouring into Simon & Schuster coffers). Most of the books in stock sell in the $2.50–$3.50 range. The Iaconis have LP language records for children ($5). They are also branching out in the adult field with foreign art books and French paperbacks. They will knock themselves out to get any foreign book you want, whether for children or adults. If you're a devotee of the current trend to teach foreign languages to children at an early age, the Iaconis will spur you on.

City Lights Bookshop   261 Columbus Avenue. A big stock of paperbacks (see p. 134). DO 2-8193.

Porpoise Bookshop   308 Clement Street. SK 2-0753. Through this narrow, cluttered bookshop strides Henry Evans, the handsome bearded proprietor who is also writer, printer, collector, and an old-time San Francisco Bohemian. Long a resident of the famed Montgomery Block, hangout of writers and artists, Mr. Evans is slightly self-conscious about his present location in the staid, bourgeois residential Richmond district. But he explains this is the "last cosmopolitan area" left in the city where you can still hear a medley of languages. (You can test his theory by walking over a block to the Miniature Restaurant, 433 Clement Street, for a bit of old Russia, including delicious *piroshkis* at bargain prices).

Although there is a varied book collection here, the emphasis is on Californiana. The store is a repository of old photos, fading California newspapers, quaint legal documents or, as Mr. Evans phrases it, memorabilia of the city. Under mountainous stacks of Palo Alto newspapers at the turn of the century, you may uncover a *sui generis* old volume on the care and treatment of vineyards. In the back can be seen his hand press on which he printed his own little booklets on San Francisco—interesting reading full of color, history, and a heavy dash of romantic nostalgia. His wife, Patricia Evans, is the author of charming booklets on jump and hopscotch rhymes which make a nice gift for a dollar. Browsers are welcome, and the proprietor will be glad at the drop of a book to get into a lively discussion on Bohemians *vs.* Beatniks.

Records

Sea of Records (116 Ninth Street, a block south of Market Street; HE 1-3519). Claims the largest stock in the West, offers new records at discount prices on the street floor, and has an unusual selection of used records in the basement. You can bring in used LPs in good condition (unscratched) and get about a dollar each, then go downstairs and shop around for rare treasures that other people have traded in. In the downtown area **Discount Records** (262 Sutter Street) has a wide selection of records at good but not spectacular prices.

Gourmet Corner

Williams-Sonoma Kitchen Bazaar 576 Sutter Street. YU 2-0295. Kitchen specialties is too mundane a description for this arsenal, where the secret weapons of the Escoffier chefs are stored. Gastronomy is king here. The recipes tacked up on the walls don't tell you how to make a tuna casserole in thirteen minutes; they all require elaborate preparation—and the special equipment displayed on the shelves. You can get just the right pan for cooking *escargots* and a crust mold from which pastry will emerge in the shape of a buxom chicken. There are pans for *rechauds,* crepes suzette, and *bourguignon.* For the best-looking hors d'oeuvres in town there are crust terrines with bird and animal heads to be filled with *pâté.* Silver skewers the French call *hatelets* will help you make a dish that looks like it came from the Ritz. There is a dazzling assortment of soufflé dishes, casseroles, tart tins, ice-cream molds, steamed-pudding tins, even pepper mills that really work (by Peugeot, the auto maker). Gleaming French copper pots are prominently displayed, and you're assured they're the slowest, evenest, and finest way to cook. The shop's epicurean flavor just by-passes gluttony. Prices are not astronomical for these wares gastronomical. There are some inexpensive items, such as good-looking aprons and earthenware dishes, also chocolate molds for a nickel.

The practicing cook can obtain valuable tools of the trade at **Thomas Cara Ltd.** (306 Columbia Avenue; SU 1-0383; see p. 66) including wonderful casseroles and *espresso* machines in all sizes. You can buy pasta machines and other equipment for Italian delicacies at **Emilio Biordi's** (412 Columbus Avenue; see p. 66).

San Francisco abounds in food stores where you can buy just the right ingredients for gourmet cooking and innumerable delicacies for hors d'oeuvres and desserts.

You can buy freshly ground coffee in exotic variety at **Freed, Teller & Freed** (1326 Polk Street) or **Joost Brothers** (1555 Fillmore Street).

At **Lucchesi's** (543 Columbus; see p. 68) you can get wonderfully fresh little artichokes as well as the fresh oregano, basil, and other herbs that will make your dishes taste different.

You can find exquisite desserts, including St. Honoré and Napoleon cakes or delicious rum cakes, at **Columbus Pastry Company** (507 Columbus Avenue). A coffee crunch cake or a frozen pudding from **Blum's** (California and Polk streets) is a traditional and delicious San Francisco dessert. Or you can pick up the best *petits fours* in town (about $2.25 a dozen) at **Fantasia** bakery (3830 California Street).

The **Ukraine Bakery** (1100 McAllister Street; FI 6-0323) has excellent strudel. But its breads, especially the dark brown Russian pumpernickel, are the Ukraine's pride. Also fine onion rolls, crunchy salt sticks, and bagels.

If you want to produce a good facsimile of Chinese oyster beef, you can buy a bottle of Hong Dong Oyster Sauce from **Tai Yick** (1400 Powell Street, corner of Broadway) for $1.25 and combine with thinly sliced pieces of flank steak.

Normandy Lane in the City of Paris department store has a dazzling variety of cheeses and cold cuts, every possible biscuit, cracker, and nut for hors d'oeuvres, innumerable imported items. **Simon Brothers** (2829 California Street) is a high-quality general food store with a big assortment of exotic, imported soups, canned *babas au rhum,* Swiss fondue, and chocolate ants. **Goldberg Bowen** (242 Sutter Street) is a complete and excellent food department store in the downtown shopping area. It carries everything, good meats, the best potato salad in town at the delicatessen counter, imported grape leaves, rare chutneys, elegant hors d'oeuvres, and even instant coffee bags.

For Antiquity Hunters

Most of San Francisco's antique shops have the disordered, chaotic appearance of grandmother's attic. In a miscellany of early Americana you are liable to come across Oriental, medieval, or even primordial finds. The shops are located in several clusters in different parts of the city, and the real aficionados tackle them systematically, neighborhood by neighborhood.

Seven or eight emporiums of the ancient are grouped together on Sutter Street just below Van Ness Avenue. Some are subdued like **Barbara Chevalier** (1199 Sutter), some shrill like **Morgan Meadows** (1201 Sutter); if you have a penchant for old gas lanterns or dripping chandeliers, the latter shop is for you. Stop off at the **Alfred B. Clark Auction Studio** (1185 Sutter). If the race is on, you will be handed a sheet like a racing form and the onlookers have that tense, rapt look. And if you feel the need for a whiff of contemporary atmosphere, drop in at **Axelrad's** (1102 Sutter) for that clean Scandinavian look.

Interspersed among the art galleries and the arts-and-crafts shops in the Cow Hollow area on Union Street below Fillmore are antique and decorator stores stacked with blue-and-white china, brass kettles, Venetian glassware, and benches. There is another pocket of elegant junk on Divisadero Street between Post and Pine. Inelegant junk is to be found in abundance in the secondhand stores lining McAllister Street below Webster; occasionally you can run across a low-priced rare item here.

The dilettante will probably find most rewarding the shops ranged along North Point Street from the Aquatic Park area up to the Marina. This is a pleasant area for walking, and a couple of shops here are fun even if you aren't obsessed with antiques.

Doppelganger   997A North Point Street. PR 5-0277. Antique shops usually have a hushed, reverent air. This one has a sense of humor, sometimes straining the "fun but in good taste" standard set up by the proprietors, two young Ivy League fugitives from advertising. A decorated bathroom serves here as a salesroom, with a collection of soap holders and signs from boarding houses on how to behave in a bathroom. The shop is a miscellany of delicious and piquant tidbits. It may strike some visitors as a bit on the precious side, but we enjoyed the whimsy.

Just be sure not to refer to the items here as Victorian, because you will be politely but firmly corrected. The proprietors prefer to call their collection "turn of the century," suggesting a light-hearted departure from the ornateness of the gilded era. The old greeting cards (original messages still discernible) have a refreshing quality of earthiness, different both from the gooey and sick, sick, sick modern varieties. There are wooden Indian dumbbells, playing cards and old games—no mechanized rocket and missile horrors. Neatly framed advertisements of half a century ago make you wonder whether Madison Avenue really has thought up anything new; a Carter's Little Liver Pill ad has a vividly vicious snake crawling around to call attention to the dangers of "Torpid Liver," much more effective than the elaborate TV medical diagrams.

The two young men who run the store take a dim view of making everything into lamp bases or planters. Their customers are mainly young people nostalgic about the good old days they never knew; maybe the store reminds them of Grandma. The excellent collection of offbeat accessories here can help liven up cleancut contemporary homes. There are no bargains, but lovers of nonsense don't mind paying for it. Oh yes, we inquired also: *Doppelganger* means two of the same likeness or seeing an image of yourself.

Merryvale 3640 Buchanan Street. JO 7-0615. Right at the edge of the Marina Green is a delightful relic of the gaslight era. This is one of the fanciest antique shops in town, but it's the building which is the real wonder. Originally constructed by the San Francisco Gaslight Company as a meter house, the main room has fifty-one by fifty-three-foot dimensions and a thirty-foot ceiling of redwood, now turned mahogany shade. The windows have traditional Georgian arches, and the weathered white walls make a striking background for the elegant collection of the Kent MacDonoughs who run the store. You see an English hunting bowl ($1200) perched on a mahogany highboy. The specialties of the house are English and French eighteen-century antiques correlated with Oriental *objets d'art* of the same period. There is also a tastefully arranged garden, with lots of cherubs amid the plants. This is a place where only those who have reached the rarefied economic perch of serious antique collectors will feel at home. But others will enjoy the magnificent room recalling

the time when men and even gas plants could have homes like
this. Safeway at one time had designs on this location, with a
plan to tear the old building down and put up a supermarket.
One can still shudder at the thought that the Safeway across the
street, decorated with atrocious murals, almost replaced this
classic structure.

Dior Hand-Me-Downs

For another off-the-usual-track shopping session, you can look
in on these stores.

Junior League Next to New Shop   2216 Fillmore Street. JO
7-1628. San Francisco society women have a reputation for
being among the nation's best dressed, but they must send their
cast-offs somewhere else; or maybe times are getting tough for
the idle rich. The collection here is rather stingy, includes some
children's and men's clothing. Worth while mainly if you would
like to take a peek at the Junior Leaguers in their crisp candy-
striped smocks.

Bergman's Next to New Apparel   1395 Sutter Street. PR
5-7440. This is the swank shop among the second-handers.
Really good woolen dresses, with big designer names, and original
prices noted to give you the feeling of a breath-taking bargain.
Tweed suits, carefully cleaned and in good condition. Lots of
cottons and sports clothes. Prices seem rather high for second-
hand status, but you could walk out with a big-name designer
creation for about forty dollars.

Kiddie Trade   622 Shrader Street, near Haight Street. BA
1-7871. An excellent place to pick up a coat or dust-catching
ruffled dress—or to get something back on the garment the child
wore once before shooting up a few inches.

Cloak and Dagger   1224 Polk Street. For men. PR 6-9485.
It's rare to find a tasteful selection of used men's clothing. This
place isn't like a pawnshop rack at all. The raffish air in the name
is reflected in the store. You can pick up a casual tweed at a
moderate price.

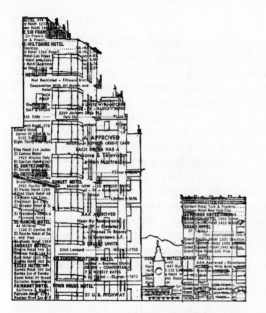

10:
LODGING
FOR THE
NIGHT

SAN FRANCISCO has always been a big hotel town, and it still is. With a couple of million visitors pouring in every year, it has to be. There are innumerable hotels and motels at every price range. These include a substantial number of moderate-priced establishments, and at least some usually have rooms available. If you want to stay at one of the city's big-name luxury hotels, you should make reservations well in advance and be prepared to pay accordingly.

If you want tradition, you ought to know that this too has a price. An older hotel with a colorful past may charge as much as a far newer and more modern hostelry; and it offers a prestige value that cannot be measured in mere dollars. Conversely, a guest at one of the spanking new hotels may run a gauntlet of scornful or at least kidding comment from San Francisco friends.

When the Jack Tar Hotel was being completed early in 1960, it was mocked in newspaper columns as an oversized juke box. To many San Franciscans it seemed that the hotel with its immodest revolving sign, its mobile at the entrance, and its garish decor was little short of a monstrosity. Old residents condescendingly referred to it as a typical Miami Beach hotel or, even more damningly, as a good Los Angeles hotel.

But here is a consoling thought for those who can't afford

tradition or aren't especially interested. They could recall to their pernickety San Francisco friends the treatment once accorded the city's most hallowed hotel. When the Palace was new, the *News Letter,* a satirical literary journal, ridiculed its garishness, its pretentious publicity claims, its newfangled gadgets with comments such as these: "A contract is already given out for the construction of a flume from the Yosemite to conduct the Bridal Veil fall thither, and which it is designed to pour over the east front. . . . The beds are made with Swiss watch springs and stuffed with camel's hair, each single hair costing eleven cents. . . . There are thirty-four elevators in all—four for passengers, ten for baggage and twenty for mixed drinks." Perhaps the Jack Tar will eventually, no less than the Palace, acquire the aura of old age. And even the new motels springing up everywhere may in time win acceptance.

In any case, a room at San Francisco's bigger and better-known first-class hotels is expensive, whether at the historic Sheraton-Palace or the respectably middle-aged St. Francis, Mark Hopkins, and Fairmont, or at the ultramodern Jack Tar. While some singles are occasionally available for ten dollars, be prepared to pay up to fifteen for a single and about twenty-five for a double at the top hotels.

It is a fair assumption that most visitors to the city will be more concerned with comfortable and reasonably priced hotel rooms than with tradition, a location on top of Nob Hill, or the utmost in luxury. Fortunately, there are scores of good hotels with singles starting at about seven dollars and doubles at eleven. Here are a few, conveniently located only a couple of blocks off the busiest downtown area:

Alexander Hamilton   631 O'Farrell Street. GA 4-5500. If you're planning to stay at least a week, you can get weekly rates and apartment suites.

Canterbury   750 Sutter Street. GR 4-6464. Near the swankier shopping section. Quite accommodating to families. Has an outdoor garden restaurant.

Richelieu   Van Ness and Geary. OR 3-4711. Off downtown area. Free drive-in facilities and family rates. Dining room. Now also has a Garden Court Motel.

Whitcomb   Market Street between 8th and 9th. UN 1-9600. Don't be put off by the ghastly green paint on the side. No additional charge for children under fourteen, and families are made welcome. Good and comfortable if not classy. You can usually find a visiting ballet company or baseball team staying here.

Restaurant and bar. Free parking available and close to the Civic Center.

El Cortez 550 Geary Street. PR 5-5000. Good furnishings in the rooms; kitchenettes available should you tire of restaurant food. There is an additional charge for garage service.

Bellevue 505 Geary Street. GR 4-3600. This has a genteel, retiring air, somewhat preferred by an older clientele, but well-maintained. Restaurant.

If the noise and bustle of city life intrigue you, there are a number of hotels to consider. You can often hear the clang of the cable cars and the chatter of the shoppers.

Californian 405 Taylor Street. TU 5-2500. Near bus and air terminal, good coffee shop, no charge for children fourteen or under, but additional charge for parking. No bar.

Fielding Geary and Mason Streets. GA 1-0980. Modern, some dinette apartments, an unpretentious lobby.

Manx Powell and O'Farrell Street. GA 1-7070. All the noise and color of Powell Street can be heard and seen from your windows, but a good, inexpensive place.

Plaza Post and Stockton. SU 1-7200. Right on Union Square and proud of its king-size beds. Good El Prado Restaurant on premises. Family rooms available with charge of $2.50 per extra person.

Stewart 351 Geary Street. SU 1-7800. Lobby usually bustling with teen-agers and action.

Non-status seekers who don't mind simply furnished rooms at sensible prices might consider a few hotels with singles starting at five to six dollars.

Maurice 761 Post Street. OV 3-6040. Where you might get a single at six dollars.

Commodore 825 Sutter Street, near Union Square. TU 5-2464. Coffee shop available.

Victoria Bush and Stockton Streets. EX 2-2540.

Colonial 650 Bush Street. GA 1-4450.

Can you get a good single hotel room in San Francisco for four or five dollars a night? Certainly, as long as you don't mind staying in what might be termed a "less desirable" neighborhood or don't object to an unpretentious exterior. There are a number of clean, respectable, well-maintained hotels in the old "tenderloin" district along Ellis and Eddy and Turk streets, also "on the wrong side of the tracks" south of Market Street. You don't have to be a live-dangerously type to stay at any one of these:

Roosevelt   Jones and Eddy streets. PR 5-6700. Refurnished rooms, family accommodations, and some singles at four dollars; doubles at five.

Governor   180 Turk Street. OR 3-2010.

Columbia   411 O'Farrell Street. OR 3-8517.

Embassy   610 Polk Street. OR 3-1404.

Franciscan   350 Geary Street. DO 2-2200.

Gates   140 Ellis Street. SU 1-0430.

Sutter   Sutter and Kearny streets. SU 1-3060.

Senator   519 Ellis Street. PR 5-0506.

Golden State   Powell and Ellis. GA 1-7264.

Pickwick   Fifth and Mission streets. GA 1-7500.

Motels are becoming as ubiquitous as the freeways and are springing up all over town. You can take your pick of motels in any price range and in any part of the city you prefer—except the immediate downtown area.

There are now several fancy motels with rates fairly close to those of the top hotels.

Del Webb's Towne House   1169 Market Street. UN 3-7100. Garish, brand new, and close to Civic Center.

Holiday Lodge   Van Ness Avenue at Washington Street. PR 6-4469. Heated swimming pool, lanais off the suites, cocktail lounge, restaurant.

Caravan Lodge   601 Eddy Street. PR 6-1380. Swimming pool and good restaurant.

Continental Lodge   Van Ness and Filbert. PR 6-7500. Free breakfast to guests; with swimming pool.

There are also glittering, modern, luxurious motels with good restaurants near the International Airport; they will arrange transportation to town as well as to and from the airport.

Hilton Inn   San Francisco International Airport. JU 9-0770.

Hyatt House Hotel   1333 Old Bayshore Highway, Burlingame. DI 2-7741.

International Inn   326 South Airport Boulevard, South San Francisco. JU 3-9600.

For the rest it's largely a matter of what part of San Francisco you'd like to stay in. They are usually clean, well run, and similar to each other as bathing beauty contestants. Rates for two usually start at eight to ten dollars, for a family of four at about fourteen dollars. Off-season rates are somewhat lower.

The city's motel row is Lombard Street, on Highway 101, right off the Golden Gate Bridge and only about fifteen minutes from the downtown area.

A-1 Motel 1940 Lombard Street. WE 1-1120.

Golden Gate Motel 2555 Lombard Street. WA 1-3105.

Marina Motel 2576 Lombard Street. WA 1-9406.

Presidio Travelodge 2755 Lombard Street. WE 1-8581.

San Francisco Motel 1750 Lombard Street. WA 1-1842.

Motel De Ville 2599 Lombard Street. FI 6-4660.

There are now an increasing number of motels closer to the downtown area, most of them near the Civic Center.

Auditorium Travelodge 790 Ellis Street. PR 5-7612.

Bay Bridge Downtown Motel 966 Harrison Street. EX 7-0657.

Downtown Motel 111 Page Street. MA 1-6006 (four might be accommodated for about twelve dollars).

Flamingo Motel 114 7th Street. MA 1-0701.

Market Street Travelodge 1707 Market Street. MA 1-6775.

Mart Motel 9th and Mission streets. MA 1-3655.

If you like the colorful atmosphere of Fisherman's Wharf and would like to look at the crab boats leaving in the morning, you might try:

Fisherman's Wharf Travelodge 1201 Columbus Avenue. PR 6-7070.

Wharf Motel 2601 Mason Street. OR 3-7411.

Another cluster of motels is along the beach, often less crowded, if you don't mind fog and are invigorated by ocean breezes.

Ocean Park Motel 2690 46th Avenue. OV 1-7268.

Pacifica Motel 1280 Great Highway. SE 1-6644.

Roberts-at-the-Beach Motel 2828 Sloat Boulevard. LO 4-2610.

Seal Rock Inn 48th Avenue and Point Lobos, right near Cliff House. SK 2-8000.

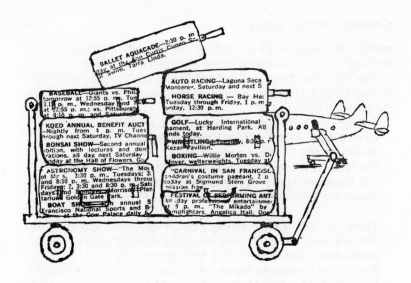

11: CITY ALMANAC

LIKE ALL OTHER tourist attractions, San Francisco is a prisoner of the nation's rigid vacation schedules. The busy months are July and August. Market Street swarms with tourists wearing cameras over their shoulders. Crowds line up at the Market and Powell Street cable-car turntable. The narrow streets of Chinatown and North Beach bulge with autos and pedestrians. Most of the hotels and motels are filled to capacity.

There's nothing wrong with a visit to San Francisco during the summer, and it's a lot better than not coming at all. Among other things, it provides an escape from the sweltering heat of most parts of the country. However, those who must have warm sun will be taking their chances. Besides, the overcrowding of tourist facilities can be a problem.

San Francisco's pleasantest seasons, to the extent the city can be said to have seasons, are the spring and fall. In April and May Golden Gate Park and Union Square blaze with flowers. Mornings and evenings are crisp, and the days warm with sun. There are even occasional heat waves when the mercury pushes close to 80 degrees. For those who really like summer, San Francisco's closest approximation comes in September and October, when the daytime temperature is usually in the 70s and when even the mornings and nights are relatively gentle.

The city's business interests and tourist agencies are, of course, anxious to spread the visitor business over the entire year. Public festivals and cultural events have been deliberately staggered to cut across all seasons. These efforts, while running counter to tradition and habit, are actually in the best interests both of the city and its visitors. The city's attractions are bright the year round.

Calendar of Events

There is almost always a parade or a festival or a gala occasion of some kind in San Francisco. Scores of national groups maintain their own religious and national observances, and cultural and civic events add to a clutter of colorful annuals. Dates vary somewhat from year to year, and you'll have to watch the weekly calendars in the Sunday *Chronicle* and *Examiner* for exact details.

January

The San Francisco Symphony Orchestra all month at the Opera House.

The annual drawing, print, and transparent watercolor exhibition of the San Francisco Art Association at the San Francisco Museum of Art.

Ceremonies by local Scots in honor of Robert Burns' birthday on the Sunday nearest January 26 in Golden Gate Park.

Horse racing at Bay Meadows in San Mateo.

Professional and some college basketball at the Cow Palace. College basketball at the University of San Francisco and at the University of California in Berkeley.

February

Chinese New Year celebrated the first day of the new moon after the sun enters the sign of Aquarius, usually in February but sometimes at the end of January.

Symphony concerts at the Opera House.

Annual exhibition at the De Young Museum by the Society of Western Artists, upholders of traditional realism and landscape painting.

Boxing matches, as well as basketball, at the Cow Palace.

March

St. Patrick's Day observed on the Sunday nearest March 17 with a parade up Market Street and High Mass at St. Mary's Cathedral (Van Ness Avenue at O'Farrell Street).

San Francisco Ballet Company.

Painting and sculpture show of the San Francisco Art Association at the San Francisco Museum of Art.

Horse racing at Bay Meadows.

April

A big month for flower-lovers. Cherry blossoms in the Japanese Tea Garden usually come out early in the month. Macy's has a flower show. Maiden Lane shops stage an open-air festival, giving away free daffodils. Rhododendrons bloom brightly in Union Square and Golden Gate Park.

Thousands of Christians of all denominations get up before dawn for the Easter sunrise services on top of Mount Davidson, the city's steepest hill.

Folk- and square-dance festival at Civic Auditorium.

Society folk and symphony-lovers turn out en masse for big fund-raising Black and White Symphony Ball.

Polo games at the Polo Stadium in Golden Gate Park, continuing through the summer, every Sunday at 12:30 P.M.

College track and field events at the University of California at Berkeley and Stanford University at Palo Alto.

For many San Franciscans this is the month the mayor throws out the first ball at Candlestick Park and they begin their trek to the ball park full of hope and confidence in the Giants.

May

Spring opera at reduced prices at the Opera House, under the auspices of the San Francisco Opera Association.

Formal opening of the yachting season the first Sunday in the month at Yacht Harbor. A major event is the El Toro race, a keen competition between tiny eight-foot sailboats.

Golden Gate World Trade Week, sponsored by the World Trade Association of the San Francisco Chamber of Commerce, with ceremonies in Union Square crowning a "Miss World Trade Week" and a series of lunches, dinners, and an International Ball.

Annual mountain play at the spectacular natural amphitheater at Mount Tamalpais.

Memorial Day Parade.

June

The Pollack Brothers circus comes to San Francisco for a brief run at the Civic Auditorium.

Midsummer Music Festival at Sigmund Stern Grove starting in

June and continuing through August. Dance performances, light opera, and classical music in a superb setting.

Colorful yacht races that can be observed from anywhere on the Marina every week end out of San Francisco Yacht Harbor.

July

Symphony Pop Concerts at Civic Auditorium all July and August.

Band concerts every Sunday at 2 P.M. during July and August at the Music Concourse in Golden Gate Park.

An all-day festival at the Marina Green on the Sunday of the July Fourth week end, with a folk-dance program, a band concert, and fog-defying fireworks.

Bastille Day celebration in Golden Gate Park on the Sunday nearest July 14. The local French persist in the quaint and strikingly inappropriate custom of crowning a Bastille Day Queen.

Union Square Fashion Shows during lunch hours; working girls and society matrons rub elbows as they watch the latest styles.

August

Ringling Brothers Circus at the Cow Palace.

Musical events continue, with Pop Concerts at the Civic Auditorium, Midsummer Festival at Sigmund Stern Grove, and band concerts in Golden Gate Park.

Preseason professional football games at Kezar Stadium.

September

Big open-air Art Festival, held in recent years at Civic Center Plaza, with the participation of hundreds of local artists and craftsmen. Always an exciting event, although the quality of the work varies wildly.

Celebration in mid-September at City Hall of Mexican Independence Day; folk dances, speeches, and big attendance from local Mexican community.

The opera season opens, with everybody who is anybody turning out and with all the ladies wearing their most elaborate gowns and jewels.

The San Francisco 49ers pull hysterical crowds to Kezar Stadium as the professional football season starts.

October

Double Ten parade in Chinatown on October 10 celebrates the overthrow of the Manchu dynasty.

On the Sunday nearest October 12 San Francisco Italians parade and celebrate Columbus Day.

Blessing of the crab fleet on the first Sunday after October 1, with Italian fishermen participating in a procession from the Church of Saint Peter and Saint Paul in North Beach to Fisherman's Wharf.

Fol de Rol Ball at Civic Auditorium, a major fund-raiser for the opera, is the season's top social event.

November

The San Francisco Film Festival, a relative newcomer, has been unveiling major foreign films, among them India's *Pather Panchali,* Britain's *The Mouse that Roared,* and the Soviet Union's *Ballad of a Soldier.*

Horse racing opens at Golden Gate Fields in Albany in the East Bay.

The Big Game between Cal and Stanford draws tens of thousands of fanatical fans in a rivalry as fierce and almost as traditional as the Harvard-Yale contest.

December

San Francisco Symphony concerts at the Opera House.

California Water Color Society show at the Palace of the Legion of Honor in Lincoln Park (see p. 144).

Christmas carols by the Grace Cathedral Choir, at Grace Cathedral (California and Taylor streets).

Christmas music by the San Francisco Municipal Chorus at the Palace of the Legion of Honor.

Children's Christmas program at Union Square (see p. 172).

Christmas program by the San Francisco Ballet at the Opera House.

The city is decked with lights. The boats at Yacht Harbor glitter, and so do the homes in residential districts west of Twin Peaks.

The football season, both professional and collegiate, winds up. The Shrine benefit East-West football game is played in Kezar Stadium.

Thousands of San Franciscans start their New Year's Eve celebrating by eating in Chinatown and then walking the crowded streets, while round-faced mischievous-seeming Chinese youngsters pelt them with confetti.

Clothes and the Man (or Woman)

While most San Francisco men rarely wear topcoats, this is one native custom the tourist would be wise to honor in the breach. A light topcoat is really a must for visitors, men or women, particularly in the evening. Don't be deceived by a balmy day; it may be quite nippy by nightfall. It is also a good idea to take along a raincoat. Even in the summer when the statistics show it rarely rains, San Francisco's low mist is low enough at night to qualify as a drizzle elsewhere. A light waterproofed topcoat can serve a double purpose for men. Neither men nor women need bother with special lightweight summer clothes. You won't wear them enough to make it worth while. On warm days women will find a cotton dress useful, but a sleeveless sundress will probably never be unpacked.

Women would do well to take along a woolen suit and a wool dress. These are always in order in San Francisco. So is a mink stole, if you have one, but a woolen one will do very nicely. The city's women favor a basic black costume for evening wear—black dress with pearls. Count Marco, a local columnist who gives the ladies advice on love, manners, and dress he claims to have learned from "my aunt, the Contessa," has waged unrelenting war against basic black, thus far without success.

Formal evening clothes are hardly necessary unless you expect to attend opening night at the opera or mix in high society. A dark suit for men and a cocktail or dinner dress for women are adequate enough for the restaurant and night-club circuit. Anything fancier might make you feel conspicuous. On the other hand, excessive informality is also considered *outré* in San Francisco. Ladies just don't go around in slacks. Men don't wear aloha shirts. A tie is required in some restaurants. But properly subdued sport shirts and jackets are quite all right for Sunday strolling on the Marina or in Golden Gate Park.

Advice to the Lovelorn

Here are a few hints for visitors who fall in love with San Francisco and want to take on the protective coloration of the natives:

Don't wander around aimlessly on Market Street looking for the action. There isn't any, or hardly any that is worth while. It just isn't the place to find good restaurants and night clubs; even interesting bars are scarce.

Escape the stigma of the tourist by leaving your camera behind —at least part of the time.

Take your time. Walk more slowly than is customary in New York or Chicago. Don't run for buses and streetcars.

Don't call the city *Frisco*. Actually, there are plenty of old-timers, particularly seamen and waterfront characters, who still do. But a tourist is likely to get dirty looks by trying to show excessive familiarity with San Francisco by giving it what he mistakenly thinks is its nickname.

Take in an opera, a symphony, a performance at one of the little theaters or an art show if you would really feel like a San Franciscan who belongs.

The Informed Tourist

Visitors to San Francisco can save a lot of time and trouble by getting in advance information that will enable them to plan their schedule.

The San Francisco Chamber of Commerce (333 Pine Street; EX 2-4511) maintains the best general information service, including up-to-date listings of events, brochures on places to see, restaurants, hotels, etc. On request the Chamber will mail a San Francisco kit which includes much of this material.

Californians Inc. (703 Market Street; DO 2-0561) has available brochures on the city as well as lists of restaurants and hotels, although its major activity is publicizing San Francisco through newspaper and magazine ads.

San Francisco Visitors and Convention Bureau (Civic Auditorium; MA 1-0652) is the organization to contact for convention information, schedules, and arrangements.

Navigation Aids

It isn't easy to get lost in San Francisco, although it has been done. Directions are simple to work out without the help of a compass or long experience as a scoutmaster. The Ferry Building, the Bay, and the Oakland Bridge are all east. Twin Peaks and the ocean are west. The Golden Gate Bridge and the Marin Hills are north, leaving only the south toward the Mission district and the Peninsula suburbs.

San Francisco has an unmistakable main street which divides the city. Slanting off Market Street toward the north are most of the familiar downtown streets—Grant Avenue, Stockton Street, Powell Street. Slanting south are the numbered streets. North of the wide diagonal of Market Street are most of the downtown hotels. South is the old Mission district.

Public transportation isn't too bad and is handier than driving in the downtown area; no parking problems. If you are taking streetcars and buses, the city-owned **Municipal Railway** (949 Presidio Avenue; FI 6-5656) maintains an excellent information service. Just phone, say where you are and where you want to go, and you'll get a clear, courteous answer. You can also get on request a little brochure, *Tours of Discovery,* which doesn't quite live up to the title but does tell you where all the city buses and streetcars go.

Maps of the city are, of course, available at all gas stations, and street maps may be purchased at newsstands. A detailed map with points of interest indicated and described is available free of charge from the Chamber of Commerce. AAA members may obtain a tour map of San Francisco as well as helpful information on Bay Area tours from **The California State Automobile Association** (150 Van Ness Avenue; MA 1-2141).

A car is almost indispensable for serious sightseeing, especially for those who want to get a sense of the Bay Area as a whole. If you have a car, try to use it sparingly. Driving through narrow, crowded Grant Avenue in Chinatown can be one of the world's most frustrating experiences. Besides, there are whole areas of the city that can be savored only if you walk around and take your time.

Drivers should be cautioned to have brakes checked frequently and to take hills in low gear. Park in gear with front wheels curbed. On steep hills use blocks. Improperly parked cars have an annoying habit of running away. Towaway warning signs are to be taken seriously. The police will have your car towed at your expense—and fine you in addition.

If you don't have a car available and can't impose on friends, one alternative is to take Gray Line tours in and around the city (see pp. 212–13). Tours start at about three dollars per person, with reduced rates for children.

A family or group that can afford it and really wants to get around would do well to rent a car. Rates start at seven dollars a day and forty dollars a week, plus a minimum of eight cents per mile. Figure on double these rates if you must have a Cadillac convertible. Rental agencies include:

Hertz   433 Mason Street. OR 3-4666.

Avis   675 Post Street. PR 5-3313.

Barrett   571 Post Street. GR 4-5300.

Conducted Tour

Gray Line Tour 1 $3.65 per person. Tour offered three times a day year round, more frequently during the summer. Phone YU 6-4000 for exact schedules. Terminal at 44 Fourth Street, right off Market. This tour gives a good bird's-eye view of the city in about three to four hours; just ignore the guide's folksy approach and corny cracks. (Recommended as against the Night Life, Chinatown after Dark, and Fisherman's Wharf Tours. You can enjoy these aspects of life more adequately on your own. Being herded in and out of night clubs for a fast drink is not one of the city's more exquisite pleasures.)

Taking this tour is like watching a tennis match; you are constantly turning your head to keep up with the guide's comments. You speed past Civic Center, learning that the City Hall dome is higher than that of the Capitol in Washington; past Van Ness Avenue, which you discover is the "old fire line" where the fire after the 1906 earthquake was stopped, and stop to look at the Mission Dolores. On some points the guide is out of date. He tells you that San Francisco's Carpenter's Gothic is probably "the world's worst architecture," ignoring the current vogue for the city's Victorian gingerbread. You drive up Twin Peaks, with due time allotted for camera fiends. You are supposed to see the view. But the guide is ready for all emergencies. He whips out picture post cards, sold in packets for fifty cents, so you can have a record of what you couldn't see through the fog. You are driven through St. Francis Wood to see how the upper half lives; once described by *Life* magazine as a typical American suburb, this area is actually closer to an exclusive London residence park.

There is a drive through Golden Gate Park, one of the city's marvels fashioned by John McLaren out of windy sand dunes. You are thoughtfully introduced to statues of Schiller, Goethe, Cervantes, and local celebrities—all erected in defiance of McLaren's attempt to keep statuary out of the Park. You do get a sense of the variety of landscaping and activity in the Park and wind up at Cliff House, where the Gray Line gives you thirty minutes to view the sea lions, buy souvenirs and snacks, and stretch your legs. After a drive through residential areas you breeze through the Presidio military reservation, where you view fleetingly the sand dunes and the glinting water of the Bay, and wind up under the Golden Gate Bridge, where you can examine close up what is probably at the same time both the most beautiful structure and the most remarkable engineering feat in the San Francisco area. You glide

past views of Alcatraz, along the Marina, and then to motel row
on Lombard where you are obligingly let off at your motel, or you
can continue downtown to the terminal.

Auto Tours

49 Mile Drive A scenic, historic, business-district block-
buster of a tour for sightseers with their own cars, worked out by
the **Down Town Association of San Francisco.** Copies of the tour
map with notes on what you see available free from the Association, 57 Post Street; DO 2-7842. This tour will take at least four
hours if you drive steadily and make only a few stops. It includes
everything—the Civic Center, the downtown shopping and financial
district, Chinatown, Telegraph Hill, a waterfront drive along the
Marina and into the Presidio, through Lincoln Park, out to the
Great Highway along the ocean, past miles of suburbs, to the Zoo,
Golden Gate Park, Twin Peaks, the Mint, Mission Dolores, even
a stretch of freeway and industrial district. In moderation, this drive
can be fun. If there are children along, it can be converted into a
"follow the arrow" game. In keeping with a maritime city, there
are sea-gull markers instead of arrows, and they are reasonably
simple to follow. But even the most seasoned traveler would pall if
the route were followed to the letter. A suggested procedure is to
omit certain sections of the drive—particularly the Civic Center,
downtown shopping and financial districts and Chinatown, which
are better covered by foot—and to break up the rest of the drive
in three parts:

Edge-of-the-Water-Drive Pick up the sea-gull markers at Grant
and Lombard at the foot of Telegraph Hill and drive to Fisherman's Wharf and Aquatic Park, stopping along the way. Then
follow the route along the bright green lawns of the Marina along
the Bay, the Yacht Harbor and into the Presidio, the big government military post. Here you will pass an old Spanish adobe
building dating back to 1776, now part of the officers' club, and you
will drive along winding roads past gaunt eucalyptus trees, sandy
hills, glinting glimpses of bay and a bold view of the Golden Gate
Bridge.

A short detour inside the Presidio (keep going on Lincoln
Boulevard until you see a gate with a bright Motor Pool sign, then
turn right) will take you to **Fort Point,** the tip of the San Francisco
peninsula and one of the city's lesser known glories. Here at the
entrance to the Bay once stood a Spanish fort, and here still stands
an old red-brick Army fort built in 1853. The San Francisco end of
the Golden Gate Bridge is anchored to the point with a massive

concrete pillar, and you can almost touch the red lace network of cable and girder above. To the right you see the city; straight ahead the narrow channel between ocean and Bay, and to the left the endless Pacific. The waves are choppy here, but an old sea wall has endured more than a hundred years. Many fishermen come here looking for bass. On the rocks are pink and orange starfish. This is a quiet but spectacular place.

Meanwhile, back on the trail, the sea-gull markers will take you to Lincoln Park near the Palace of the Legion of Honor. Next are Cliff House and Seal Rocks, where you can stop a while and then quit or take the Great Highway south along the ocean. At this point you can call it a day. Skip the part of the drive past the Park Merced and Stonestown apartment and shopping areas.

Park Tour Save for a separate day a drive through Golden Gate Park and the Zoo suggested on the tour map; but you can reverse the directions, taking in the Park first (see p. 159). If you stay in the city any length of time you will want to make several trips to the Park, and a relatively quick exploratory drive to begin with won't hurt.

Hills and History You can pick up the markers at the Stanyan Avenue end of Golden Gate Park and drive up Twin Peaks, then continue past Buena Vista Heights, where you will see tile-roofed houses on some of the city's steepest streets and an untamed little park with a sweeping view on top of the hill. This might be a good opportunity to take in Mission Dolores, which deserves a leisurely tour rather than a quick stop (see p. 28).

Tour by Water

Harbor Tours, Inc. Pier 45, Fishermen's Wharf. DO 2-5414. One-hour tour, $1.50, mainly the city skyline and glimpses of the two bridges. Two-hour cruise, $3, a considerably broader expanse of bay. Reduced rates for children on both tours. There are daily trips, but frequency depends on season. Call for exact schedules. If you have a friend with a sailboat or a motor launch, you can skip this. Otherwise, it is a must. In the old days you could see the city from the Bay any time you wanted to from a ferry. Now you have to take one of these sleek excursion boats. The two-hour cruise is definitely recommended.

There is no other way to get the same view of the city cool and airy between the perfect frame of the two bridges, or the sense of the grace of these giant structures, or the feel of San Francisco as a narrow peninsula surrounded by the pulsing waters of ocean and

Bay, or the sudden blast of cold air through the Golden Gate that creates fog and fights off heat. The only thing you see a bit too much of is Alcatraz; the grim fortress does not improve on closer acquaintance. The two-hour trip takes you past Sausalito, Belvedere, Tiburon, towns with tiered houses perched precariously on hills and which acquire from a distance the timelessness of Mediterranean villages.

Returning to the pier, you see close up Yerba Buena Island, tunneled by the connecting link between the two spans of the Bay Bridge; man-made Treasure Island, which is now a Navy training base; the cities of Oakland and Berkeley against the East Bay Hills; the docks busy with tugs and freighters and luxury liners; and the proud Ferry Building watching over the port.

A Gallery of Views

Mt. Olympus   17th and Clayton Streets. Climb the stairs off 17th Street, or take the No. 43 bus at 14th and Market streets to Upper Terrace and then walk up this quiet residential street to the top of the hill. Although somewhat hard to reach, this 570-foot hill smack in the center of the city, with a panoramic view in every direction, is the favorite of many San Franciscans. Why the hill is called Mt. Olympus is open to dispute. You can take the obvious explanation that from its summit unfolds a sight fit for the gods. Or you can accept the local legend that it was named for a crippled Irish milk-peddler who served the neighborhood and was known as "Old Limpus." Most people who come here ignore this issue and just refer to the windy height as Statue Hill after a statue of a woman with a sword that once stood here on a thirty-foot pedestal. The figure of the lady was removed after it disintegrated gradually but not gracefully; the pedestal remains. Once you get here and start looking around the question of nomenclature becomes quite unimportant.

California Palace of the Legion of Honor   Lincoln Park in the extreme northwest corner of the city. A No. 2 Clement bus which you can catch downtown on Sutter Street will get you to Clement Street and 33rd Avenue at the edge of the park and a brisk walk to the grandiosely named museum. You should take this one in even if you aren't interested in the museum's collection of Old Masters or even if you don't appreciate eighteenth-century French architecture represented by this classic pile, which is approached through a Roman arch and double rows of Corinthian columns. Here you are near the western end of the Golden Gate. From the walks around the museum, or even closer from the park across the golf course, you can see Land's End where the narrow gorge becomes ocean.

Top of the Mark   Mark Hopkins Hotel, California and Mason streets. California Street cable car from lower Market Street, or Powell Street cable car from Market and Powell. Or just walk up California or Powell. Some crotchety old-timers say they have never been to the Top of the Mark, but their number is few indeed. Most San Franciscans secretly enjoy taking visiting friends to one of the city's best-known bars with a justly celebrated view. Try going week days before the cocktail hour to avoid the crowds. Drinks are not exorbitantly priced, and they aren't pushed. But don't just sit there guzzling. Take highball in hand and walk around the glass-encased tower to see the city stretch out before you on three sides, and on the fourth side the ocean.

Coit Tower   Top of Telegraph Hill. Take the No. 39 bus at Columbus and Union at Washington Square. Or follow the signs and walk. Try to avoid driving. The long line of cars clogging tiny Pioneer Park at the top of the hill makes it almost impossible to stop and look around at the views of the Golden Gate and the Bay or to savor Telegraph Hill with its mixture of brightly painted, cliff-hanging little homes, rows of old flats, and new modernistic apartment houses. If you want a more panoramic view, climb up the stairs to the top of the tower or take the elevator. (The tower is open daily 10 A.M. to 4 P.M., Saturday and Sunday to 5:30 P.M. Elevator service is twenty-five cents per person.) Walking will allow you to examine the rather grim Depression-day murals executed by WPA artists. Coit Tower is a monument to one of San Francisco's early characters, Lillie Hitchcock Coit, who started running after fire engines when she was ten years old and never quite stopped. She attached herself to Knickerbocker Engine Company No. 5 and for the rest of her long life continued to attend its annual banquets in a fireman's red shirt and helmet. A smoker, a hard-riding horsewoman, a sharp poker-player, crack rifle shot, and devotee of other unladylike pursuits, Lillie somehow remained in the bosom of San Francisco society. When she died in 1929 she left $50,000 for a monument to her beloved firemen, which you can see in Washington Square while waiting for your bus—and $100,000 which was used for the once-white, now graying, fluted column which bears her name.

Twin Peaks   Drive up Market Street to Twin Peaks Boulevard. The No. 37 Corbett bus from Castro and Market will take you part-way up the slope of the hill. Twin Peaks is one reason San

Franciscans rarely feel encased in a concrete cage. Through accident or whim, Market Street aims straight at this double summit. From the drabness and bustle of the street you can always look up and see the hills gay and green on a sunny day or dark and mysterious in the fog or at twilight. From the top of Twin Peaks you get one of the most magnificent views not only of the city but of a fairly sizable chunk of the Bay Area. The Indians had a legend that these were once man and wife. But they quarreled and the Great Spirit in anger smote them apart. The romantic Spaniards called the Hills *Los Pechos de la Choca,* "The Breasts of the Indian Maiden." The reference was supposedly to the lovely and virtuous daughter of a local chief. The name will seem apt to anyone looking up to Twin Peaks from the heart of the city.

Vista Point Take first turnoff from Golden Gate Bridge on Marin side. You may want to combine this view of the city and of the Golden Gate with other trips into Marin County (see p. 219). But after seeing the Marin hills and the Golden Gate from the San Francisco side, you may want to reverse the view and look at San Francisco from the north. Even the slight distance across the Golden Gate lends the enchantment of fog and haze which makes the view of the city from almost anywhere in Marin County an endless delight.

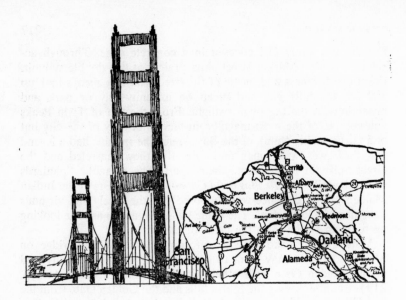

12: BAY AREA TOUR

ONE OF San Francisco's most enduring joys is leaving it—briefly. There is always some new and different and inviting place to go in the Bay Area or in outlying Northern California. It is possible to spend a lifetime of week-end exploration without exhausting the possibilities. But to live in the city without at least trying to cover the area on week ends is not to be a San Franciscan at all. And to visit San Francisco without sampling the surrounding pleasures is not really to visit San Francisco.

Even during the working week, San Franciscans have an intuitive sense of the area beyond. That is why they can ignore as irrelevant the statistics that prove the city rivals Manhattan in density of population, why they can dismiss as misleading the maps that show San Francisco hemmed in on the tip of a narrow peninsula. They have only to look out toward the ocean or Mount Diablo to the east or Mount Tamalpais to the north to get, without particularly thinking about it, a sense of space and beauty. They know that within easy reach of a short automobile drive are winding roads and pleasant small towns, parks and beaches, forests and mountains that man has not yet succeeded in ruining.

Every week end all year long San Franciscans in the tens of thousands visit the area around on short and long trips. And the

best advice to visitors is to do likewise. Now it is possible without a
lot of trouble to take a Greyhound bus north into Marin or south
toward the peninsula or a Key System bus east to Berkeley and
Oakland. It is also possible to take Gray Line tours in almost every
direction. Many visitors get around this way, and manage to see
quite a bit. It is a lot better than not doing it at all. But you can't
really browse and linger and explore without a car. If you are
autoless and brash enough, you should impose on friends by bor-
rowing their car or getting them to drive you around. If you have
enough money, you should rent one.

Northern California auto maps are available from any gas station. You can get more detailed information and brochures from:

California State Chamber of Commerce   350 Bush Street. EX
2-1400.

California State Automobile Association   150 Van Ness Avenue. MA 1-2141.

Californians Inc.   703 Market Street. DO 2-0561.

Jaunts for a Day

Marvelous Marin   That's what the Chamber of Commerce calls
Marin County, and it really is. There is hardly a more beautiful
drive than north on US 101 across the Golden Gate Bridge into
Marin; that is, if you don't stay on the highway. Some Marin builders and developers have displayed remarkable ingenuity in failing
to take advantage of the natural surroundings, and the Bay shore
and the hills are scarred by atrocious suburban tracts. But much of
Marin is still untamed or at least rural rather than suburban. All of
it somehow remains beautiful, and most of it is charming. It is
warm and sunny, and once you are over the bridge the fog miraculously disappears.

The old-timers tell you that **Sausalito** (about twenty minutes
from San Francisco off 101) was just a fishing and yachting village
and a small artists' colony before World War II—and that then
came the great Marin shipyards and the bustle of war workers and
building and expansion, and after that the tourists from San Francisco and from all over. They say it has never been the same since
and that they don't venture out of their homes on week ends. But
even if you know all that you forget it every time you see Sausalito
nestled in an arm of the Bay with a view of the city white in fog
and barren hilly Angel Island, the masts of the boats in the Yacht
Harbor and the little town climbing steeply up the hills from the
water. You still think you are in a Mediterranean fishing village.

You can have a drink and listen to jazz right out on the

water at the **Trident,** a new night club opened by the Kingston Trio. From this spot you have a fine view of the Bay and of San Francisco sparkling and clear in the night. Walk a couple of blocks along the waterfront to the **Trade Fair,** an international bazaar on one of the historic ferries, the former Southern Pacific steamer *Berkeley.* The selection is overwhelming, the prices somewhat on the high side. However, if you don't like shopping you can just sit on a bench or a barrel at the open end of the old ferry and look at the bridge and the city. You can stop in at **The Tides,** a combination coffee shop and bookstore, with emphasis on highbrow paperback titles, or you can loiter at the **Village Fair,** a cluster of little art and gift shops against the hill; there is a pleasant little coffee shop—with a view, of course, on the second floor. Or if you prefer sailing yachts and motor cruisers simply walk along the dock and do your window-shopping that way, picking the boat of your preference.

Belvedere and **Tiburon** (a few miles from Sausalito off 101) were also just villages a few years ago. Now the Tiburon peninsula, a hilly spit of land east of Sausalito, is a swank suburbia. There are old houses hanging on top of Belvedere Island—not really an island—and modern, expensive houses on the Belvedere Lagoon below, where a home is a combination yacht dock and goldfish bowl. But Tiburon's main street retains a village atmosphere, with a few older bars and hangouts surviving among brightly antiqued new shops and cafés. Stop in at **Sam's Anchor Cafe,** which has resisted both modernization and phony Victorian decor and is still a pleasant restaurant and bar overlooking the water. Sam's Dock, where yachtsmen really pull up for a drink and a salad or sandwich, is a delightful place to while away an afternoon. It is on Raccoon Strait facing Angel Island and has a splendid view of the city and of the yachts and the freighters and the oil tankers in the Bay.

This is one side of Marin, and a pleasant enough one. But to the west and north lies another Marin, almost untouched by the burgeoning suburbia and the new towns springing up and old ones doubling and tripling between each census. From all over Marin you see Mount Tamalpais; its undulating shape reminded the Indians of a sleeping maiden, and that was what they called it. At the base of the mountain lies **Muir Woods National Monument** (you hit the turnoff from 101 past Sausalito), dedicated to John Muir, the California naturalist and conservationist who tramped all the mountains and valleys of the state. Here is a grove of great

California redwoods; some of them were scarred by a fire a couple
of hundred years ago, only an incident for trees two thousand years
old. Theodore Roosevelt and Gifford Pinchot and other conservationist big guns helped save this grove from destruction by a water
company. Although this is an ever-popular spot for visitors, there
is enough space for the solitude of a quiet walk.

While San Franciscans for some reason rarely visit Muir Woods
unless they have out-of-town guests, many do drive frequently to
Mount Tamalpais (just follow the signs when you turn off 101).
This is where Sierra Club hikers limber up on Sunday mornings for
more serious summer mountain-climbing by taking the steep fire
trail to the 2600-foot summit. You can drive a winding road to the
top. Or you can compromise with a relatively gentle two-mile walk
from the entrance of the park to Bootjack Camp, where you can
stop for a picnic lunch or a cigarette. Mount Tamalpais is protected by a 960-acre state park from commercial exploitation. It
offers overnight campsites, secluded walks on narrow trails, and a
sudden refuge only about forty minutes from the city.

(*Note*. You can break up this Marin tour for two afternoon or
morning trips, doing Sausalito and Tiburon on one, then Muir
Woods and Mount Tamalpais. If you try it all on one day, an extended walk on Tamalpais might be overdoing it.)

The East Bay If you want to regain your lost youth, one
harmless way to try is to visit the **University of California** campus
at Berkeley, and thousands of old Cal grads in San Francisco
keep doing it all the time. (Turn off at University Avenue from
the Eastshore freeway after you cross the bridge.) When you
walk around the campus, stop at the new modern and spacious
Student Center (Bancroft Way and Telegraph Avenue) or linger
at the Campanile Tower, a university landmark for almost fifty
years. You can drop in at International House, a center for
students from all over the world with emphasis on Asia, and at
the university library, one of the best in the country. You won't
see the cyclotron (which isn't on exhibit) and you won't meet
Cal's horde of Nobel Prize winners. But at least you will get a
whiff of a great university and a sense of a new generation of
students. You can take in the off-campus student centers by
walking south on Telegraph Avenue, the main street for the
university crowd. There are big bookstores along the way, coffee
houses frequented by students, handsome gift shops, and a lively
twin of art film houses, the **Studio** and the **Cinema Guild** (see
p. 155). You can also browse at the **Sather Gate Book Shop** (2335

Telegraph) or at **UC Corner** (2350 Telegraph), a combination bookshop and general store. Have a café espresso or take in a movie and make believe you are one of the students.

The hilly eastern part of Berkeley, dominated by Cal's more than twenty thousand students and its vast faculty, still has the atmosphere of a university town. The teaching staff and other professional people live up in the hills, and a drive up the rambling roads will give you a sense of a pleasant and generally unpretentious suburbia as well as some sweeping views of San Francisco and the Bay. But Berkeley is also a factory town, as you can see driving along the Eastshore freeway. The flat western part of the city has a large working-class and Negro population, and this is Berkeley's link with the other cities and towns of the generally industrial East Bay area.

Oakland used to be called San Francisco's bedroom. Now it is almost equally true that San Francisco is Oakland's bedroom. There is heavy commuting both ways. The East Bay is more than a bedroom. It is also a workshop for the Bay Area. Oakland, the biggest East Bay city with a population of over 350,000, has always remained in the shadow of San Francisco and has never developed a colorful or distinctive personality of its own. But Lake Merritt (off MacArthur Boulevard) has been turned into an attractive recreation area, surrounded by some handsome modern buildings, notably the new Kaiser headquarters. **Children's Fairyland** (see p. 163) in **Lakeside Park** is far superior to anything of the kind in San Francisco, and families with children will find a visit to the park rewarding. There are also several good regional parks in the East Bay. **Tilden Park** (follow signs off University Avenue in Berkeley) has good facilities for fishing, swimming, tennis, boating, and picnicking. It even has a trout farm where any child is virtually guaranteed a couple of fish. If you want to get a sweeping view of the Bay Area, you can drive twenty miles east of Oakland up to **Mount Diablo,** where there is a state park on the slopes of a 4000-foot mountain.

A visit to **Jack London Square** (at foot of Broadway in Oakland) is optional. The square boasts a bust of London, but is otherwise strictly commercial with a Jack London Yacht Sales Company and a Sea Wolf Restaurant. Although a couple of the restaurants have some London photographs, there is no museum devoted to Oakland's greatest writer and there is no place on the square you can even buy one of his books. A block off the square is the **First and Last Chance Saloon** (50 Webster Street) where London wrote, or studied the dictionary, on the round table in the corner. Johnny Heinold, the proprietor, had the shrewd business sense to leave everything just the way it was in London's time. The only additions are dust, dirt, and thousands of calling cards on the ceiling. While having a beer you can look through chicken wire and cobwebs at some faded London photographs.

(*Note.* One possibility is what AAA calls a grand circle tour of the three Bay bridges. You can drive first across the San Francisco–Oakland Bridge, north along the freeway to the Richmond–San Rafael Bridge, and then back on the Golden Gate Bridge to San Francisco. This is a drive of about fifty miles and you can do it in a few hours even with a couple of stops along the way. But it isn't recommended unless your time in San Francisco is extremely limited.)

The Peninsula You won't really have the feel of San Francisco unless you have been in its major suburbia, "The Peninsula," a catch-all referring to the almost continuous string of cities and towns to the south on the thirty-two-mile peninsula of which San Francisco is the northern tip. You can get there quickly enough on the Bayshore Freeway past Candlestick Park, the International Airport, and factories and jerry-built tract homes. All along the freeway to San Jose you see signs of the electronics and other factories that have sprung up all over the peninsula and the Santa Clara Valley to the south, which only a few years ago was devoted chiefly to prune and apricot orchards. You can drive more slowly on El Camino Real, the old "King's Highway" of Spanish times, which takes you right through suburban Millbrae, Burlingame, San Mateo, Redwood City, Menlo Park, Palo Alto. Closer to the freeway are the cheaper, less expensive homes of the new industrial communities. On the fringes of the Camino Real are the more expensive homes and estates in Hillsborough, Menlo Park, and Atherton.

If you don't have time for expensive exploration, your best bet is Palo Alto. Stop off at **Stanford University,** the western equivalent of the Ivy League, substituting palm trees and Moorish-Spanish architecture for the East's Gothic campuses. Stanford now has the new modern buildings of the medical center and is dominated by the Hoover Library tower. You can see suburbia in action by driving a few blocks farther on the Camino Real and making a left turn to the **Town and Country Shopping Center,** a pseudo-rustic cluster of shops featuring all the smart things to buy, from Hispano-Suiza sports cars to the latest fashions and the newest and most intellectual paperbacks. If the kids are along and need to be bribed or soothed, there is a **Stickney's** restaurant here featuring gargantuan hamburgers and excellent barbecued meats. For more adult fare, there are several fine eating places on El Camino Real's restaurant strip. **Charm** (2821 El Camino in Redwood City) is one of the few Northern California restaurants offering Northern Chinese food, and for French food try **L'Omelette** (4170 El Camino in Palo Alto). To sample the peninsula's intellectual atmosphere, drop in at **Kepler's Books** (825 El Camino in Menlo Park) which features a large selection of good paperbacks, a coffee shop, and discussion meetings on such controversial topics as capital punishment and the House Un-American Activities Committee.

If you're not in a hurry, the most enjoyable way to get down the peninsula is to take the **Skyline Drive** (State Highway 5), which starts at the end of the Great Highway past San Francisco's beaches and Fleishhacker Zoo. This is country road almost all the way along the coast hills and ridges past wooded mountain lakes only a few miles from the city. You can turn east at any point to connect with any of the peninsula cities or you can continue to connecting roads with the San Mateo County Memorial Park or the Portola State Park or, farther along, the Big Basin State Park, all with fine groves of redwoods. This route will also take you to the sandy beaches in the Santa Cruz area, about seventy-five miles south of San Francisco.

Along the Coast You can get some idea of the rugged Northern California coast with a relatively short drive either north or south of San Francisco on S 1, a road that challenges the driver with endless hairpin curves. Don't try to average more than thirty miles an hour. If you go south, start the same way as on the Skyline Drive, taking the coast road where it veers to the right. In only a few miles, although it seems more, you're driving at the edge of the jagged rocks of Pedro Point with the ocean pounding on the cliffs. There are beaches all along the way, but you have to walk down trails to most of them. Try Montara Beach, thirteen miles out of San Francisco.

Stinson Beach to the north (you hit it on S 1 off US 101) is a sandier, more sheltered beach than the ones you'll find by driving south. But it is several miles farther, and the road is even more winding. If you keep going north along S 1 (although you can get there faster via the Sir Francis Drake Highway) you'll see the desolate mesa of the Point Reyes Peninsula and Drake's Bay, which was long confused with San Francisco Bay. This is windswept country barren of trees, something of a geological freak since it is a remnant of a great land mass now covered by ocean. In sharp contrast, although only a few miles away, is the long narrow finger of Tomales Bay, sheltered by trees, with good beaches and picnicking facilities in a state park. All this, incidentally, is still another aspect of Marin County. There is a strong move, backed by some newspapers, to turn the whole Point Reyes Peninsula into a national park.

Wine Tour   The greatest single one-day junket in the San Francisco area is probably the Napa Valley wine tour. But for this you have to be lucky enough to be around in late September and October. While the wineries are open most of the year, the tour isn't as much fun when they're not in operation. The idea is to go when the leaves on the vines are sprinkled with red and yellow, when the grapes are being pressed and turned into wine and sifted through elaborate systems of pipes and vats. Even the air in this little narrow valley smells of wine then. There are guided tours of the wineries, and elaborate explanations of the differences between the various wines. But even those who don't enjoy the wonderful aromas and the sight of the great oak casks in cool cellars can always taste the wine. There is ample opportunity for sampling. You may run across a sweet (not cloying) Semillion or a dry Johannisberger Riesling you've never met before. Napa at the start of the tour is only fifty-three miles from San Francisco (north on US 101, then east on S 37, which runs into highway S 28 to Napa). Count on driving about 150 miles during the day.

If there are youngsters along (you'll enjoy it too), you've got to take in the Christian Brothers' **Mont La Salle Vineyards** eight miles northwest of Napa. A Roman Catholic congregation devoted to the education of boys and young men, the Christian brothers support their activities by the production of wines in their medieval-type monastery high in the hills, and they show off the wares with secular verve and salesmanship. The tour includes a lingering look at the fabulous display of corkscrews—from cumbersome old gadgets to the sleekest, latest models, collected by Brother Timothy, long the chief winemaker.

A few miles north (on S 29) is a neo-Gothic castle, the **Inglenook** winery, founded in 1879 by an adventurous Finnish sea captain. Tradition is the big thing in most of these small, good wineries. Inglenook still belongs to the family, and there is great pride both in the quality of the wine and in the fine old casks from Germany's Black Forest in which they are matured. Try the **Beaulieu** winery (on the Silverado Trail out of Napa; you can also cross from S 29). It looks like an old French estate, and it is. It has been run by a French family and its descendants ever since it was started at the turn of the century. The Marquis and Marquise de Pins, the present owners, live here part of the time, when they are not being social lions in San Francisco or visiting French wine-growing areas. Oldest of the wineries is **Charles Krug,** dating back more than a century. The winery buildings (also on the Silverado Trail) are of native stone and set amid the great Krug oaks, long-time Napa Valley landmarks.

Actually, you won't go far wrong if you wander into any of the other fine wineries in the valley. They all put on a good show and are generous with samples. They display their wines, but don't push them. The only possible risk of this tour is a pleasant but harmless glow.

Valley of the Moon If you don't take the wineries too seri-ously, a good side trip which might be combined is to the Sonoma Valley, Jack London's Valley of the Moon (signs point the way to Sonoma, east of Napa, from S 37). Sonoma, forty-five miles from San Francisco, is still a pretty, sleepy place. The city square is the old plaza of the Spaniards, with several adobe buildings still intact on its fringes. Of course, there is now a monument to the ragged Bear Flag rebels who here overthrew the Mexican regime and established their own short-lived republic. A few miles from here through the valley is Jack London's old ranch, now a state park (seven miles north to the Glen Ellen cut off, then a half-mile past Glen Ellen). His fabulous Wolf House is now just a ruin and he never lived in the house built by his widow, which is now used as a museum. There are some London mementos here, certainly more than at Jack London Square in Oakland. But it is considerably less than an adequate London museum. The principal joy of this trip is driving through the still quiet and pastoral Sonoma Valley be-tween wooded hills.

Weekend Trips

Monterey Peninsula More than fifty years ago George Sterling and other writers and artists discovered that this was the most strikingly beautiful stretch of California coast and they settled down for concentrated spells of serious work in the little village of **Carmel**. (You can get there on S 1, but the fastest route is on US 101 past Gilroy and then right on S 156, about 125 miles and a three-hour trip.) Even a generation ago when Lincoln Steffens lived there and Robinson Jeffers built his stone tower overlooking the ocean, Carmel was only an artists' colony. Now the artists have almost been overwhelmed by retired military personnel and tourists.

But they are still ahead in their long battle against modern conveniences. Carmel has no street numbers and few street lights. The main streets are lined with little shops and restaurants, very smart and also quite expensive. But don't be diverted too long from the beautiful white sand beach, lined by windswept cypresses.

Between Carmel and Monterey is the seventeen-mile drive, a private toll road winding past the Pebble Beach golf course and lodge and other retreats of the wealthy. It also covers one of the really beautiful stretches of rugged California coast. But you can get much the same untamed feeling at **Asilomar Beach** (a state-owned resort in Pacific Grove, just north of Monterey). And probably the most spectacular area of all is **Point Lobos State Park** (four miles north of Carmel on S 1), where state rangers have somehow managed to keep intact a wilderness area where you can wander at will among cypress groves and down little trails to tiny beaches hemmed in on every side by cliffs and rocky caves through which the waves surge.

When you get to **Monterey,** don't expect John Steinbeck's Cannery Row. The canneries are still there, but they aren't operating most of the time. Cannery Row is now the site of several swank restaurants. More than any other Northern California town, Monterey retains at least a whiff of the old Spanish atmosphere, of the time when it was the Mexican capital in the state. The old adobe custom house and other relics near the waterfront are well preserved. Monterey has a Fisherman's Wharf, almost as honkytonk as San Francisco's. It has a little Wharf Theater and an artists' colony and some interesting coffee houses and art galleries. With its location on a beautiful bay, it suggests in some ways a smaller San Francisco.

Mendocino Coast   As the Monterey Peninsula has become increasingly popular, artists and devotees at large of the California coast have been frequenting the Mendocino County coast, some 125 to 150 miles north of San Francisco. (You can go all the way on S 1, or with fewer twists and turns on US 101 to Cloverdale and then west on S 28.) This is old lumbering country, and the beaches are littered with timber. It is a great place for driftwood collectors. Fort Bragg is the major town of the area. But probably the most attractive place to stop is Mendocino City to the south, an old lumber town with an antique Masonic Hall and white-steepled churches that are straight out of New England. Russian Gulch and Van Damme state parks are also in this area along the coast, convenient for camping or picnicking.

(*Note.* The California coast is foggy much of the summer, and the fall or early winter is generally a better time for these trips, if you can arrange it.)

Redwood Highway   As you drive north out of San Francisco, US 101 signs alternate with Redwood Highway signs. You are hardly permitted to forget that the highway takes you through the redwood country, and everything north of Golden Gate Bridge is loosely described as the Redwood Empire. But the signs don't really begin to take on substance until you drive about 150 miles, just past Willits. For the next hundred miles or so, you drive by some sixty memorial groves of redwoods, good for just looking and loitering, and a succession of state parks where you can camp and picnic. The agitation of the Save-the-Redwoods League back in 1918 was successful in keeping the great trees from going the way of the buffalo. Now the redwood area, crisscrossed by the Eel River (which lives up to its name), is one of the state's major vacation resorts, with good facilities for fishing and swimming. You can stay at the numerous and excellent but crowded state parks or at motels in any of a number of resort towns—Garberville, Layton-ville, and Benbow. Take it easy and stop along the way. This is one of the most beautiful stretches of road in California.

Gold Tour   If you have a weekend to spare, you can drive up and down S 49 (the number isn't accidental), looking for ghost towns. This is a favorite for male children of all ages. It is a con-siderable drive if you're going to be serious about it. The gold country is an immense belt in the Sierra foothills, 300 miles long and 20 miles wide. It is about 150 miles east of San Francisco both to the north and the south. You can't possibly cover it all in a weekend or a week. A good compromise is to head to Placerville (on US 50 out of Sacramento), an old gold-mining town, and then head north on S 49 for eight miles to Gold Discovery State Park. This is where John Marshall found gold at Sutter's Mill in 1848, and there is a good little museum with relics in the park. If you're really determined, you can keep going north to Grass Valley, a wonderful little town with old storefronts with wood canopies ex-tending out over the sidewalk. Or instead of going north you can head south to Angels Camp, which Mark Twain made famous in his Jumping Frog story, and to Columbia, once one of the greatest of the gold-mining centers, now the best-preserved of the ghost towns with a state park keeping intact old buildings and relics. There are also neglected and decrepit ghost towns all through this area and you stumble across them as you drive, especially on side roads.

The Parks   You haven't really seen Northern California unless you take in one of the great national parks, which overshadow in size and grandeur even the tremendous network of excellent state parks. The national parks are substantial empires with millions of acres. They are winter resorts and summer resorts. They have hotels, cabins, tents, recreational facilities of all kinds. They are also forest and wilderness areas preserved almost intact against civilization. All four of the major national parks—Yosemite, Sequoia, Kings Canyon, and Lassen—are on the wild western slopes of the Sierra Nevada mountains. They are within range of a week-end trip, although considerable driving is involved. Yosemite is the closest, 183 miles to the southeast; Sequoia and Kings Canyon about 100 miles farther in the same direction; and Lassen is 250 miles from the city at the northern end of the Sierra.

Each of the parks has its ardent devotees who prefer one to all others. Yosemite is the most popular; the valley thronged during the summer by those who just like scenery and fresh air, the High Sierra above challenged by the serious hikers and campers who are legion in California. At Sequoia and Kings Canyon the main camping grounds and recreation areas are higher up and surrounded by California's big trees, the great sequoias which are related to the redwoods but are even older and bigger. Lassen is a geologic marvel, strewn with rocks thrown helter-skelter by relatively recent volcanic eruptions and with bubbling mud and boiling lakes. It also has quiet streams and lakes and meadows, and shares with all the parks endless trails for walking and hiking. All four parks are open the year round and have winter sports facilities. (*Note.* Ski enthusiasts also use winter-sports facilities somewhat closer to the city. Detailed brochures are available from the State Chamber of Commerce and the California State Automobile Association (see p. 219).

The park systems (there are some good county and regional parks as well as state and national parks) have brought inexpensive vacations within the reach of most Californians. A camping trip at one of the parks costs little more than staying at home, and it is just as desirable and refreshing to the prosperous doctor or businessman as it is to the plumber and the carpenter. The availability of the parks has turned innumerable San Franciscans, along with other Californians, into outdoor enthusiasts. They are hikers, mountain-climbers, skiers, fishermen, yacht and motorboat fiends, or just nature-lovers and camera fans. Wildflowers are so popular that one major oil company has made a big thing of distributing booklets about them at its gas stations. The outdoors is part of the way of life for San Francisco, as it is for most of California.

INDEX

INDEX

Note to first-time visitors: look up *Tourists* in the index for helpful hints.

233

THINGS TO REMEMBER

THINGS TO REMEMBER